Skiing Mechanics

JOHN HOWE

Poudre Press

The author most gratefully acknowledges the technical and editorial assistance provided by Dr. Juris Vagners. Dr. Vagners, as well as being an Associate Professor of Aeronautics, Astronautics and Applied Mathematics at the University of Washington, is the head of the Biomechanics Subcommittee of the Professional Ski Instructors of America. He has long been a recognized leader in the physical analysis of skiing as well as an outstanding instructor and skier. His suggestions and corrections were most valid and helpful during the period in which the manuscript was completed.

Original Title: Skiing Mechanics
Copyright © 1983 by John G. Howe

First Edition

T1/83

Illustrations by Frank Campione

ISBN 0-935240-02-0

Printed in the United States of America

Poudre Press
Box 181
Laporte, Colorado 80535

A co-production of:

Poudre Press
Laporte, Colorado 80535

and

The Newport Press
Santa Ana, California 92705

CONTENTS

To Debbie...
        super skier, super wife.

FORWARD

IN A WORLD OF SPACE TRAVEL, home computerization, working robots and ever-expanding technological capabilites, the design of snow skis still remains an art. The design of these seemingly simple implements of pleasure and recreation is practiced by talented engineers in the employment of large companies, where resources would allow application of current engineering technology, as well as by engineers who are essentially the company by themselves with very limited resources. One is often hard put to distinguish between the products and how they perform. The fascination of the design problem itself is such that more than one designer returns on personal time to their own 'garage research and development company' after leaving the employment of known ski manufacturers in search of other challenges.

Why this fascination with the problem of designing skis? Because the simplicity is deceiving — the good ski is much like a good musical instrument in that how well it performs depends on how it is used. So even though the designer must understand and appreciate the underlying physical laws governing the mechanics of composite materials and structures (even as the violin maker must know acoustics), that alone is not enough. The mechanics of use — skiing and skier — are just as important in achieving a good ski design. And the mechanics of human movement in skiing are complicated indeed.

So the challenge is laid down. Design a ski that will be responsive to the demands placed on it by the user, stimulate improvement and yet will be forgiving and easy to use when the skier does not wish to pay attention to the task at hand. To succeed in meeting such vague performance criteria, designers rely heavily on user feedback, their own understanding of the mechanics of skis and the mechanics of skiing.

This book is the product of such activity — a view of skiing mechanics from the perspective of a ski designer, himself a long-time skier. John Howe brings many years of practical experience with skiing and the art and science of ski design to the subject. The task of writing this book was made difficult not only by the complexity of the subject, but also by the desire to find a level of presentation which is understandable yet technically sound. Because the human body is a complicated collection of non-rigid limbs with joints capable of incredibly varied movement patterns, just the task of writing down the mathematical equations of human motion, as defined by the laws of physics, is very difficult. If we add the varied terrain and snow conditions we ski on, the task becomes virtually impossible. And yet, much understanding is to be gained from even simple models of skiing and skiers. This book deals with such models and the interpretation of skiing mechanics that such models allow.

The technically sophisticated reader may be tempted at various times to seek a more rigorous and precise derivation or analysis than that chosen by the author. This was certainly the case for me the first time I read the material; based on that experience, I strongly urge anyone so tempted to proceed. Each time I found that *simplicity and rigor* were extremely difficult to achieve but that my own understanding of the mechanics of skiing grew as a result of the effort. So it seems that for the technical audience, the book serves as an excellent departure point in solidifying concepts. For those who perhaps do not have a technical educational background, the book will serve as an introduction to the underlying mechanical principles, how they might be applied to analysis of skiing mechanics and the interrelationship of skiing mechanics with ski design.

Thus, this book should prove to be a foundation and a steppingstone for future work on skiing mechanics as well as an introduction to a technical treatment of the subject. It should stimulate a re-examination of one's understanding of skiing mechanics and result in a deeper appreciation of the subject.

JURIS VAGNERS, PhD.
Chairman, Biomechanics Committee
Professional Ski Instructors of America
and
Department of Aeronautics and Astronautics
University of Washington

INTRODUCTION

Howard head once told me, "A ski is a rascal and an enigma." Howard, as a post World War II engineer, was one of the first to tackle the design of a ski from an analytical approach. He had at his disposal high strength aircraft aluminum, honeycomb cores, and a vivid imagination. His success at commercialization is history, culminating with an election to the Skiing Hall Of Fame. His warning has stayed with me to this day.

This book is not about the Head Ski Company. Instead, it is a collection of the thoughts, observations and calculations that have accumulated in my mind and office for the last 23 years. During the last 12 of these years, I have had the responsibility for product design for the Head Ski Company (now the Head Sports Products Worldwide Division Of AMF). I do not profess to know all the answers about skiing. On the other hand, I feel I have substance to publish which will help the serious aficionado better understand the complexities and questions of this fascinating sport. Possibly because of the puzzles of skiing, publications to date have been limited to a variety of periodical articles, many excellent photo books, and very few (in English, they can be counted on one hand) worthwhile, basic analyses of the sport of skiing. The translated *Teach Yourself To Ski* and *Skiing: An Art... A Technique* by Joubert, *How The Racers Ski* by Witherell, and *World Cup Ski Technique* by Major and Larsson appear to be the best English language books that lead to modern skiing in the eighties. It is hoped that my book will complement these references by supplying more analytical explanations to the subjective thoughts they present.

Writing on skiing must be like tackling the history of the world. Where do you start? How do you organize such a mass of intermixed facts, premises, and exceptions to the rule? How do you make something which is necessarily complex, understandable to readers with a wide variety of educations, interests and

backgrounds? I have elected to approach this problem by hitting it head on. This will not be a simple book since there are not simple answers. The analytical approach used is necessarily difficult to understand if the reader is not working every day with algebra and trigonometry. However, the equations and calculations are needed as background for those who really want to understand what's happening. Of course, great emphasis will be made towards relating the analysis to the subjective feelings of the skier, in everyday language.

In the way of organization, the first part of the book is prepared as a background or basic reference necessary for the mechanics presented in later chapters. The concepts presented must be developed slowly on a solid base of terminology and understanding about skiing. These early chapters are written in a manner which is integrated and biased with my personal feelings about the sport. Hopefully, they are not 'rehashes' of old publications on physical terms and ski terminology. Chaptery 1 is the necessary refresher course in basic physics, but completely slanted towards the needs and language of the skier. Chapter 2 covers the ski as it has evolved in the 1970's. Chapter 3 investigates the human part of the system; including strength, a few comments on the mental approach to skiing, and equipment other than the ski. The third part of the ski-skier-slope system is covered in Chapter 4. This chapter explains largely why skiing is as mysterious as it is. The infinite variety of possible environmental situations prohibits a simple analysis and a dogmatic approach to equipment and technique.

The actual mechanics of skiing; the forces, velocities, vectors and accelerations that are concerned are prefaced in Chapter 5. This chapter is intended to be a simplified look without the equations as in the chapters that follow. Chapters 6 and 7 cover the skier movement in a quasi-straight direction down the hill and in a traverse across the hill. Chapter 8 introduces centrifugal force as the second most important force to the skier (after gravity). The close relationship between ski side cut and the turn is covered in detail in Chapters 9 and 10. Finally, all of the other forces and their synchronization throughout the turn make up Chapter 11.

The selection of proper visual support for this text is difficult. Traditionally, high speed photography or photomontages have been used. The danger of these is that observations can be very misleading, since so many motions and forces are occuring in a very short time. This book will instead use artist's 'stick figures' and sketches to accurately present simple force diagrams.

Skiing seems to be one of the few sports which can occupy our energies until we're exhausted. By this, I mean the vastness of conditions, experiences, environments, and challenges present an everchanging kaleidoscope to test our senses and abilities. We are willing to expend fortunes and careers grappling with the elusive puzzle of sliding down frozen moisture on a pair of boards. In skiing, there must be some psychological release from a subconscious frustration of being grounded and laboriously slow compared to other members of the animal kingdom. Water skiing, sailing, bicycling and sailplaning, to name a few other sports, provide similar sensations; but none offer the extreme variety of situations to challenge us as snow skiing does.

The ski slope is the final laboratory. The various schools of instruction and students of the sports are there continuing their curriculum — some seriously, some purely for escape and enjoyment. Hopefully, my thoughts will help.

JOHN G. HOWE
February 22, 1982

chapter 1

A BACKGROUND IN MECHANICS FOR SKIERS

MECHANICS IS THE BRANCH OF PHYSICS dealing with the motion of bodies and the interaction of forces acting upon bodies. Several subdivisions of mechanics are statics, dealing with stationary bodies; dynamics, dealing with moving bodies; and biomechanics, which is concerned with the mechanics of the human body itself. The mechanics of skiing is concerned with all of these branches.

The subject is understandably complex. There are too many possible combinations of forces, masses, movements, and resistances to allow simple singular equations that will encompass all that could happen during a single turn. This does not, however, preclude a basic understanding of the primary forces and their interaction. The advanced skier, racer, instructor and coach has to be concerned, sooner or later, consciously, with the mechanics of the descent down the mountain. The beginner has to rely on one of the above for direction or be hopelessly lost the instant that the skis start to slide.

The pure theoretician would try to approach the mechanics of skiing with an all-inclusive set of equations. These would be so complex and full of differential and integral calculus that the average person would be immediately lost. The other extreme is for the nontechnical author or expert to try to put into words a subjective interpretation of the feelings and forces encountered while skiing a particular technique. Frequently, great liberties are taken with the second approach. Forces are used to "cause" accelerations or motions entirely contradictory to classical mechanics. A good example is the erroneous term "upunweighting." How can a mass be moved up away from the pull of gravity while simultaneously decreasing the gravitational pull it feels toward the ground?

Sir Isaac Newton laid the foundation for modern skiing with several basic laws of motion. Violations of these laws are the cause of problems. Anyone attempting to thoroughly understand skiing should know these laws and the terms used in their proper, intended meaning. In order to get the most out of this book, the reader should be familiar with the following terms, definitions, and units of measurement.

Force

Figure 1—1

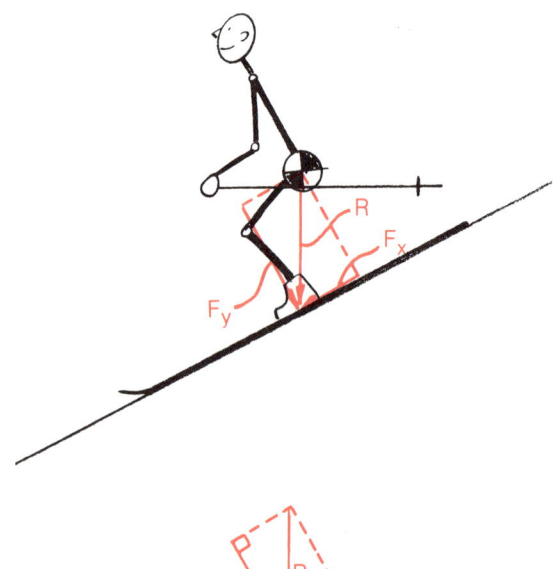

Force is a push or a pull acting between one body and another body. For every force, there is an equal and opposite counterforce. If a free light body pushes against a heavy body, the light body will be pushed backwards. If a free heavy body pushes against a light body, the light body will be moved. If neither body can be moved because of great weight or immobility, the force is still there acting as a *static* situation. If either (or both) of the bodies can move, we have a *dynamic* situation. We (and everything on the surface of the earth) are always acted upon by the force due to gravity which is tending to pull us towards the center of the earth. A skier is able to exert forces against the slope through his skis or poles.

Forces are *vectorial* quantities, that is, they have a magnitude and also a direction of action. They can be represented by arrows (vectors) with obvious direction and magnitude indicated by length. Any singular force vector can be resolved into two or more component vectors acting in different directions but through the same point in space as the singular force vector. Conversely, two or more singular force vectors acting in different directions but through the same point may be represented by a singular force vector called the resultant. This resultant has exactly the same effect as the singular forces acting together.

In Figure 1—1, force (R) acting on the snow surface could (as far as the snow surface is concerned) just as well be two separate forces (F_y) and (F_x). Likewise, the separate pair of forces (F_y) and (F_x) could just as well be represented or replaced by a singular resultant (R). By representing the forces with magnitude and direction as vectors it is possible to picture them graphically, and by completing them as a parallelogram to determine the singular resultant vector.

In the traditional English system, the unit of force has been the pound. In the new SI (the International System of Units) system, the unit of force is the Newton. One pound is equal to 4.45 Newtons.

Mass

Mass is very closely related to weight. The mass of a body is constant anywhere in the universe. It is determined by the total of all atoms of matter that make up that body. The weight of that same body is the force acting upon that certain mass by a specific gravitational field. For instance, we are most familiar with body masses at the surface of the earth where the gravitational pull is constant, therefore, we sometimes speak of mass in terms of weight. The quantitative relationship between mass and weight is determined by a constant equal to the acceleration due to gravity.

$$(1\text{—}1) \qquad \text{Mass} = \frac{\text{weight}}{\substack{\text{acceleration due to gravity} \\ \text{at the surface of the earth}}} = \frac{\text{weight}}{32 \text{ ft/sec}^2}$$

The units of mass are pound-seconds squared per foot. This cumbersome term has been shortened to "slugs" by American engineers. In the SI system, the unit of mass is the kilogram.

Wherever possible in this book, the more familiar term of weight will be used since we are skiers concerned with pursuing our sport on the face of the earth where the gravitational pull is constant.

Acceleration

Newton's second law explains simply that if a force acts upon a mass, it will be accelerated.

$$(1—2) \quad \text{Force} = \text{Mass} \times \text{Acceleration} = \frac{\text{weight}}{32 \text{ ft/sec}^2} \times \text{Acceleration}$$

Because forces are vectorial (magnitude and direction), so are accelerations, and we are again concerned with "how much" and "in what direction." The acceleration is the change in motion that will occur. Acceleration is a change in velocity (also again a vectorial quantity). As you start up from the stop light, the engine of your car applies force through the wheels to the ground, thus accelerating the mass of your car from a velocity of zero to some terminal velocity. This final steady velocity is determined by the condition at which all counteracting forces such as gravity, wind resistance, and rolling friction exactly equal the driving force coming from the engine.

The units of acceleration are "distance per time squared," usually "feet per second squared." Of course, deceleration is just negative acceleration or slowing down.

Velocity

When there are no forces acting on a body, or when the forces active upon a body are equalized, the body has a constant velocity. Newton's first law states that a body at rest tends to stay at rest, and a body in motion tends to stay at uniform motion in a straight line unless acted upon by an outside force. In other words, no acceleration or deceleration will take place. A body standing still has a constant velocity of zero. The units are "distance per time," such as "feet per second" or "miles per hour."

Torque

If a force is applied to a body through a lever arm, it is called torque. Because the force is not applied through the axis of rotation or the center of gravity, any movement possible takes place as some form of rotation. The units of torque are the units of "force times the length of the lever arm," such as "foot pounds" or

"Newton meters."

Work

If a force is applied against a body and the body *moves* a finite distance in the direction of and during the time the force is applied, the product of the force and the distance is called work. No actual work takes place if there is no movement. However, in a biomechanical sense, the static or isometric flexing of a muscle still causes one to become tired.

The units of work are the units of force times the distance *only* in the direction over which its force is applied which gives the typical work units of foot pounds. If a ski lift (or the skier himself) carries the 170 pound skier 1,000 vertical feet up the mountain, then 170,000 foot pounds of work are done. If it only takes one pound of force to push the 170 pound skier *along the level ground*, then only 1,000 foot pounds of work would be done in 1,000 feet of travel.

Power

Power is work being done in a specific amount of time. This is an important concept to understand. Obviously, if you take 3 days instead of 3 hours to mow your lawn, a different type of exertion is involved, although the work involved (pushing the lawnmower a certain distance) is the same. Similarly, if you climb up a mountain you have to exert a force equal to your weight (to counteract gravity) over the vertical distance ascended. The time rate at which you climb determines the power you expend during the period involved during the climb. For instance, if you climbed the 1,000 vertical feet in 30 minutes, your rate of doing work would be:

$$(1-3) \quad \text{Power} = \frac{170,000 \text{ foot pounds}}{30 \text{ minutes}} = 5,666.67 \ \frac{\text{foot pounds}}{\text{minute}}$$

A standard unit for power is the horsepower, which is equal to 33,000 foot pounds per minute. So, in climbing the mountain you would be generating:

$$(1-4) \quad \frac{5,666.67}{33,000} = 0.172 \text{ horsepower}$$

This is about all the power a man can put out for a continuous period.

Energy

Energy occurs in two forms. *Potential* energy is the

(mechanically) stored latent ability to do work. A coiled spring or a skier standing at the top of the slope both have stored energy capable of doing work. *Kinetic* energy is the energy of motion, such as with a skier moving down the mountain, and the change in kinetic energy equals work done. Since energy and work are related, they have the same units such as "foot pounds." Note that potential energy does not infer the rate of speed at which the work will be done. Kinetic energy, however, is the ability to do work due to the mass and the square of the velocity of a moving body.

$$(1-5) \qquad \text{Kinetic energy} = \text{mass} \times \frac{\text{velocity}^2}{2}$$

Another example of energy is the chemical energy that can be stored in a battery. This energy can be used quickly to result in a lot of power, or it can be used very slowly thus providing very low power. You have a certain amount of chemical energy stored in your body. You can expend it quickly climbing up the mountain, or you can walk slowly all day. Energy intake is quantified as the caloric content of our food. Each Calorie of food has a potential energy of 3,088 foot pounds of work, although far less than this is actually done by the body due to inefficiencies of conversion from one form of energy to actual work. If we consider a 170 pound skier descending a slope at 44 ft/sec (30 mph), he has converted some of his potential energy into kinetic energy. In this case:

$$(1-6) \qquad \text{Kinetic energy} = 1/2 \frac{W}{G} V^2 = 1/2 \frac{170 \text{ lbs.}}{32 \text{ ft/sec}^2} (44 \text{ ft/sec})^2$$

$$= 5142.5 \text{ ft lbs.}$$

If both skis are reverse bent with a total bending deflection of 0.894 inches (which requires 30 pounds of force each for a stiff ski (see Chapter 9)), the energy absorbed by the skis is:

$$(1-7) \qquad \text{Spring energy} - \frac{1}{2} \text{Bd F} = \frac{\frac{1}{2}(0.894'')(30\#)(2 \text{ skis})}{12''/\text{ft}}$$

$$= 2.23 \text{ ft lbs.}$$

From this example, it can be seen that bending the skis takes only a fraction of one percent of the kinetic energy of motion. However, it still is desirable for a racer to try to recover this energy at some point later in the turn.

On the other hand, if the skier (or racer) were to skid sideways — say 20 feet while generating a total lateral force (F_{TL}, see Chapter 8) of 100 pounds — this would represent considerable work done (or energy lost) of:

$$(1—8) \quad \text{dissipated energy} = F_{TL}\text{(distance in direction of force)}$$

$$= 100\#\,(20') = 2{,}000 \text{ ft lbs.}$$

This represents a loss of energy and velocity that can only be recovered after the skier slowly accelerates again.

Centrifugal force

In any discussion of mechanics, one must always decide on how to view and interpret the fundamental law that:

$$(1—9) \quad \text{Resultant of applied forces} = \frac{W}{32.2}a$$

$$= \text{mass} \times \text{acceleration}$$

There are two schools of thought on the subject. One proposes that the term 'force' be reserved only for applied forces, such as gravity, muscular force, frictional interaction, magnetic force, air drag and so on, and speak of the terms *mass × acceleration* as 'inertial resistance' or 'inertial effects.' If this approach were followed, we always write the law of motion as above. The second approach is to identify the inertial resistance as 'inertial force' and to think of inertial forces as acting to reduce problems of motion to problems of force equilibrium. That is, inertial force is always in vectorial equilibrium with the applied force.

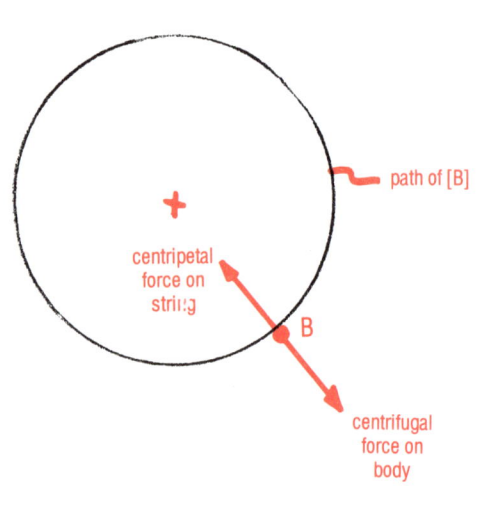

Since motion can be quite complex, various forms of inertial force are possible. The best-known of these is the *centrifugal force* which we experience in any curved motion. The centrifugal force corresponds to the acceleration normal, or at right angles, to a curved path. This normal component of acceleration is called the *centripetal acceleration*, and the *centrifugal force* acts in the opposite direction to the centripetal acceleration; that is, outward at right angles to the curved path.

Recalling that acceleration results if we have forces acting, we see that a force towards the center of curvature of a curved path must act in order for the body to move in the curved path. A simple illustration is obtained by swinging a body on the end of a string — the body will move in a circular path because of the pull on the string towards the center of the path. Note that if the string is held tightly, the path is circular as shown in Figure 1—2a, or more complex if the string is gradually let out (Figure 1-2b).

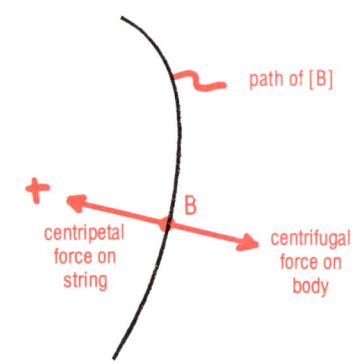

An understanding of this concept is critical to understanding the later discussion of ski turns, which can trace different arcs on the snow as a result of different conditions.

Inertia

Inertia is another name for the tendency of a body to follow Newton's law; eg. to stay in a given path at a certain velocity unless acted upon by an outside force. Unfortunately, inertia is also the name used to describe the cross sectional area of a beam (eg. the "Cross sectional moment of inertia"). This can be confusing, so one must infer or clearly state which type of inertia one is talking about.

Momentum

Momentum is the quantitative expression to describe a moving body:

$$(1-10) \qquad \text{Momentum} = \text{mass} \times \text{velocity} = \frac{\text{wt}}{32 \text{ ft/sec}^2} \times \text{velocity}$$

Obviously a heavy skier has more momentum than a light skier traveling at the same velocity.

Within the framework of the above definitions, the mechanics of skiing can now be investigated. The total spectrum of skiing could be construed to be any form of sliding on some medium while standing on one or two sophisticated boards attached to the feet. Some of the mechanical principles are common to water skiing, cross-country skiing, and alpine or downhill skiing. For this reason, there is no formal attempt to limit the thoughts presented to only alpine skiing. However, to avoid getting too far afield and involved in too many exceptions to the rule, the only concern of this book is alpine skiing, where the force of gravity is the *major* moving force. This is differentiated from cross-country skiing where muscular forces are the most important consideration or water skiing where a boat provides the pull.

The danger of any discussion of the mechanics of skiing is either over-simplification so that all the important factors are not considered; or over-complication so that the writer gets lost in exceptions to the theme and the reader cannot follow the mathematics anyway. The attempt following will be to maintain a balance between these two extremes. Hopefully, there will be enough presented to be useful to the readers with wide backgrounds of education and also be immediately applicable to their skiing needs.

The approach used will be to first identify and tackle specific maneuvers as single entities. Then, the individual blocks will be brought together to make a dynamic sport. All types of motion, turning and sliding, flow together to constitute the unique creation

15

of that particular sequence or run down the mountain beginning and ending with a stationary position. If alpine snow skiing were as simple as checkers or croquet (or even tennis or water skiing) the analysis of the mechanics would be simpler. However, with the wide variety of slopes and snow surfaces available, the subject gets very complicated.

chapter 2

SKI PROPERTIES AND CONSTRUCTION

THERE ARE MANY VARIABLES involved in ski design and construction. Most of these have been defined frequently in other ski publications, so any repeat here will be brief unless serious exception to presently accepted thinking is taken. In general, the development of a ski is a rather mysterious compromise of many conflicting philosophies or design objectives. Since there are no accepted text books teaching ski design, there are many different approaches used. Some manufacturers are seriously exploring ski design on a systematic, technical level equal to that used with other high quality goods. This includes sophisticated laboratories, computer analysis and design, and statistical evaluation of structural and performance testing. Other manufacturers take a more artistic approach to ski design — they rely on strokes of imagination and the use of material and design that are not completely supported by the accepted scientific method.

An analogy might be a painting compared to a technical drawing. Who is to say which one is more right or suited to the task? The majority of ski design and manufacture is probably a blend of these two extremes — a bridge between a modern, technical world of manufacturing, and a product necessary to fill an esoteric, human activity.

In addition to performance, the ski designer also must consider durability and cost. The interaction between these three design restraints is biased certain ways for certain customers; but in total, a modern commercial ski must have all these; good skiability, the integrity to hold up in a very adverse environment, and a cost acceptable to a mass market.

Longitudinal Ski Stiffness

A ski is stiffness designed first; that is, the longitudinal bending stiffness must be such that the proper pressure will be distributed over the snow for the terrain, snow conditions, skier weight, and anticipated speed. Immediately, the compromises can be seen. A ski too stiff for a light skier on a highly moguled slope could be too soft for a heavier skier trying to hold a precise, high speed carved turn on ice.

In addition, stiffness distribution (variations in flex along the length of the ski) and stiffness balance (one end is stiffer or softer than the other) are important and do much to give the otherwise similar skis widely differing characteristics.

Soft flex

—results in a pressure distribution based around the foot.

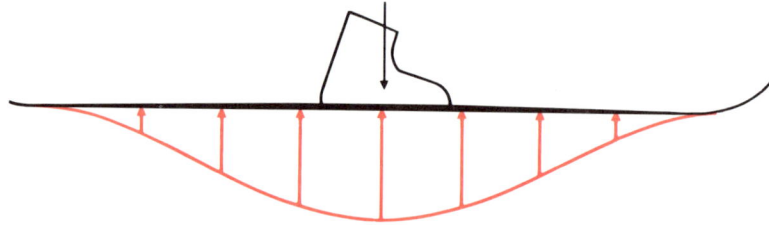

This ski is much better through moguls and will flex into a tighter turn on a concave surface.

Stiff flex

—results in a pressure distribution biased towards the ends of the ski.

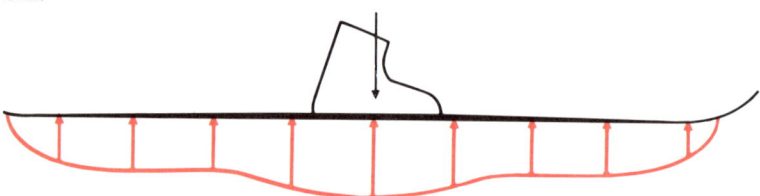

This ski is more stable at high speeds and does not change direction easily with foot swivelling techniques.

Stiff forebody, softer aft-body

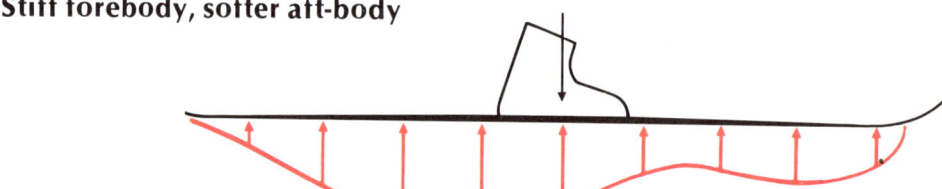

This ski will initiate turns quickly and tend to release in the tail, especially if the weight is forward (oversteer).

Soft forebody, stiffer aft-body

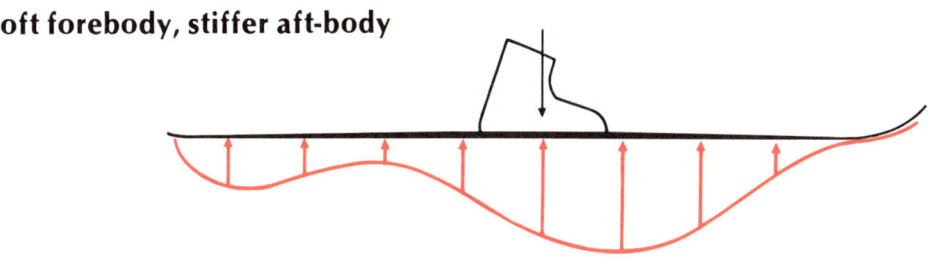

This ski will be vague in starting turns and will tend to run straight as soon as weight is pressed back toward the end of the turn (understeer).

Stiff center, soft ends

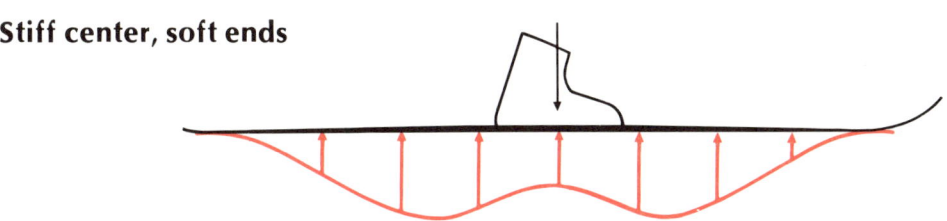

This ski tends to feel stiff and is difficult to carve tighter turns with, but has a greater stability at high speeds. This is characteristic of giant slalom skis (or downhill skis when the tails are stiff).

Soft center, stiff ends

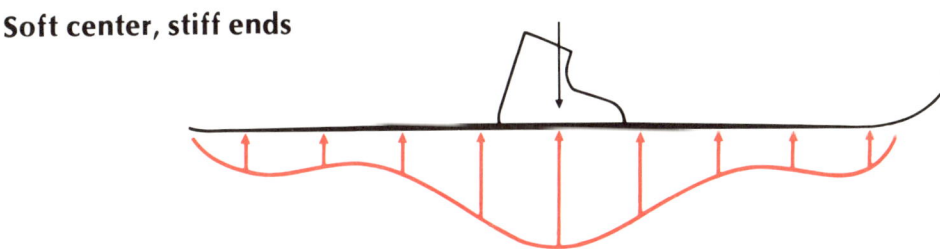

This ski will carve round, tight turns but be less stable at high speeds. This is more characteristic of slalom skis.

The stiffness of a ski can be measured in a number of ways. Of prime consideration, however, is an understanding of the interaction of camber with stiffness since most tests eliminate the camber effect and then, to truly understand the total stiffness of the ski, the observer must be sure to factor camber back in. For instance, the skier on the hill feels the resistance offered by the ski against being pressured into an arc. A soft flex ski with high camber will offer the *same* resistance at *one* particular arc as a stiffer flex ski with low camber. If one were to measure the flex of the ski above without considering camber, he would be mislead in his assessment of how the ski will feel in actual skiing conditions.

In spite of this phenomenon, most tests (such as ASTM F498-77) measure stiffness alone with camber zeroed out before the test. This test, as well as equivalent tests used by manufacturers, are good for evaluating the ski in a one zone test (support both ends, load in the middle) or as a two zone test (cantilever support in the middle, load each end independently). Sophisticated manufacturers go far beyond simple one or two zone tests for design purposes. The ski has to be broken down into six to ten zones and evaluated on expensive laboratory stress-strain machines in order to truly evaluate the complete stiffness distribution of the ski.

Ski Camber

In its relaxed position, the ski is constructed in a graceful arch This is done to provide a slight initial force against the snow at the ski extremities, which in turn gives the ski sensitivity at the ends for turning as well as stability for straight running. As described above, the camber is intimately interrelated with the longitudinal ski flexibility and, therefore, one cannot be described or discussed without consideration of the other. A soft flex, higher cambered ski is better for varied terrain and snow conditions. A stiffer flex, lower cambered ski has a narrower range of bending for a wide range of loads applied and, therefore, lends itself to higher speed skiing and longer radius turns. Even the location of camber must be considered in ski design. If the point of maximum camber is moved fore or aft from the boot location, it will interact with the flex distribution of the ski to make the ski tend to overturn or underturn. Camber is typically measured with the ski sideways to a flat reference surface in order to eliminate the effect of the weight of the ski. Typical values of camber are ¼ to ½ inch per ski.

Longitudinal ski stiffness is varied in the ski design in a number of ways. The quickest and simplest is to vary the thickness of the ski while keeping the materials constant. This is usually done by a mold or core change, depending on the type of ski construction. Ski stiffness varies approximately as the square of thickness, so this method is very effective. Most of the ski's stiffness is provided by the thin structural skins just under the top and bottom plastic surfaces. A variation in these skins (whether

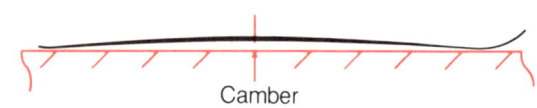

Camber

metal or fiberglass) in thickness or width will change the ski's stiffness proportionately. The ski's core construction and density will also influence ski stiffness as will the type and cross sectional area of the steel edge.

Torsional Stiffness

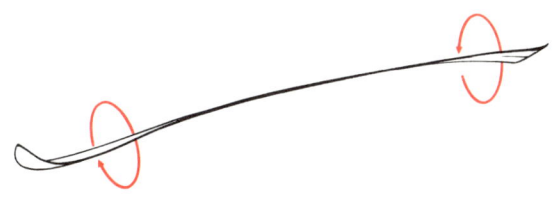

The torsional stiffness is the resistance to twisting of the ski. It is quite independent from the longitudinal bending stiffness of the ski. Torsional stiffness is necessary to keep the ski holding and carving precisely, even when it is longitudinally bent into a reverse arc.

At first, it would seem desirable to have a ski with maximum torsional stiffness. However, a ski must be able to release laterally (sideways) as well as hold on hard surfaces, and if the torsional stiffness is too high, this cannot be done smoothly. The control extremities of the ski's side cut also become too sensitive. As would be expected, skis with higher torsional stiffness are better for ice and expert skiing. (Softer torsion skis are more forgiving for recreational skiers and are easier on "grippy" snow conditions.)

Torsional stiffness is measured by clamping the ski in the center and applying a twisting torque at either end. The torsional stiffness design of a ski is not as easy to vary as longitudinal stiffness, especially if the longitudinal stiffness is to be kept constant. Only internal material changes in the construction of the ski can vary the torsional properties to any meaningful extent. Box construction skis and skis with metal laminated skins tend to be stiffer in torsion. Fiberglass laminated skis or skis with rubber layers are soft in torsion. Skis with cracked edges tend to be stiffer in torsion since for equivalent longitudinal stiffness, the cross section of the ski has to be thicker to achieve the proper longitudinal flex.

Lateral Stiffness

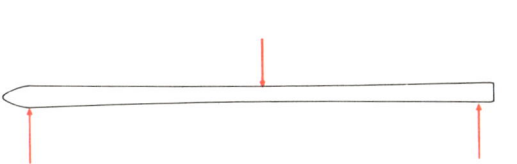

The third way a ski can flex is sideways. Over the past years, there has been much controversy regarding the magnitude and meaning of this mode of ski flexibility. This camp finds it difficult to understand where any forces come from that are substantial enough to effect lateral bending. The only such force conceivable is the side component due to knee angulation as discussed in later chapters. This force is small compared to the force required to laterally release the toe of a binding which, in turn, is small with respect to the force required to substantially deflect the ski sideways. In other words, if there were any side forces of any

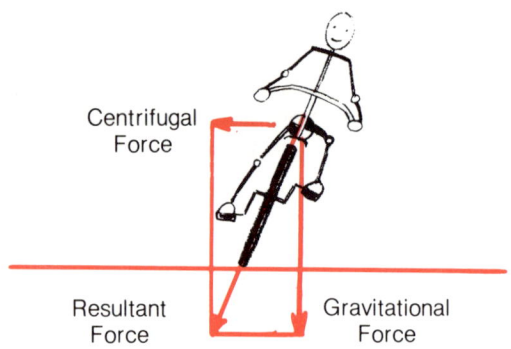

Centrifugal
Force

Resultant
Force

Gravitational
Force

magnitude, the anti-shock or release mechanism of the binding is purposely designed to absorb these shocks so they cannot appear in the ski long enough to have an effect on the ski's direction.

An anology is the bicycle as it leans into a turn much like a skier. The resultant of forces pushes against the ground along the plane of the wheel and, therefore, a bicycle wheel has and needs little side strength (unlike an automobile wheel which must support side forces since it is always in a vertical position).

Ski Geometry

There are many dimensional variables of a ski which may or may not be independent of the materials used in construction. These variables are in many ways interrelated and interact with the other properties of the skis to give the ski its total personality. There is an ASTM standard (F472-76) for geometric terms and definitions. This standard will be used as a reference in the following discussion:

Side cut

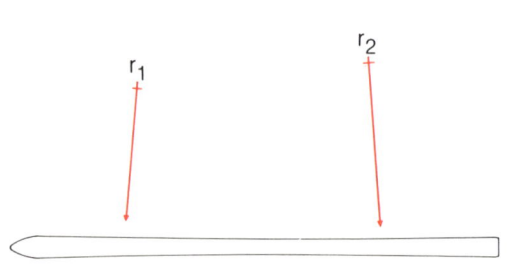

r_1 r_2

This is the most important dimensional variable since it largely determines how a ski will turn. As a ski is placed on its edge and pressed against the snow/ice surface, the side cut forces the ski to deflect into a reverse bend and carve or skid a turn depending on a number of other factors. This one subject is so important to a technical understanding of skiing that Chapter 9 is completely devoted to it. The radius of side cut might vary between the forebody and aft-body of the ski. One manufacturer (Kaestle) even varied it from one side to the other. This radius of side cut for typical skis varies from 3,000 inches down to 1,800 inches. If it is high, the ski tends to run straight and carve very long turns. If it is low, the ski is much better for turning, but will tend to be unstable at high speed and climb uphill sharply on any traverse.

Width

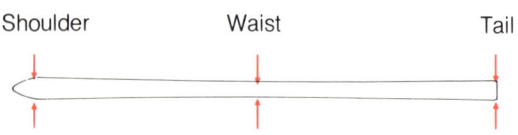

Shoulder   Waist   Tail

Interrelated with side cut is the actual width of the ski. In other words, a ski can be wide or narrow, but still have the same arc or side cut. Like all the other ski design variables, width is a compromise. A narrow ski is easy to get on an edge and feels more precise on hard surfaces. However, too narrow a ski will lack the required buoyancy in softer surfaces and could catch outside edges in soft snow or drag the side of the boot in some situations.

Typical ski widths at the narrowest part of the ski vary for adult skis from 2½ inches to as wide as 3 inches for some models of short skis.

The location of the waist dimension is also an important variable in ski design. It varies from half way between the shoulder and heel for older ski designs to up to 10 inches behind this point for some racing skis. This type of ski will tend to complete a turn more quickly when the skier's weight is pressed onto the aft-body of the ski.

Taper

Also interrelated with side camber and width is the angle of taper of the side camber. A quantitative value for this variable is the difference between the shovel and the heel width divided by 2.

Greater taper in a ski tends to make the ski very sensitive to starting turns but not as good for holding in the aft-body in the later part of the turn. Less taper makes the ski difficult to turn, even with substantial side cut.

Side camber

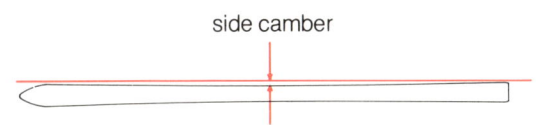

Side camber is the actual dimension between the side of the ski at the narrowest part and a straight line between the heel and the shoulder. In a conventional ski, it could vary from 0.2 inches to 0.3 inches. Side camber plus length constitute another way of describing side cut and will be discussed in detail in Chapter 9.

Ski length

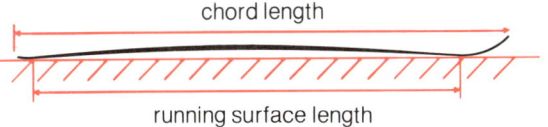

The two lengths of concern are the total length of the ski and the running surface length. By standard definition, the total length is the chord length or the straight line distance between the ski extremities. Some manufacturers, however, continue the European practice of using the developed parts length as the normal length of the ski. When the ski is pressed against the snow/ice surface, the contact area is called the running surface length. This length is usually close to the same as the geometric length between the shoulder and heel of the ski.

A great deal of controversy continues over the ideal length of a ski. However, there cannot be too much argument about the following facts:

- *A shorter ski has less leverage against the skier. Therefore, some of the skiing forces exerted against the body are less and the skier has a better chance of over-powering a ski which inadvertantly is pushed or heading in the wrong direction. This would infer that short skis are safer and easier for recovering from mistakes.*

- *A shorter ski will tend to carve a tighter radius when put on*

23

an edge. The mechanics discussed in Chapter 9 *show in detail the effect of the ski length on the radius of turn.*

Opposed against the above two favorable pluses for a short ski is the consideration that a long ski is more stable and less liable to be deflected from straight ahead or long arc carving motion. There is also some psychological, macho, stigma that long skis are the sign of a tougher, stronger, better skier.

Out of the confusion and conflicting objectives, the following thought is offered regarding length:

The type of skiing, including speed, terrain, snow conditions and radius of turn, should determine the ski length — not skier's height as in the past. This determination would be tempered somewhat by the strength and ability of the skier. In other words; fast, high speed cruising demands a longer ski, regardless if a 110 pound girl or a 210 pound man is on the ski. However, tight trees or mogul covered hills require shorter skis. The difference in skier's weight (more than a difference in height) will influence the final optimization of a ski flex, but the length is determined by other factors. The accompanying chart is a better graphical representation of these thoughts (note that skier's height, except as related to weight, isn't included in this chart).

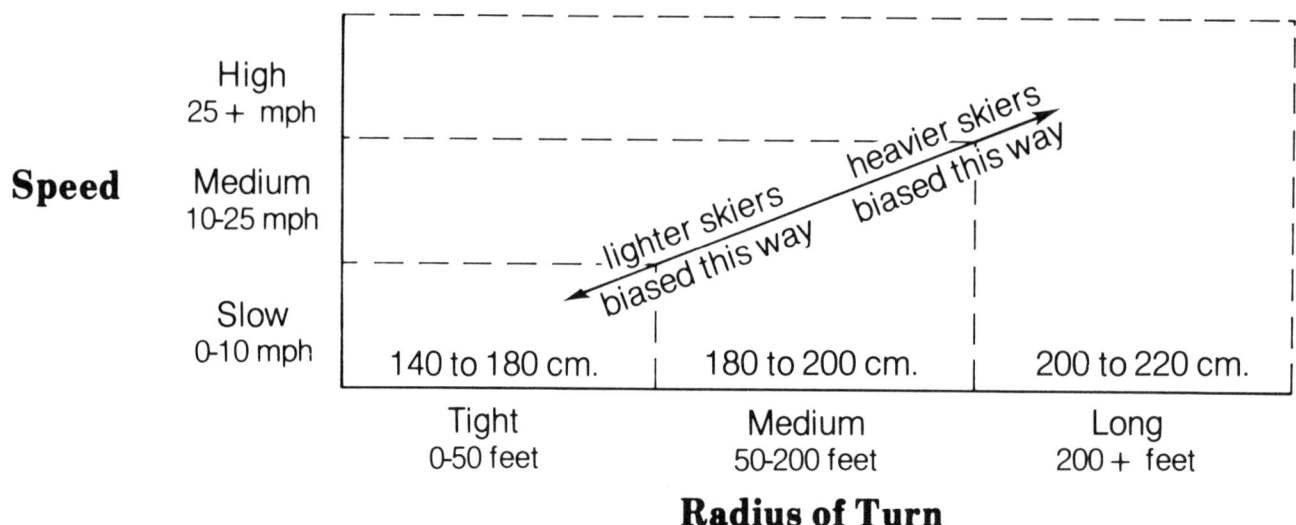

The lengths recommended in this chart have empirically evolved over years, and agree with the theory presented later in this book. The extremely short or long skis in the chart tend to be specialized for their purpose. (You wouldn't want to run downhill on ballet skis or vice versa). In the middle third are the all-around or compromised skis, best for every day skiing but obviously not as good for specialized use as the extremes in length.

Ski thickness

A ski is stiffness designed first; i.e., it is designed to have the proper longitudinal flexibility. To achieve this desired flexibility requires radically different ski thicknesses depending upon the materials used. Stiff (high modulus) materials like aluminum require a thinner ski than more flexible (lower modulus) materials like fiberglass. Therefore, it is the material design of the ski that determines the ski thickness with slight variations possible if a very stiff or very flexible ski is desired. The use of a cracked edge will result in a much thicker ski because the stiffness contribution by the edge is lost and the ski must be made appreciably thicker to compensate for this fact.

Ski thickness is somewhat related to ski damping. This is because the more flexible materials that result in a thicker ski also strain (or move) further for every vibration of the ski. In so doing, the material fibers absorb more energy and damp the ski quicker. Another school of thought teaches that the thinner (metallic type) ski can move sideways through powder easier. This seems like a nebulous justification for thinner skis. The sum conclusion from this discussion on thickness is that the property is a result of the ski construction and doesn't have as much effect on the final ski properties as most of the other design variables.

Splay

Tip and tail splay are the distances between the ski extremities and the actual contact points of the ski with the ski pressed flat.

A ski with long tip and/or tail splay will actually have a shorter running surface and ski like a shorter ski. On the other hand, the long, gradual intersection of the ski with the snow will result in less resistance and more speed as the ski plows ahead through the snow. Like so many other variables, this variable is a compromise, but tends to average about 5 cm. for the tail and 20 cm. for the ski shovel. These distances are referred to as the tail surface area and shovel surface area in ASTM F472-76 standards for alpine skis.

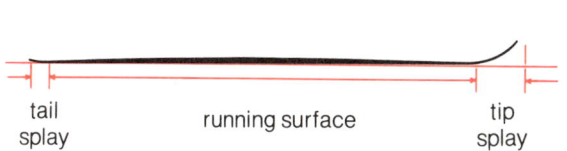

tail splay   running surface   tip splay

Roll back

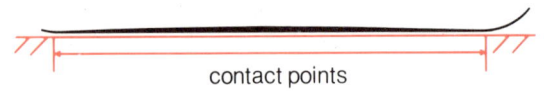

contact points

When the ski is pressed down, the contact points move inward until the ski is flat, thereby determining the splay. This distance between the contact point when the ski is arched with camber and then pressed flat is called *"roll back."* It will be 1" to 2" for a conventional ski. Greater or lesser amounts infer an abnormal, and perhaps defective, ski since it will intersect the snow either too abruptly or too gradually.

Tip and tail height

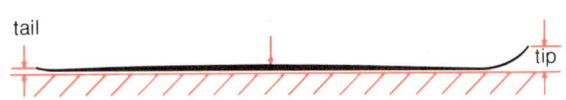

tail

tip

These two details of ski geometry are more a matter of tradition than of functional detail. The shovel of the ski needs to turn up to 2 to 4 inches to intersect the snow and uneven surfaces. The tail turn-up is ¼" to ½", or only enough to allow the ski to slide backwards. The exact amount of turn-up doesn't seem important and varies between manufacturers and models.

Damping

As a ski is flexed, energy is absorbed in the ski. This energy will cause the ski to spring back when the force causing the flex is released. If the outside forces or resistances to motion are removed, the ski will continue to flex back and forth (vibrate) until the original internal energy stored in the ski is dissipated.

There are two ways this energy can be dissipated, externally against surrounding media (air and snow) and internally as structural fibers and other material parts of the ski move microscopically against each other. As long as the ski is used in soft snow and kept in contact with the snow and the total ground surface, damping is not of great importance. In fact, there is a theory that a poorly damped ski, such as the original HEAD metal ski, is better in soft snow because it will vibrate more and shake loose from the grip of the surrounding snow. Another premise is that a ski with minimal damping is faster for the same reason.

In contrast, when the snow is hard and icy, an undamped ski will bounce around excessively, especially at higher speeds or if there are chatter marks to start the motion. If a ski is intended for this use, damping is extremely important and should be maximized. This is done with the internal construction of the ski. Common techniques are the use of rubber shear layers between components, fiberglass (which has more natural damping than aluminum) and foam cores. The design danger of all these materials is the possibility of too much torsional flexibility, since this usually accompanies greater damping. For this reason, the ski designer must be careful how he uses these materials, and somehow make provision in the design to maintain proper torsional stiffness. The use of a cracked edge will also add some damping to the ski because of the elimination of the very undamped steel contribution to ski stiffness and energy absorption. This technique has the added advantage of simultaneously increasing torsional stiffness (because the ski has to be slightly thicker) rather than decreasing it as do the other methods.

Materials of Construction

Most of this information is available from the manufacturers. Only generalizations and major points of interest will be mentioned here.

The ski is a very complex beam that is to be used over great bending deflections. Because of weight limitations, the required performance dictates some type of heterogeneous construction; e.g. very stiff structural members are displaced from the neutral bending axis of the ski by a lighter weight core material. This is precisely the principle of an 'I' beam.

By displacing the structural members away from the neutral axis, they are forced into greater strain and, therefore, build up more resisting force for a given bend or radius of curvature (r). If the structural members are in the core or closer to the neutral axis, they are not stretched or compressed as far for a given bend radius. They would thus be less effective than their weight and cost would justify. Therefore, a lower weight, lower cost core material is used to space the structural members apart. The structural members have traditionally been high strength aluminum or unidirectional fiberglass. Just any old aluminum or other than primarily unidirectional fiberglass will not do the job. Very high quality wood can be (and certainly has been) used for skis. Wood has properties somewhat between synthetic structural laminates and the lighter core materials. It therefore serves both functions, although a thicker ski is necessary which, in turn, requires segmented edge segments. This is because a continuous edge will be too stiff and won't take the stretch (strain) necessary when displaced so far from the neutral axis.

High tensile steel and titanium could also be used for structural laminates in a ski but they would have to be thin. Cost and the problems of drilling holes to mount the bindings are prohibitive, although some skis have used high tensile steel wires. The stiffer (higher modulus) space age filament materials like carbon, boron and Kevlar* have not worked out well for ski construc-

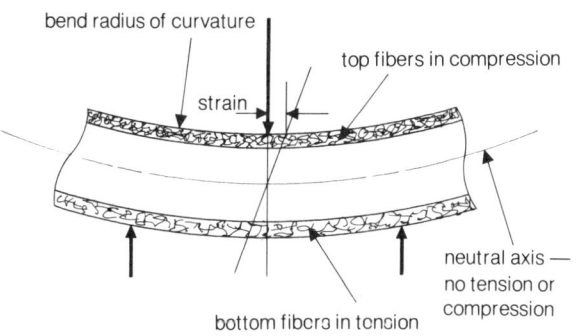

bend radius of curvature

strain

top fibers in compression

neutral axis — no tension or compression

bottom fibers in tension

*du Pont trade name

tion because they won't stretch enough before breaking or have poor compressive strength.

One very important design consideration for ski construction is that the structural elements plus the steel edge be thermally compatible; i.e. their expansion and contraction rates must be such that high temperatures during molding and low temperatures during skiing do not cause significant stresses and camber changes in the ski.

The bottom edges, in contact with the snow, have universally been high strength steel with a yield point higher than 200,000 PSI. This is necessary so the edge won't take a permanent set as the ski is flexed. All the ski manufacturers today use high carbon steel to achieve this, although from time to time special alloys of stainless steel have been used. Apparently the extra cost of the stainless steel was not justified by the anti-rust feature because these edges never remained on the market very long. The hardness of the edge must be high, commensurate with its yield strength, but not so high that a good quality file cannot be used. Between Rockwell 'C' 45 and 50 is the normal hardness range for all steel edges.

If the edge is cracked or cut periodically, it can stretch much easier and, therefore, does not contribute to the ski's bending stiffness. A continuous edge will provide about 30% of the ski's stiffness (and vibrational characteristics). A cracked edge reduces this figure to about 2%. The cracked edge still has to be hard, however, or rocks and dirty snow would dull it prematurely.

The edge dimensions vary among manufacturers. The width exposed to the snow is generally about 2 mm. (0.080 in.) although edges as narrow as 1 mm. (0.040 in.) have been used for racing skis to reduce the amount of steel sliding on the snow and the cross sectional area of the steel which, in turn, reduces the stiffness contribution caused by the edges... more like a cracked edge.

In years past, various alterations to edges have been used, such as concave grinding, scallop grinding (bread knife) and stepped or angled edges. These schemes have always proved too "grabby" or ineffective; so today, only the basic 'L' edges, either continuous or cracked, have survived.

Today, the running surface of the ski is universally high molecular weight polyethylene. Over the years, virtually every type of moisture resistant plastic has been tried, but only special grades of polyethylene have the best combination of sliding ease, toughness, weight and cost. Even more expensive materials, like Teflon*, are not as good because they do not provide enough friction to melt the snow crystals and allow the ski to slide as easily as polyethylene. On non-snow surfaces, however (such as synthetic ski decks), the lower coefficient of friction of Teflon justifies the extremely high cost and special bonding techniques required. Another characteristic of polyethylene is its molecular similarity to wax. This allows intimate blending of the wax into the polyethylene with even better moisture resistance because the wax

*duPont trade name

completely fills every pore in the base material.

The molecular weight and hardness of the polyethylene is varied for certain types of snow conditions where the last percentage point of speed is required. A contemporary downhill racer will have different skis for varying snow conditions, not only for the flex characteristics but for the base polyethylene used.

Top plastic and side plastic is primarily for scuff protection and cosmetic appearance. Various materials, such as ABS (acrylonitrile butadiene styrene), paper based phenolic, and polyurethane have been used. The material has to be tough and compatible with the manufacturer's process and the type of ski construction used.

The core material of a ski depends primarily on the type of construction. Something has to hold the top and bottom structural members at the proper distance from each other and force them to go into tension and compression. The core can be wood, light weight synthetic foam or structural ribs alternated with air spaces or very light core material. All these techniques are in use today. If the ski is a complete wrap or box construction of structural laminate material, the core is not too important and can be quite light. However, if the ski has only top and bottom laminates of structural material, the core must take all the shear stress and interlaminar forces itself and, therefore, needs to be heavier and stronger. If the core is somewhat elastomeric, as a polyurethane foam, it will allow the structural skins to slide very slightly between themselves and therefore provide energy absorption (in the core) and better damping than with the more brittle wood core.

Nearly every type of ski construction requires additional reinforcement in the foot pad area to firmly anchor the binding screws. The ASTM ski committee has developed a specific standard (ASTM F474-76) for this subject. The exact location of reinforcement and the screw pull out strength required are established as a guide for all manufacturers.

Construction Methods

Over the years, virtually every imaginable way to make a ski has been tried. Very elaborate sculpturing with solid or laminated wood was used prior to World War II. Synthetic construction was initially developed after the war by Howard Head. This was the beginning of modern ski technology, and the basic laminated ski is quite common today with fiberglass or aluminum skins and wood or foam cores. Radical departures from this type of structure were initiated by William Kirchner of K2 with the wet wrap fiberglass ski and Hub Zemke with the Hexcel prepreg and honeycomb core ski. The Europeans have not been quite as revolutionary; instead, most manufacturers have evolved the Head type laminated ski into an infinite variety of shapes, sizes and detail constructions. Two exceptions in Europe are Volkl of East Germany and Dynamic of France. These companies have also developed excellent wet wrap skis. Gaston Haldemann, a French ski designer originally with Rossignol, perfected hollow tubes and ribs as the core function of the ski.

The structural laminate in a modern ski is either aluminum or fiberglass. The fiberglass can be of three distinctly different forms, each within a matrix of epoxy resin.

- Precured   As a dimensionally stable, fully cross-linked structural laminate used in lieu of the aluminum laminates. The European laminated skis and Olin in the United States are of this type.

- B-staged   The fiberglass has been impregnated by a special epoxy which can be subsequently softened with heat and pressure and finally hardened to the desired final form. The Hexcel, Hart Honeycomb and Head XR-80 are of this type.

- Wet Wrap   The fiberglass is impregnated with liquid eopxy resin just as the ski is made. In this type of ski, the semi-wet fiberglass is usually wrapped completely around the wood or foam core, thus giving the box construction. Head HRP, K2, Volkl and some models of Dynamic are made this way. Rossignol also makes some models with a wet laminate construction.

This discussion will not dwell further on the intricacies of each type of construction. The ski world is full of variations and each manufacturer will tout his as being the superior way to make skis for various reasons. Actually, it is the pragmatic result that is of concern to the skier. The total personality of a ski is what the skier feels. This personality is a blend of all the components and geometry used which yields the desired (and sometimes unexpected) end result. A ski is so complex, especially considering bottom and edge tuning, that unless they have deteriorated to a commom level of mediocre condition and performance, like a rental car, no two pairs of skis really feel quite the same.

Compromises in Design

So far in this chapter, the ski has been defined and the important components and design considerations have been named. This is not to suggest that there is some perfect design resulting in the world's *"best ski."* There can be no such thing because the end use of the skis is not precisely established, nor is it even close to being consistent. The ski is only one part of the skier—boot—ski—snow condition—terrain system. Since the other parts are not consistent, how can there be any one type of ski? Virtually every aspect of design becomes a compromise, albeit biased towards one expected combination of skier type and end use.

Flex needs to be stiffer for the heavier, faster skier; softer in moguls and soft snow. Torsional stiffness needs to be high to hold on ice, yet soft enough to release when a skid is needed. Length... long enough for stability, short enough for maneuverability and safety. Side camber is a definite compromise. How do we ask the same structure to track straight on a traverse yet carve into a turn when put on edge? Even weight needs to be light enough for quickness yet with sufficient inertia to move steadily through a variety of extraneous, disturbing forces. The point is made: *the ski is necessarily complex and varied because of the nature of the sport.* Hopefully, subsequent chapters will shed some light on the total subject.

Bottom and Edge Condition

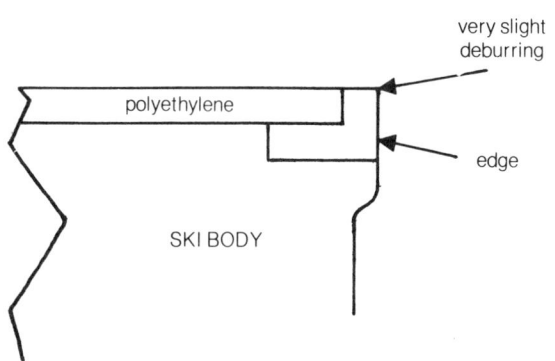

very slight
deburring

polyethylene

edge

SKI BODY

A discussion on skis cannot be made without comment on the condition of the running surface and steel edges. The final performance of a ski can be masked or ruined by faulty bottom and edges. It is amazing how much space in the ski magazines has been devoted to this subject, and how many skiers still ignore it.

A smooth gliding quality of the base is even more important for turning than for maximum speed. Wax should periodically be ironed into the base and the excess scraped off. This is a simple operation which can be handled in any ski shop if the skier himself isn't up to it. Excessive gouges or base damage will certainly interfere with smooth gliding and turning and should be repaired prior to waxing.

The steel edges should be square cornered and deburred. To achieve this is a more complicated operation than waxing. Usually, the polyethylene base has to be made lower than the edge by grinding or scraping by hand. Then the two edges are simultaneously flat filed back down to the slightly lower base. These two steps are alternately repeated until the steel edge is perfectly flush and square.

Fine emery paper should then be used to polish and deburr (actually slightly round) the edge right at the very corner. When the ski is properly prepared, a straight edge across the base will allow no light to pass, even out at the corner of the edge.

Good quality skis prepared properly can actually grip or hold on ice too much! If this is the case, slight additional rounding of the edge is done on the hill with a pocket stone until the compromise between edge holding and edge releasing is exactly right for the skier's particular preference.

Those skiers who envy the experts effortless holding on ice and very hard snow can never hope to achieve the same performance without perfect edge preparation. Sharp edges and smooth bases are a necessity for correct skiing and prerequisite for appreciation of the mechanics involved. Final hand preparation is required for every commercial ski if the maximum response is to be realized.

chapter 3

PHYSIOLOGICAL FACTORS, SAFETY, AND OTHER EQUIPMENT

OF ALL THE RECENT BOOKS published on skiing, most dwell heavily on the physiological rather than the mechanical considerations of the sport. Gallwey's *Inner Game Of Skiing*, McCluggage's *The Centered Skier* and even Ruedi Bear's and Warren Witherell's excellent technical books devote many of their pages to the subjective aspects of skiing. One cannot argue with the need for a proper mental attitude and psychological well-being as prerequisites for superior neuromuscular performance. However, these cannot be used as total substitutes for a proper technical understanding of the endeavor. A great pianist does not perform only on the basis of perfect mental and physiological preparation. These are the finishing touches to years of painstaking, solid foundation building. Likewise, a skier (or tennis player, or runner, etc.) will not achieve a stellar performance solely because he has the right mental attitude and his #2 self is in control. This might make the difference between winning or losing at the front of the pack; but getting there in the first place can only be the result of painstaking, objective preparation.

This chapter is prefaced with this thought because the theme of this book is the basic mechanical approach to skiing and most of the mental approaches will be left to the psychologists and other authors. On the other hand, there are several physiological aspects that need to be presented and discussed because of their direct and important context in this book.

Physical Conditioning

Skiing is a very dynamic sport. The movements and forces involved come first from, or act directly on, the body as part of the overall system. It is the author's belief that every skier beyond the beginner-intermediate level is performance limited by personal strength. In other words, after the rudiments of the sport are properly learned, each skier can only progress as far as individual strength will allow. The later chapters show how properly made turns require very high compressive forces on the leg and thigh muscles. As a skier upweights and laterally projects from a high speed carved turn, the total force to be carried through one flexed leg can easily approach 300 pounds, if the skier could handle this much load. All serious competitors learn very quickly that aggressive summer strength-building programs are absolutely necessary.

All types of physical conditioning are required for skiing:

- A static, or isometric, type strength is absolutely necessary to cope with the steady state and dynamic forces involved.

- A strong cardiovascular endurance is needed to be able to repeat the exertions required for minutes (in a race) or all day (as in safe, recreational skiing).

- Balance and coordination are certainly necessary as so much is happening so quickly.

- Flexibility of the body is required for safety as well as the ability to cope with awkward situations and changing terrain.

In spite of popular belief, there are probably better preparatory exercises for skiing than skiing itself. Improvement of muscular strength and endurance requires pushing to the limits, as well as repetition. No skier wants to be at the 'limits' of strength or endurance while negotiating an exciting slope at 30 mph. Therefore, it is better to push to the limit during the off season. This is the time to run, lift weights and participate in other dynamic sports that place a premium on movement and coordination.

The point cannot be made strongly enough that proper alpine skiing requires more physical strength and endurance than the average American has. The greatest improvements in a person's skiing can be effected through a serious summer training program. Fortunately, there are many other benefits from such a program. A better overall feeling, more energy, better sleeping and eating habits and probably a longer life; all go hand in hand with a continuous year round physical conditioning program aimed primarily at improved skiing. The health and physical well being of life-long, serious skiers is very apparent when they are compared to sedentary people of the same age.

Mental Attitude

There is a great deal of truth to all the mental approaches to skiing. In any dynamic endeavor things happen too fast for the participant to be able to think about all that is going on. We can only think, consciously, about one thing at a time. Skiing should be basically subconscious so we can concentrate on where we are headed, how pretty the scenery is, how to go faster... or slower, or how to consciously integrate one change of technique into our movements. However, if we get our cerebral inputs too much involved with the flow of what's happening, the natural and subconscious movements will become impeded and things will start to become inhibited. The important thing in learning a dynamic endeavor is to systematically understand and practice the correct fundamental steps and store them away into the subconscious... one by one. Sooner or later, they'll come together in the right order and a quantum jump in ability will happen. Usually when you are struggling to achieve a certain step, only fatigue and boredom occur at the time. If you keep trying, the progress comes later, when you are refreshed and your subconscious has had a chance to organize all the input. True improvement (or change) can only come after a conscious struggle. This is because we are creatures of comfortable habit and *not* being able to ski is a habit *before* we learn the new habit of being able to ski.

This has been an engineer's view of a subject in which he is not trained; but after 44 years of painful struggling with many different challenges, he has observed a certain common denominator to all learning processes. "You've got to pay the pain price."

The other mental consideration worth mentioning is the esoteric reason for the popularity of skiing. During a descent down a mountain with good snow, cooperating equipment, adequate physical conditioning, and proper technique, everything comes together. There is no other sport that offers the senses the same combination of quiet freedom of mobility, fresh air, and a challenge to our life preserving instincts. There is so much happening that is beautiful and pleasant that daily burdens and problems really can be forgotten and then reexamined later through a rosy looking glass. It is unfortunate that it can all come to an abrupt halt with a fall or an uncomfortable chill. There is no need for these intrusions. Advanced skiers who know exactly what they're doing will go a season without falling. Being warm is just a matter of investment in proper clothing.

Sharing a beautiful run with a friend is also pleasant, but skiing is really an individual sport. If you're skiing with someone else you must be careful not to collide. Also, it is extremely rare that two people want to ski exactly the same pace and terrain on any given day. With skiing, you don't have to find an opponent to challenge your ability. There's always a bigger mountain or a more difficult snow condition to provide a new puzzle. Social skiing is a dilution of the very best skiing has to offer.

Skiing should be a quiet, gentle, personal experience. This is true for alpine skiing as well as cross-country. Yet, the exhibitionists and egotists, as well as greedy commercialism, have driven many to the solitude of the forests. Fortunately, there is usually room for every one on the mountain, but the different needs and outlets used by different skiers are obvious. This could be a point not worth mentioning if it weren't for safety's sake. One of the challenges of skiing is being able to ski within the limits of one's ability. But to ski abnormally fast on a slope used by cautious beginners or even experts is a crime. Usually it is the poor skier who is able to negotiate the beginner's hill in a pseudo-racing crouch that terrorizes the public and causes serious accidents. This is rarely seen on the steeper slopes because the dangerous skier would only harm himself first.

Instead, a common sight on the expert slopes is the masochistic struggler who is completely over his head. Instead of enjoying skiing by staying within his limitations, he (or she) ends up sliding, skidding and falling down the expert slope. This, not short skis per se, is what causes moguls. By not carving turns, and therefore dissipating all the available energy in a short space, the struggling skier skids and slides. As soon as one skids and then stops sliding, a pile of snow builds up. The next skids in the same place. Very quickly, the slightly better skier, and finally the expert, must turn in the same trough. The only thing short skis have done is allow the poorer skier to ever get on the steep slope in the first place. Then, the short skis allow the better skiers to continue to negotiate the tortured terrain, but only in the established troughs. Finally, the moguls are so deep and tight that long skis physically will not fit into the trough and one must be able to just ski on the high spots or find a smoother hill. The incessant pounding from a mogul field is similar to motocross racing. Only the young can take it... for a while. It is not the most enjoyable skiing. It wouldn't happen in the first place if the initial skiers on the slope were able to continue to make turns at random locations instead of quickly skidding off smooth places and piling up piles of snow (moguls) for those following to amplify.

This digression into mogul making really started with a discussion of mental attitudes resulting in lesser skiers on steeper hills. Both physical and mental considerations lead into the next subject.

Safety In Alpine Skiing

By now, it should be apparent that skiing is not a simple sport. It is probably one of the most complex (and therefore challenging) of any of the leisure recreational pastimes. It follows, then, that one cannot very well learn to ski by oneself... anymore than self-learning to fly an airplane without self-destruction. There is too much happening at high speeds. Careful preparation in the form of physical conditioning is a prerequisite. Proper equipment is next. Lessons from a competent instructor are absolutely necessary. Finally, a proper mental attitude towards personal ability vs. the slope and conditions is as important as with driving a car or flying a plane. Violation of one or more of these four simple rules greatly increases the chance of a fall and injury... either to yourself or someone you may run into.

Proper equipment will help, but it will not guarantee protection from violations of the needs of physical strength, instruction, and good thinking... yet the sport is cursed with lawsuits against equipment manufacturers and ski areas when the skier really bears the blame. This phenomenon is reaching everybody's pocketbook in the form of higher ticket prices.

If only each skier would automatically advance in skills, one step at a time, with full mechanical and mental understanding of what is to be accomplished, then once it has been established what one is doing and where it can be done, and stays within those limitations, the skier will be far safer and happier too. A good analogy is the 'aerial' discipline of freestyle skiing. Both approaches were used by different competitors; ie. a systematic, safe, controlled learning process versus a 'get a little high and go for it' attitude. History has shown how the second group has ruined the sport for the first.

This discussion may seem out of place in this book, but a better understanding of the mechanics of skiing before and during skiing will help contribute to safety as well as increased skill and pleasure.

To summarize; the preconditioning of the body, as part of the mechanical system, is an absolute necessity. Good equipment is next. Shorter skis will help, because in an emergency they exert less leverage against the leg. Good safety bindings in proper adjustment are helpful, although they should not be relied upon as a panacea for out-of-control skiing. Accidents can happen even after bindings release. Ski brakes help the 'windmilling' problem, but they don't help the people under the lift or the ones searching for their ski in deep powder. The best bet is to keep your skis on and ski intelligently; ie. with proper initial instruction, awareness of personal limitations, and a semblance of understanding of the mechanics of the sport.

Teaching Methods And Techniques

Because of the complexity of skiing, there has not been total uniformity of teaching methodology. But, in the past few years, the student has a better chance of receiving consistent ski instruction between one ski area and another. The P.S.I.A. (Professional Ski Instructors of America) and C.S.I.A. (Canadian Ski Instructors Alliance) struggled with this problem for many years, systematizing their teaching methods and establishing standards for certified instructors. Unfortunately, however, there have been sweeping revolutions in skiing technique and many schools and instructors are drifting somewhere between the new and the old. The author has personally been through the old positive (follow through) rotation days of the Arlberg school. Then came the complete change to exaggerated counter rotation as popularized by Stein in the 50's and the reverse shoulder days of Austrian dominance. In the early 60's we were Canadian certified using "up-unweighting" and twisting angulation. Then came down-unweighting, the concept of carving, wide stance, GLM and, finally, independent leg action. No wonder the student can be confused.

If one looks back in retrospect, however, a clearer path can be seen. There is excellent correlation between the accepted technique of the period and the equipment being used. No one was referring to the ski as a "carving tool" prior to the 60's. Before then, the ski was a rigid encumberance to be struggled with. Any changes in direction required a skid on good snow and a complete removal of the ski in soft. The 'ruade' and other types of jump turns were the vogue in soft snow until the metal laminated ski made possible the extreme flexibility necessary for the ski to actually bend through a turn in the powder.

In order to withstand tremendous sideways forces and keep skidding (in a skidding technique) to a minimum, the racers used very stiff skis. This would at least spread the sideways force over the whole ski length and have the force act upon as much of the snow/ice surface as possible. The icier the condition, the stiffer the ski would be. The leather boots in this era didn't help matters. They were either too stiff and hurt or quickly became soft so most of the connection between the body and ski was lost. The solution was to take long leather straps and wrap them around and around... leg and boot. This was the binding. Everyone had their personal technique of wrapping.

The 1960's saw a technical revolution in skis and boots that was continued through the 70's. Concurrently, teaching methods and the resulting ski techniques have changed considerably. Competition and forward thinking coaches led the way. At times there was a 180° difference in thinking between racers (coaches) and ski instructors. Now that period is pretty well behind and there is excellent consistency between what the racers are doing and what the up-to-date ski schools are teaching. Recent racers do become instructors and good instructors can certainly race. This is important to the recreational skier because there is only a gray distinction between racing and advanced recreational skiing which is the goal of all aspiring skiers.

Racing forces the skier to make a specified turn at a certain predetermined place on less than ideal snow conditions. Once a skier has mastered most slopes and conditions, racing is an excellent test of real ability as well as the best way to advance beyond the average ceiling of recreational ability. Nastar racing has become very popular with the public in the last ten years. Advanced Nastar and more difficult sanctioned racing should become more popular with adult, recreational skiers as the general public skill level continues to improve.

The evolution to a modern technique alluded to refers basically to a down motion at the beginning of the turn which, in turn, allows a better chance of pressing the ski into an edged (body and knee angulated), carving turn. The subsequent up motion really should be thought of more as a finish of the preceding turn than, as in the old days, as a beginning of the next. The remainder of this book is devoted to explaining the mechanics of these principles.

Boots, Bindings And Poles

There are three basic concerns in skiing; the skier, the skis, and the hill. There are also three lesser, but still important, factors in the total equation that need to be discussed briefly. Other authors, noticeably Witherell in *How The Racers Ski*, devote many pages to these subjects.

The boots should allow forward movement of the lower leg while maintaining the plane of movement parallel to the ski. In other words, the knee should be perpendicular over the flat ski as it presses forward. The forward resistance to flex should be fairly soft to allow substantial leg movement. On the other hand, the initial movement should not be so loose as to negate an intimate feel with the ski. The resistance to forward flex should steadily increase as the knee is pressed forward and not sharply increase all of a sudden at some point in forward flexure.

Rearword movement of the leg should be limited to just less than a vertically locked position. If the leg can be easily locked vertically as in standing, the skier will have to lean too far back in order to apply leverage to the rear of the ski. This is a delicate balance between being able to stand comfortably and ski correctly. The better, higher performance boots opt for skiing. Too much forward lean with the boots flat on the floor is wrong since it would put the knees much too far forward when the skis are inclined on a hill.

Sideways stiffness in the boot should be quite high so that any slight changes in angulation can be directly transmitted to the ski as edge control. However, several boots from the past, notably Rosemont and Raichle (red, clamshell), were too rigid laterally because of their fiberglass construction. This eliminated any possibility of compliance and shock absorption between the edged ski and the leg.

Modern safety bindings are extremely complicated and sophisticated. If one were to locate all of the binding patents in the world, the stack would probably be two feet high. Out of these concepts have come very few, popular, successful bindings on the market today. The design objective is simple; keep the boot on the ski until an abnormal force, applied for a significant duration of time, requires a release. The commercial approach to the problem still follows one of two schools of thought: metal to metal release with some form of plate, and metal to boot release without an intermediate plate. In the past, the difference in boot design and materials have justified the plate as the only defined structure that could be predictably located and released. More recently, however, largely due to the efforts of ski safety standardization committee work, there have been tremendous strides made toward defining the boot sole as the "plate" function. This makes the plate, as a separate member, redundant to the boot sole.

Regardless if there is a separate plate, or the boot sole is functioning as a plate, there is a certain interaction of forces between the rigid "plate" and the flexing ski. This is especially true as ski designs have become more flexible in the midsection. This interaction forces the boot to exert a compressive force in the binding when the ski is bent. It is conceivable (albeit highly doubtful) that this may happen exactly at the time a release is needed. The solution to this problem is a well designed binding with a heel that can move aft slightly as the ski is bent; or a Spademan binding that attaches to only the center of the boot. Unfortunately, the Spademan binding requires that a plate be attached permanently to the boot sole and there can be a slightly unnerving feeling of toe movement between the boot and the ski. This difference has no bearing on the mechanics of skiing, as long as there is not a looseness or decoupling between the body of the boot and the ski.

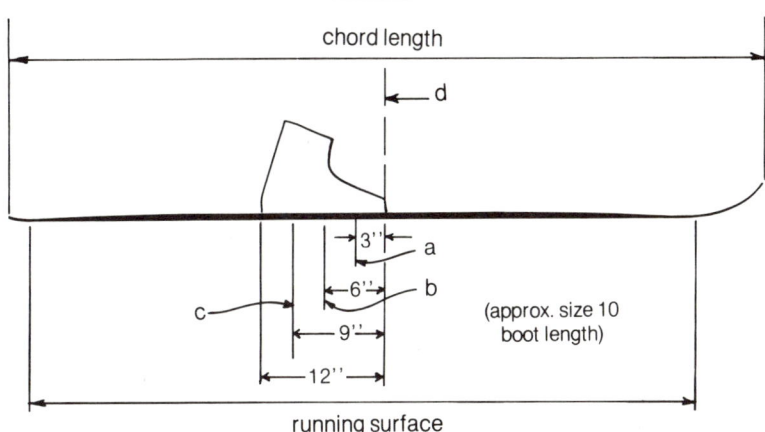

a = midpoint of running surface and ball of foot.
b = midcavity boot location mark
c = approximate center of skiing forces and narrowest point of the waist.
d = midpoint chord length and approximate toe of boot.

Binding adjustment is also a personal thing. The personal weights, strengths, abilities and styles of skiing require different settings. The best bet is to err on the lower setting side and gradually tighten the setting if there are any premature releases. Binding release testers are good, but they still have to be used based on a norm and not a particular individual.

Binding placement standardization has been proposed by the ASTM ski safety committees. Most new boots have a midpoint boot mark that should be aligned with corresponding marks on the ski. This has the advantage of placing small or large boots in the same centered position on the ski. As a general rule, this midboot location is about 6 inches behind the mid-chord length of the ski (6 inches behind the toe of a normal boot) and 3 inches behind the ski running surface midpoint. The result is that the center of forces acting through the leg, ankle, and boot concentrate on the ski about 9 to 10 inches behind the mid chord length of the ski. This coincides nicely with the typical narrowest point in the side cut, although it is usually behind the flex center of the ski. The flex center is the point near the center of the ski around which equal torques at either end will give equal deflection.

The proposed standardization consists only of each complying ski manufacturer showing on his skis where he feels the mid cavity boot location should be. The actual mid points of running surface, flex balance, and waist location vary between manufacturers and models depending on the intended market and the designer's philosophies.

Also, by ASTM standardization (F474-76) the total binding area of the ski has been locally strengthened to insure that the binding screws will not pull out. If the bindings are placed using the proposed midboot location marks, the binding screws will be well within the reinforced area of the ski.

The ski pole is the only part of the equipment which hasn't changed much in the last fifteen years. Aluminum alloys and tube drawing processes have not changed. The less expensive poles use lower cost alloys and are subject to bending. The higher priced

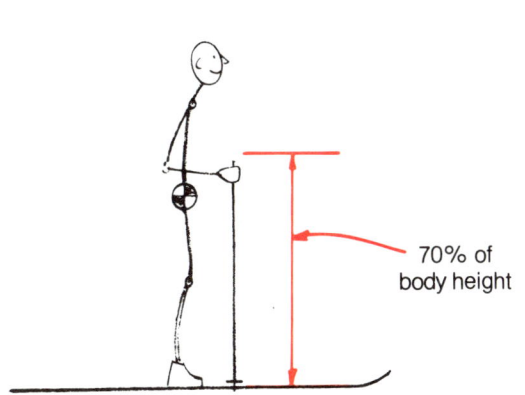

70% of body height

poles use heat-treated, aircraft alloys and will not bend, but are sensitive to cracking at a deep knotch. Baskets have become a little smaller. Breakaway handles have been developed. There have also been minor innovations in tips and shock absorbing handles. None of these, however, are involved in an analysis of ski mechanics.

Ski pole length is one subject open to some question. In the last three decades, pole length has varied from very short to very long, to finally, something in between. The best rule of thumb is that with the arms relaxed and bent 90° at the elbow, so the forearm is horizontal, the pole should penetrate the snow to the basket. Another way of quantifying pole length is that it should be 70% of body height.

chapter 4

THE PLAYING FIELD

THE THIRD PART OF THE SKIER—SKI—SNOW SURFACE system is the snow/ice surface, including the terrain and environment that skiing is done on (in). This is the most elusive aspect of any discussion concerning the mechanics of alpine skiing. The infinite number of combinations of slopes and snow conditions make any one ski design somewhat specialized. But, it is this variety of conditions, combined with other elements of skiing, such as clear fresh air, physical invigoration, visual beauty, the social aspects (or opportunities for isolation), and the thrill of controlled speeds, that make skiing one of the most enjoyable endeavors pursuable by man.

With most product designs, the engineer at least has some quantitative definition of the end use of his design. This is not the case for the ski designer. He is faced with a myriad of needs and conditions that frequently contradict one another. His only approach is to concentrate on the primary variables that are related to ski design and have a direct bearing on the mechanics of the sport. The theoretical approach covered in the remainder of this book is built on the assumption that the ski slope is a smooth, hard, planar surface inclined to the horizontal at some angle. Any skier knows that this is hardly the case in real life for more than a few feet. If it is the case, alpine skiing can become boring unless there is competition (like tennis) or the hill angle becomes substantial. Truly, the beauty and challenge of alpine skiing is the creativity required to handle the deviations from the textbook case... once the rudiments of the sport are learned. The remainder of the book does cover the textbook case of a smooth planar surface, but before getting into the mechanics, we need further discussion on the total environmental spectrum. This will put the theory in the correct context.

Snow Conditions

Snow is a crystalline, solid form of moisture. It can be pure, sparkling beauty or a frigid encumbrance. In its new fallen, soft state, it will not support the high pressure of man's weight on his feet alone. Man soon found that if he distributed his weight over a larger area and reduced the pressure, he could travel on the new snow. It was also logical to some ancient creative traveler that this larger-area device be long, narrow, smooth, and turned up at its leading end so he could slide as well as walk. In the old days, as soon as the snow was packed hard, the traveler would discard the wide area traveling devices and revert to his feet (or his horse) or use a sliding device with a much narrower runner. A narrow, hard runner was all that was required to support his weight if the snow became very hard.

A modern skier is faced with the whole spectrum of snow conditions; from the deep, new powder to solid white or blue ice. Each blend of conditions presents a different problem and challenge to the skier and the designer of his skis. Usually, any new snow is quickly packed by machines and skiers to a fairly hard, smooth surface. It continues to harden as days go by until new snow comes, the old snow is chopped up by machine, or the skiers start to quit because the sport is unenjoyable. The addition of rain or high moisture man-made snow will encourage the hardening so that some type of pulverization is frequently needed. Also, as soon as some areas of the slope become so hard that skidding becomes more common, then the conditions rapidly deteriorate to a checkerboard of icy, skidded patches and piled up softer snow. The advanced skier who can carve his turns on sharp edges can negotiate the changing surface. The poorer skier who is skidding most of the time becomes very much at the mercy of the inconsistent snow/ice surface which he himself has helped to make.

The complete skier needs to know how to adjust his technique and equipment needs to any type of possible snow conditions. The following is an attempt to categorize them as well as the related ski design and technique.

Soft Snow... This is deeper than two or three inches and the buoyancy of the ski begins to be a factor in the way the ski bends, as opposed to just the carving effect of the edge. The best skis here are wider and softer in flex. Torsional stiffness and damping are less important and it is better if these are reduced somewhat, especially if the snow is heavy. The problem of skiing in soft snow is one of making the skis bend through the snow and turn. If the snow is light, shallow, or the radius of turn and speed are high, or the hill angle steeper; the turning problem is minimized. If the snow is deep, or heavy, and/or the hill is shallow and speed is low; then excessive movements are required to turn.

Normal Packed Snow...   This is snow that has been packed or has been 'skied out' for a day or two with overnight cold to further harden it. Good man-made snow would also fall in this category. This is the easiest surface to ski on since it is possible to get good lateral adhesion against the skis and, thereby, reduce skidding to a minimum. It is also less tiring and technically demanding than the extremes of snow conditions. The ski design is best if compromised to a conventional side cut, damping, width and flex. This means that the same design can be used fairly well in soft snow and ice, although it is not biased towards these extreme conditions.

Icy, Hard Surfaces...   Warm weather, lack of snow, and heavy traffic tend to shift conditions toward hardpack and ice. Therefore, the challenge of ice is more prevalent than that of deep and heavy powder. Many ski designs are biased to accomodate the harder conditions. Also, since racing requires this type of surface, any racing skis or quasi-racing skis need to be designed accordingly. Specifically, the skis are narrower, torsionally stiffer, and damper. The turning radius will be more dependent on the theoretical case of the side cut arc intersecting with a hard, planar surface. Therefore, the side cut will determine the type of turn intended; ie. long radius or short radius. The longitudinal flex of the ski will become stiffer and the optimum flex will depend largely on the skier's weight. The pressure distribution against the hard surfaces needs to be just high enough at the ski extremities to provide control and stability, but not so much as to release prematurely at the tip or tail, or to be too stiff in concave surfaces. The ski technique becomes a challenge of holding instead of initiating turns. Very precise edge control and a quiet upper body are required. Good angulation and timely, instantaneous weighting of the skis is also required.

There are many variations of the three basic snow conditions. The real challenge of skiing is when the variations are mixed in the space of a few feet. The expert skier knows intuitively how to 'read' these conditions and make quick adjustments in his body forces against his skis. To conclude; a more precise, carving technique is much better in changeable conditions than a skidding technique which places extra emphasis on the widely varying lateral adhesion.

At one time or another, skiing has been tried on water, artificial surfaces, hay, pine needles, sand, and with rollers on a dry, hard surface. Only the water skiing and skateboarding have survived as legitimate sports. The natural dual state (solid—liquid) of water provides a lubricity and unique feeling that make snow skiing what it is. As soon as the dry outer layer of sand or sawdust is scraped off, the wet layers underneath are very slow. The use of rollers does not give the subtle blend between carving and skidding that is necessary for energy dissipation or making turns with other than carved radii.

Terrain

Added to the blend and complexity of snow surfaces is another infinite range of terrain that the snow surface covers. Pitches, angles, rolls, and any combination offer enough challenge for any creative skier. Continued adjustments of technique are required. All the nicely worked out understanding of the mechanics becomes academic because things are happening too fast. This is not to under-value the mechanics. It is to point out that there is no time for static forces and body positions. A proper understanding of the mechanics should be worked out beforehand. As terrain changes become extreme, some of the optimum mechanics reverse completely; ie. instead of upweighting at some point in a turn, the skier would be better to down-unweight.

The fundamental terrain parameter is that of hill angle. This angle of steepness is called (a) in the subsequent mechanics and is included in all of the equations involving the forces between the skis and the slope.

A consistent hill angle is modified by concavity or convexity (in its extreme, called a mogul). The deviations in forces due to these terrain changes are covered in detail in the following chapters. It is especially important to understand temporary, terrain-caused increases or decreases in force by the skis against the slope so that complimentary, concurrent changes can be made with the thigh muscles. This insures proper contact with the slope throughout the turn.

Speed

Velocity is relative. If the terrain is smooth and wide open, high speeds are easy. If visibility is bad and the terrain or snow surface are inconsistent, even a few miles per hour becomes an exciting challenge. Unlike driving a car, a skier can quickly approach whatever speed is comfortable or exciting to himself personally. Part of the creativity of skiing is the continual modification of speed to cope with or challenge the dual variety of snow conditions and terrain.

Velocity enters directly into any theoretical discussion of the mechanics. In fact, with regards to wind drag, kinetic energy, or centrifugal force; velocity enters as a squared term. In other words, twice the velocity has four times the effect. This is an especially important concept because we are intuitively used to things being linear in their effect; e.g., while you may feel that a higher speed simply causes a higher centrifugal force for a given radius turn, theory shows us that, in fact, this happens more emphatically than we would expect.

Maximum speed is not extremely important to the recreational skier; however, to the racer, it is everything. Races are won or lost by very slight differences in average speed. A one percent variation at 30 miles per hour over a one minute course will mean the difference of 26.4 feet or 0.6 seconds at the end of the run. It therefore is extremely important for the racer to ski very smoothly and efficiently and strive for a higher average speed. This might sound naive, but this type of skiing can be quite different from excessively aggressive or erratic skiing.

Visibility

The skier's eyes are an integral part of his information loop. The feedback to his central computer, through the sense of sight, is an absolute necessity. Even a blind skier needs a guide. Anyone who has skied in a "white out" of fog or snow knows the helpless feeling of being unable to differentiate between sliding, falling, and which way is up or down. Flat light and poor visibility are variations of this problem that severely challenge the skier's abilities. A reference such as a tree, track or another skier will help considerably. The shadows cast by trees along the edge of the trail are a hindrance on sunny days, but a definite help on poor days when the sun's rays are reflecting off from millions of moisture particles. Night skiing represents another visibility problem, especially for the myopic skier. There are no easy solutions to any of the visibility problems. Different colored lenses may help in certain visual environments, but the improvement will not be great.

The speed and cold associated with skiing infers some type of eye protection. This will not necessarily improve visibility except to prevent the eyes from watering. Conversely, the goggles or glasses have a tendency to fog and may add to the visibility problem. The only solutions here are special anti-fog goggles with, if necessary, an anti-fog coating on the lenses.

Temperature

Water changes from solid to liquid at 32 °F (0 °C). Below this temperature snow is good, ice is bad. Above this temperature, snow is bad and ice is good. As the temperature gets very low, the snow ceases to provide the lubricity for the ski to slide until a "break point" is reached and the speed obtained generates sufficient friction. Warmer, wet snow is terrible for sliding, especially if it's machine-made snow which includes oil and it, in turn, collects on the surface.

Full range skiing can involve any of the above conditions, and you should know how to cope with each. Proper waxing will help considerably. A smooth, waxed ski base is best at normal skiing temperatures between about 10°F and 32°F. Below 10°F the hard snow crystals don't melt to provide lubricity except at higher speed. It is therefore better to remove all the wax when it is very cold. Steel or copper wool can be used for this. Above 32°F, if the snow has been alternately melted and frozen into large ice kernels called corn snow, there is no problem with sliding as long as normal wax is used. If the snow is new powder, thawed for the first time, it is the slowest surface imaginable. The only hope for speed is to wax with a yellow paraffin and use 'steps' or other surface roughness to break the suction caused by the excess moisture.

One of the greatest satisfactions of skiing is beating the combined challenge of temperature, visibility and weather by being properly conditioned, clothed and outfitted to enjoy skiing in its most natural state. This always occurs at a time when most skiers have been beaten indoors and the lifts and slopes are deserted. Cold and the other environmental hindrances add to the challenge of skiing after mastering the mechanics of the perfect turn in perfect snow.

Competition

The true competition of skiing (like sailing, climbing and running) is its form of 'mini-living'; ie. compressing the challenges and unknowns typical of life itself into a few hours to see how we can innovate to cope with them. Our morality and human frailness can be tested without having to take a fatal step. This is an 'alone' trip and only we know the personal score. The mountain itself is the opponent. We may master it under certain conditions, but at another time it will gain the upper hand; especially if combined with some of the other adversaries mentioned above.

There is no real measure of how we are meeting this challenge as compared to our fellow skiers unless we ski through the same situation and compare speed or style. The common yardstick has traditionally been the time required to negotiate a specific course. Since soft snow varies from skier to skier and trees are hard, flagged courses on prepared snow have become the accepted race course. Skiing differs from other sports in that formal competition is only pursued by a small percentage of total participants. This is probably because there is enough challenge already presented by the combination of all the other variables. However, as more and more skiers master most of the environmental challenges, human competition should become more and more prevalent to test the skier to the limit.

The perfection required to excell in competition accentuates the need for a better understanding of all the mechanics related to skiing. The racer has always led the way to better skiing. Older techniques were frequently at odds with the optimization of force and movements. It was the racer who made the breakthrough in each progressive step, moving from the old open christies to the parallel, and from the skidded skiing of the 50's and 60's to the independent leg movement, down-up, and carved skiing of the 70's.

The forces involved in skiing are the same for the recreational skier and the racer; therefore, the mechanics should be the same. The exception is that the racer is concerned with maximizing speed and minimizing energy loss. The recreational skier may wish to dissipate a considerable amount of energy via skidding at specific times. There are several fine books written regarding ski racing. A further discussion of this subject will be referred to these excellent author-coaches who are well recognized in their field.

chapter 5

A PREFACE TO THE MECHANICS

THE PURPOSE OF THIS CHAPTER is to present an overview of the principles developed in the later chapters, but without the algebraic analysis.

Alpine skiing, in its most simple form, consists of gliding straight down the fall line with the skis flat against the snow. The force due to gravity pulls the skier down the slope with only sliding friction and wind resistance to limit his speed. The skier will accelerate until the sum of these resisting forces equals the component of gravitational pull *in the direction of travel*. This concept is fairly simple and its comprehensive analysis is primarily of concern to the downhill racer.

The next level of complexity is to place the skis on their uphill edges and traverse at some angle across the fall line. This introduces two more factors; the angle of traverse and the angle that the ski running surface is edged against the slope. The traverse is usually treated as motion in a straight direction but, since the skis have side camber and the slope is a fairly hard, packed surface, the skis will tend to carve uphill. This is truly a carved turn, although usually of very long radius. As long as speed is low and the hill is not extremely steep, centrifugal force is not a factor. As speed and/or hill steepness increase, however, centrifugal force begins to become significant.

The centrifugal force may add to or subtract from the force due to gravity and suddenly the algebraic analysis begins to become complicated. Likewise, the situation on the ski hill also becomes less clear, and from here on it is hoped that a more comprehensive algebraic analysis will guide us to a better understanding of the sport.

So far we have not thought of the traverse as a turn, although it is usually (and easily) curved. This long radius track made by the ski on its edge is only dependent upon the geometry of the ski and the angle at which the ski is edged. This is much like a car with the steering wheel locked into only one very long turn up the hill. This would be a very panicky feeling if we were not free to deviate from the set course. As accomplished skiers, we really expect to be able to turn at any radius, anywhere on the slope, in any snow conditions and at any velocity... yet the ski wants to make only one very long, carved turn. To make the skis deviate from their natural carved turn, we have to initiate any number of additional forces and establish some type of skidding mode.

We have heard and read much about the elusive 'carved turn.' Some would argue that it is not truly possible, but a ski tracking on its edge is carving. If a ski is skidding, it is dissipating energy and is much more sensitive to variations in the snow surface. It is like a car skidding sideways around a corner instead of tracking cleanly. Therefore, it is the underlying premise of this book that carving is desirable and, whereas it is not always exactly achievable, at least should be approached as closely as possible.

Now, we have two types of turns under consideration; the natural carved turn that the *ski* wants to make and ALL the turns *we* want to make. The challenge of modern, accomplished skiing is to bring these two types as closely together as possible as frequently as possible as we descend the mountain. We do need to skid sometimes in order to dissipate energy (in the form of speed). Therefore, it would be nice to understand the mechanics of skidding as well as pure carving.

One unique phenomenon about skiing is that the compaction and lubricity of the snow crystals allow us to easily drift back and forth in the gray area between carving and skidding. By carving in one part of the turn and skidding in another, we can vary the radius at will. The subsequent chapters show a proposed mechanical analysis of the interaction of the primary forces involved as we vary the turn radius. The last chapter adds the secondary forces at our disposal. These are usually necessary in order to vary the turn radius as desired and, at least, can be used to enhance the efficiency of the turn.

The arguments have been made that a skier is either a 'skidder' or a 'carver'... or a racer never skids. It might be better to say that a certain skier's style is characterized by a habit or tendency (conscious or subconscious) to skid or carve. The two styles are quite different and easily distinguishable between the form of a racer (or expert free skier) and the average recreational skier. The average recreational skier is severely encumbered by the habit of skidding, and by practicing these habits repetitively he only reinforces them and will never change his style and ski like an 'expert.' Yet, if he is properly instructed and understands the mechanics of what is happening, he can begin to reestablish his movements into a carving style of skiing. This is usually a difficult task because it will mean making some movements just the opposite or at different parts in the turn than in the past. He may start his new learning process systematically, but as soon as fear or some other preoccupation takes over his mind, the body will naturally revert back to the old habits. It therefore takes a dogged persistence, as well as good physical strength, to master the correct movements. A clear cerebral picture of what is happening is usually helpful, and it is with this intent that the remainder of this book is offered.

chapter 6

THE MECHANICS
OF STRAIGHT GLIDING

G RAVITATIONAL FORCE IS ACTING upon all of us, all the time. Consider the skier in figure 6—1 on the following page.

In the straight gliding case, the direction of travel is considered to be the steepest inclination of slope or the fall line. In this direction, a snowball will roll. Travel at some angle to the fall line is called traversing, and is covered in Chapter 7. In straight gliding, the component of force pulling the skier down the mountain, *in the direction of travel*, is dependent upon the skier's weight and the steepness of the hill. This force is ($F_g \sin \alpha$). As the hill gets steeper, ($\sin \alpha$) increases and this basic force also increases.

The skier will accelerate according to Newton's second law due to the action of gravity ($F_g \sin \alpha$) on the skier's mass ($M = F_g/g$). The acceleration will generally be retarded by the forces of snow friction, air friction or drag, or braking force; and may be aided by the added physical force of poling or skating. These observations are summarized in the force equilibrium equation:

$$(6\text{—}1) \qquad \frac{F_g}{g}\, a = F_g \sin \alpha - F_f - F_w$$

where, for the present, we assume that the skier is not braking, poling or skating. The skier will continue to gain speed until the sum of the frictional forces equals the force pulling the skier down the hill and a maximum speed is reached (assuming the skier is not braking). At that time, the acceleration (a) is zero and we have

$$(6\text{—}2) \qquad F_g \sin \alpha = F_f + F_w$$

The air friction force (F_w) is a function of the frontal area of the body (A), the streamline shape of the body, the velocity in the

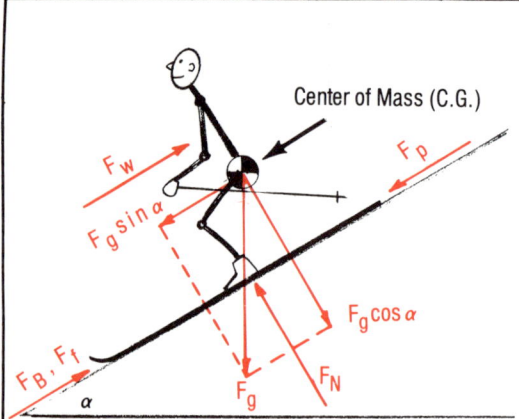

Center of Mass (C.G.)

F_w

$F_g \sin \alpha$

F_p

$F_g \cos \alpha$

F_B, F_f

F_g

F_N

α

Figure 6—1

F_g = gravitational force; ie. weight of skier (including boots and skis) assumed acting through skier's center of mass (CG).

F_f = friction (sliding) force

F_w = air frictional force

F_p = added physical force; such as poling or skating.

F_T = total force on the snow; perpendicular to the snow ($F_T = F_g \pm F_D$).

F_A = boot toe reaction force.

F_B = braking force.

F_C = top of boot reaction force.

F_D = temporary inertial force caused by vertical acceleration of the skier's mass.

F_N = normal reaction force; equal and opposite to ($F_g \cos \alpha \pm F_D$).

$F_g \cos \alpha$ = normal force perpendicular to the slope.

$F_g \sin \alpha$ = force to accelerate mass (F_g/g) in the direction of travel.

a = acceleration of the CG in the direction of travel.

a_v = acceleration of the CG in the direction perpendicular to the slope surface.

V = velocity in the direction of travel.

g = acceleration due to gravity (a constant on the earth's surface equal to 32 ft/sec²).

α = angle of inclination of the slope.

X_1 = perpendicular distance between the center of wind resistance and the CG.

air past the body (V), and the density of the air (ϱ).

$$(6-3) \qquad F_w = C_D \frac{\varrho}{2} AV^2$$

In textbook mechanics, the sliding friction force is dependent upon the coefficient of friction and the gravitational force (weight) perpendicular or normal to the hill. The friction of a ski sliding on snow is significantly more complex than that, but we will use the simplified equation:

$$(6-4) \qquad F_f = C_f F_g \cos \alpha$$

If we were to combine equations 6—2, 6—3, and 6—4; we would arrive at the following expression at maximum speed:

$$(6-5) \qquad F_g \sin \alpha = C_f F_g \cos \alpha + C_D \varrho A \frac{V^2}{2}$$

or, rearranging and solving for V:

$$(6-6) \qquad V = \sqrt{2F_g \frac{(\sin \alpha - \cos \alpha \, C_F)}{C_D \varrho A}}$$

Several real life examples of 6—6 might be:

$$C_D = 0.5, A = 5 \text{ ft}^2, \varrho = 0.0023 \text{ \# sec}^2/\text{ft}^4$$

$$C_F = 0.03, \alpha = 10°, F_g = 150 \text{ pounds}$$

where solving for V we have

$$(6-6a) \qquad V = 86.7 \text{ ft/sec}$$

or, by leaving all other factors constant and changing the skier's weight (F_g) from 150 pounds to 200 pounds, we again solve for V and find:

$$(6-6b) \qquad V = 100 \text{ ft/sec}$$

From this analysis, it would appear that the heavier skier with the same frontal area and aerodynamic shape would reach a higher maximum speed during straight gliding. This conclusion also makes sense if we consider only equation 6—6. Since weight (F_g) would be expected to increase as the cube of any linear dimension change, and area (A) only as the square of a linear dimension change for a similarly shaped body, then we would

X_2 = perpendicular distance between ($F_g \sin \alpha$ or CG) and the slope surface.

X_3 = perpendicular distance between the reaction force F_N and the CG.

X_4 = perpendicular distance between the reaction force and the boot heel.

X_5 = perpendicular distance between the toe and heel of the boot.

X_6 = perpendicular distance between the boot heel and top of the boot.

C_F = coefficient of friction (0.02 to 0.1 by test).

C_D = drag coefficient depending on the shape of the body (0.2 to 1.0 by test).

ϱ = air density = 0.0023 lb. sec²/ft⁴
Note: Air density would decrease to 0.0017 lb. sec²/ft⁴ at 10,000 ft. and also decrease by 4% as temperature increases from 10° to 30°F.

M = mass = F_g / g

expect the numerator of 6—6 to increase faster than the denominator, as all the linear dimensions increase in the similar bodies. In real life, a solid, chunky skier should make a faster downhill racer than a long, lean skier.

There are many other conclusions that could be drawn from equation 6—6; for instance,

1. Since (V) is dependent upon the square root of a number of variables, there is a rather abrupt terminal speed for all skiers, even with substantial changes in the variables. This is of interest to the recreational skier. It means that there's not much holding this skier back at slow speeds except for his own efforts at dissipating energy or staying on a flatter (less α) hill. At higher speeds, wind resistance makes a big difference and it is difficult to go much faster than the slope of the hill will allow. This is one reason why experts seem to ski more effortlessly. They have wind resistance helping them at higher speeds and they don't have to use as much muscular energy to keep their speed down.

   Another example is that if you start a straight run (schuss) higher and higher up a hill, you don't go proportionately faster. You might think that since you approached your own comfortable speed limit starting way down the hill, that it would be impossible for you to start schussing higher up the hill. Yet, in reality, even if you started much higher, you might reach a speed only a little higher than in the first case.

2. The racer, on the other hand, is extremely interested in even minute increases of speed. The racer tries to decrease frontal area (A) and the drag coefficient (C_D) by assuming the best possible "egg" position. National team racers have used wind tunnels to optimize (C_D) and have found that just a hand out in the air stream can significantly increase (C_D). A downhill racer can also use a drastic increase in (A) to slow down just by standing up and "windchecking."

3. It is also interesting to see the effect that changes in air density (ϱ) due to altitude and temperature have on maximum velocity. The best chance for a speed record on skis will be at high altitude on a warmer day — assuming there is not a negative effect of temperature on the coefficient of sliding friction (C_F).

4. The whole subject of sliding friction (C_F) is very complex. It diminishes in importance as the hill gets steeper and (cos α) decreases. Proper waxing is much more important when racing on flatter courses. Also, in real life (C_F) will vary with many factors; such as the skier's weight, velocity, the way the skis are ridden, the type of snow crystals, the snow temperature, and the shape of the skis. It has been found that usually (C_F) decreases very sharply on very cold snow above a certain velocity. At this point there is enough friction generated to melt the snow crystals so they cease to drag on the bottom of the ski like dry sand. On

wet snow, the suction of too smooth a ski base acts as a drag as the ski surface "wets" with water.

5. If the skier were to introduce a braking maneuver by forcing the skis into a snow plow or skid, a new force (F_B) is introduced which is significantly larger than (F_w) and (F_f). In this case, the latter two items become comparatively insignificant and at any low constant velocity:

(6—7) $F_B = F_g \sin \alpha$

From this equation we infer that all braking force is absorbed through the leg muscles. It is also proportional to the steepness of the hill. Again, the expert who can ski faster and has wind resistance (F_w) helping is considerably less tired at the end of the day than a struggling beginner, even in the same physical condition. Similarly, (F_f) is much higher in deep snow, which explains simply why it is so much easier to ski steep hills in soft snow. The snow holds you back and controls your speed.

6. At slow speeds, and at the start of a run, where there is little wind resistance and, if no additional physical force (F_p) is added, such as from poling or skating, the small amount of friction force (F_f) is far less than the basic force ($F_g \sin \alpha$) available to pull the skier down the hill. Therefore, the net difference in these two forces will accelerate the skier:

(6—8) $F_g \sin \alpha - C_f F_g \cos \alpha = Ma = \dfrac{F_g}{g} a$

As can be seen, the skier's weight (F_g) cancels out, and the acceleration is equal to:

(6—9) $a = g(\sin \alpha - C_F \cos \alpha)$

In other words, without muscular effort, a skier's acceleration from rest is only dependent on the angle of the hill and the coefficient of sliding friction. If we take the lowest measured value of sliding friction for a ski on snow ($C_F = 0.02$), equation 6—9 becomes:

(6—9a) $a = 32 \text{ ft/sec}^2 (\sin \alpha - 0.020 \cos \alpha)$

or, for zero acceleration:

(6—9b) $0 = 32 \text{ ft/sec}^2 (\sin \alpha - 0.020 \cos \alpha)$

and rearranging, and setting either term equal to zero:

$$(6\text{--}9c) \qquad 0.02 = \frac{\sin\alpha}{\cos\alpha} = \tan\alpha, \; \alpha = 1.15°$$

On any hill steeper than $\alpha = 1.15°$, sliding will continue once started. This is one explanation of the unique beauty of skiing; like a wheel on a hard surface, (C_F) is very low and movement can take place on a very shallow hill angle.

7. If physical force (F_p) is added in the direction of travel, the equation of motion becomes:

$$(6\text{--}10) \qquad F_g \sin\alpha + F_p - C_F F_g \cos\alpha = \frac{F_g}{g} a$$

Or, by rearranging:

$$(6\text{--}10a) \qquad a = g\left[\sin\alpha + \frac{F_p}{F_g} - C_F\cos\alpha\right]$$

In this case, the ratio of (F_p) over (F_g) shows that the additional physical force (F_p) due to poling or skating must be proportional to the skier's weight (F_g) in order for a heavier skier to accelerate as fast as a light skier. Also, acceleration can now take place on the level where $(\sin\alpha)$ is equal to zero as long as (F_p/F_g) exceeds $(C_F\cos\alpha)$.

The Normal Reaction Force Center And Its Location

Figure 6—2

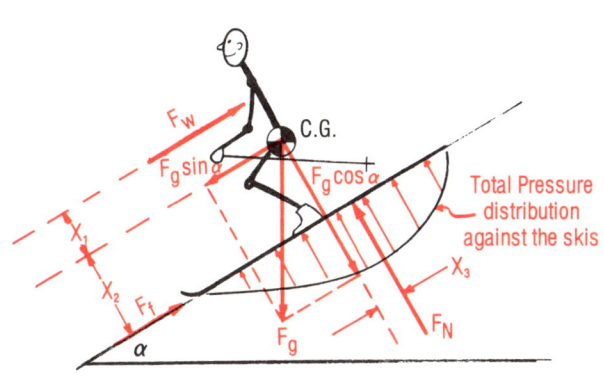

Total Pressure distribution against the skis

Up to this point, we have not concerned ourselves with the skier's vertical position over the skis. We will now investigate the mechanics of the body stance in terms of the external forces that are acting upon the skier/ski system during straight running. For the purpose of simplification, we will not include internal muscular caused forces (F_p) or temporary vertical forces (F_D). These will be added later.

The gravitational force (F_g) is constant, always vertical, and always acting through the center of gravity. The wind resistance (F_w), as was shown earlier, is dependent upon many factors. The sliding friction (F_f) is a function of the ski surface and the snow surface. Finally, the reaction force by the snow surface against the skis (F_N) and its location (X_3) is dependent upon the other three forces. This reaction force (F_N) is a singular, concentrated force representing the entire pressure distribution against the ski.

The action of $(F_g\sin\alpha)$ will cause the skier to accelerate until it is

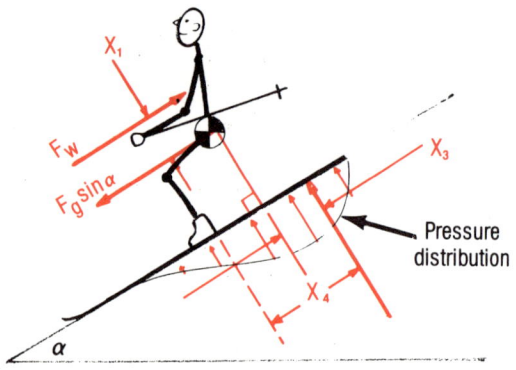

Figure 6—3
Skier standing tall and leaning backward (sliding friction negligible).

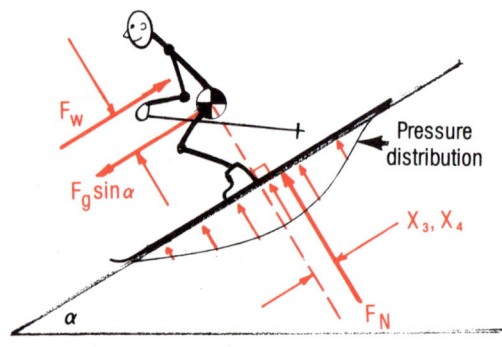

Figure 6—4
Skier standing tall and pressing forward (sliding friction negligible)

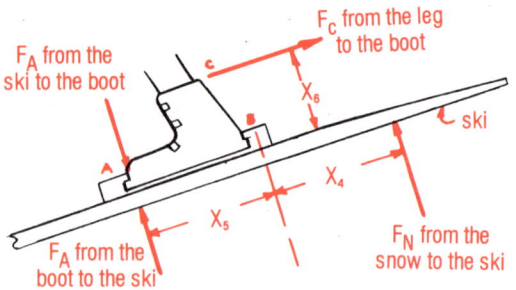

Figure 6—5
As the distance X_4 increases, there is a greater twisting moment exerted against the boot/leg system. For the ski to remain in equilibrium, the normal reaction force (F_N) and its moment arm (X_4) to the boot heel must be balanced by a toe reaction force (F_A).

opposed equally by a summation of the two resistances (F_w) and (F_f).

For a smooth slope, and as long as the skier maintains his muscular rigidity so that he does not collapse or tip over, the location of (F_N) from the C.G. as shown by (X_3) will be automatically determined by the magnitudes of the external forces (F_w) and (F_f) and their perpendicular distances from the center of gravity. There are more and less favorable places for (F_N) to occur, so we will investigate this subject in greater detail.

For tipping equilibrium, the summation of moments about the C.G. must be equal to zero.

$$(6—11) \qquad F_w \cdot X_1 = F_f \cdot X_2 + F_N \cdot X_3$$

In real life, there are an infinite number of possibilities for the stable equilibrium situation; as represented in figures 6—3 and 6—4. In both these situations, provided sliding friction is negligible with respect to wind resistance,

$$(6—11a) \qquad F_N \cdot X_3 = F_w \cdot X_1; \quad \text{or } X_3 = \frac{F_w}{F_N} \cdot X_1$$

At the terminal velocity, when (F_w) is equal and opposite to ($F_g \sin \alpha$) and, since (F_N) is equal to ($F_g \cos \alpha$), we have:

$$(6—11b) \qquad X_3 = \frac{F_g \sin \alpha}{F_g \cos \alpha} \cdot X_1 = \tan \alpha \cdot X_1$$

In other words, as the hill angle (α) increases, the tangent of (α) also increases and (X_3) increases in magnitude with respect to (X_1).

In figures 6—6 and 6—7, we have the situation where the wind resistance (F_w) isn't causing a tipping moment around the C.G., but the sliding friction (F_f) causes a counter-clockwise moment by acting through the perpendicular distance (X_2). For tipping equilibrium, the reaction force (F_N) has to move in front of the line through the C.G. and perpendicular to the slope.

$$(6—11c) \qquad F_N \cdot X_3 = F_f \cdot X_2$$

We could go on and on investigating various combinations of (F_w), (F_f), (X_1), and (X_2), but the thing we're even more interested in is the distance (X_4) between the normal reaction force and the boot. As this distance (X_4) increases, there is more and more twisting moment, or leverage, exerted against the boot/leg system. For the ski itself to be in equilibrium, the normal reaction force (F_N) and its moment arm (X_4) to the boot heel must be balanced by a toe reaction force (F_A). By taking moments around (B), we have:

$$(6—12) \qquad F_N \cdot X_4 = F_A \cdot X_5$$

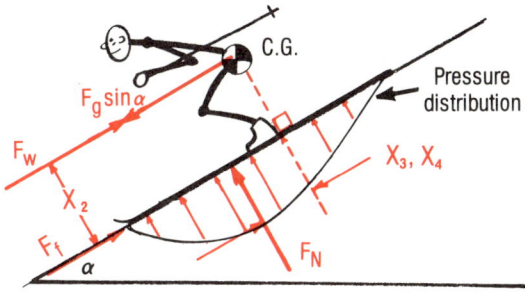

Figure 6—6
Skier crouched so that (F_w) and ($F_g \sin \alpha$) are colinear and (F_f) is similar in magnitude to (F_w). Skier pressing forward.

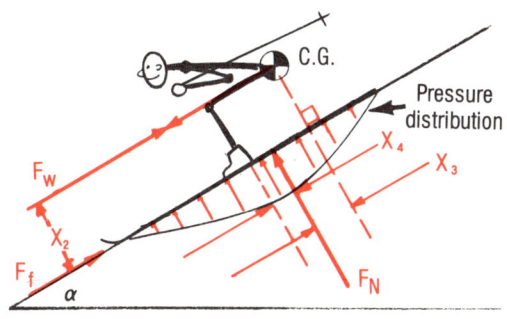

Figure 6—7
Skier crouched so that (F_w) and ($F_g \sin \alpha$) are colinear and (F_f) is similar in magnitude to (F_w). Skier pressing backward.

Figure 6—8
In real life situations, the distance (X_3) between the reaction force (F_N) and the line through the CG and perpendicular to the snow surface is quite small.

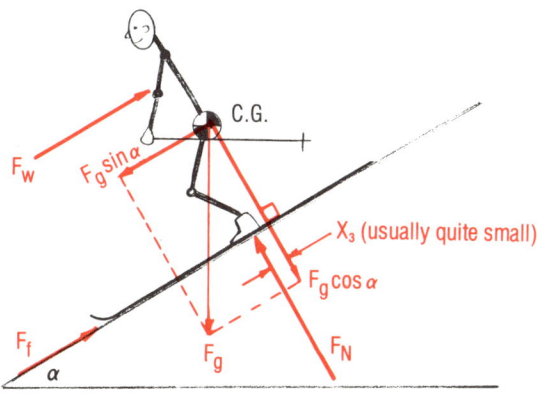

Now we can readily see that (assuming the boot contacts the ski at (A) and (B), if the skier adjusts his body position to have (F_N) act in a line through (B); the lever arm (X_4) reduces to zero and the vertical toe reaction force (F_A) must also be zero. We can also see that the skier can, by adjusting his body position fore and aft with respect to wind resistance (F_w) and sliding friction (F_f), select virtually any normal force reaction location (X_4) and vertical toe reaction (F_A). Needless to say, it is most comfortable to keep (X_4) small and the location of (F_N) somewhere between (A) and (B). The skier uses the ability to vary (X_4) and (F_A) to control fore and aft leverage on his skis, to cope with terrain, and to enhance turning. Additionally, if we consider the forces in the same boot, we can now see that by taking moments around (B) of the forces acting on the boot:

$$(6—13) \qquad F_A \cdot X_5 = F_C \cdot X_6$$

(C.C.W. BOOT TOE FORCE = C.W. TOP-OF-BOOT FORCE)

If the skier adjusts his body position to increase the normal reaction force distance (X_4), then he must pay the penalty in increased boot toe reaction force (F_A) and top of the boot reaction force (F_C) against the leg.

Clearly, this analysis represents a large percentage of the total problem of binding and boot design. The boots must be designed so that the skier *can* achieve the intended body position and desired location of (F_N). Also, the boot must be comfortable to absorb and distribute the boot force (F_C) on the skin or calf, depending upon its direction. The binding must be set to absorb normal vertical reactions at (A) and (B).

In real life, for reasonable hill angles, skier velocities, and sliding friction; the distance (X_3) between the reaction force (F_N) and the line through the C.G. and perpendicular to the snow surface is usually quite small. This is because, although (F_w) is usually two to five times the magnitude of (F_f), the moment arm (X_1) is considerably less than the moment arm (X_2). This leaves very little net tipping moment around the C.G. to be balanced by (F_N) and its moment arm (X_3). The importance of this statement is that the line of action of (F_N) is commonly quite co-linear to the perpendicular component ($F_g \cos \alpha$) of the force due to gravity. As stated earlier, force (F_N) represents the summation of all the pressure between the snow and the ski, and ($F_g \cos \alpha$) is the total gravitational force perpendicular to the snow; then (F_N) and ($F_g \sin \alpha$) must also be equal and opposite in magnitude.

Assuming that the skier adjusts his body position to keep the reaction force (F_N) acting near or through the boot; and assuming that (X_3) is usually small in real life situations, then it follows that the perpendicular component due to gravity ($F_g \cos \alpha$) can be considered to act in a line also through the approximate

a) C.G. forward

b) C.G. back

c) C.G. neutral

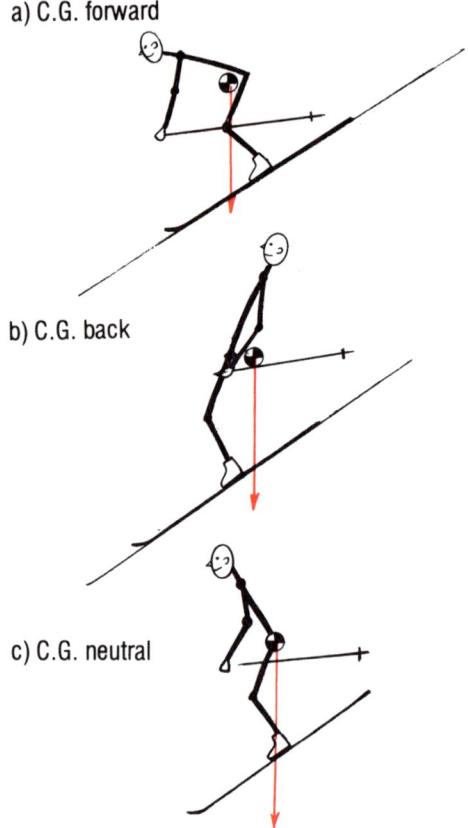

Figure 6—9

Figure 6—10

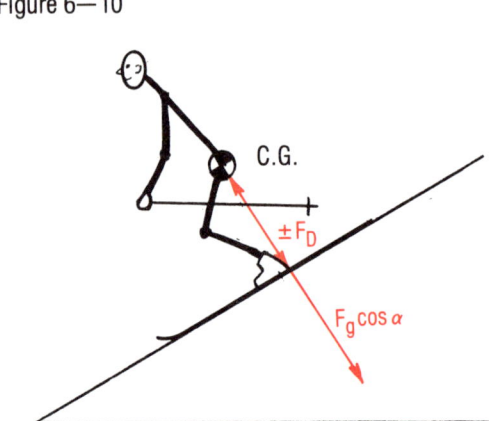

C.G.

$\pm F_D$

$F_g \cos \alpha$

location of the boot. This conclusion is important for following discussions, because the perpendicular force ($F_g \cos \alpha$) will be used extensively and considered as acting through the area of the boot.

Upper Body Position

The argument has now been made that it is desirable to keep the reaction force (F_N) acting near or through the boots. The skier can locate (F_N) by shifting his body position back and forth to position his C.G. He can also position the C.G. by bending the upper body, and the heavy head and shoulder weight, back and forth.

In figure 6—9a, the C.G. is well forward; but the butt is way back and there are excessive bending stresses in the back required to support the head and shoulders. Diagram (B) shows a vertical upper body which brings the C.G. back, but with the knees pressed abnormally forward. Diagram (C) shows a more relaxed, natural stance for straight running with approximately the same angle at the ankles, knees and hips. The skier in (C) is in the best neutral position to reposition his C.G. in all directions to cope with sudden changes in terrain or sliding friction.

Muscle Caused Temporary Forces

By suddenly extending or relaxing his thigh muscles, which in turn accelerate the body mass up or down, the skier can add or subtract a temporary, dynamic, inertial force (F_D) against the snow surface. This temporary force (F_D) acts in a direction between the hip and ankle joints and would, therefore, be in the same direction as ($F_g \cos \alpha$); which is also acting through the ankle and boot. In a steady state condition, the legs and thigh muscles are carrying the compressive force ($F_g \cos \alpha$). When they are relaxed, this force ($F_g \cos \alpha$) accelerates the upper body mass downwards toward the slope. When the legs are suddenly extended, the additional force (F_D), over and above ($F_g \cos \alpha$), accelerates the body mass upward and away from the slope.

The skier has the ability to suddenly add extra force (upweight) or decrease the force (down unweight) against the snow surface. A proper understanding of the meaning and timing of this quick muscular effort will have a great effect on the skier's skill. This concept is important during straight gliding to counteract terrain-caused force changes. It is very important in turning, since it allows the skier to momentarily sharply decrease or increase the force between the skis and the snow/ice surface at the proper time

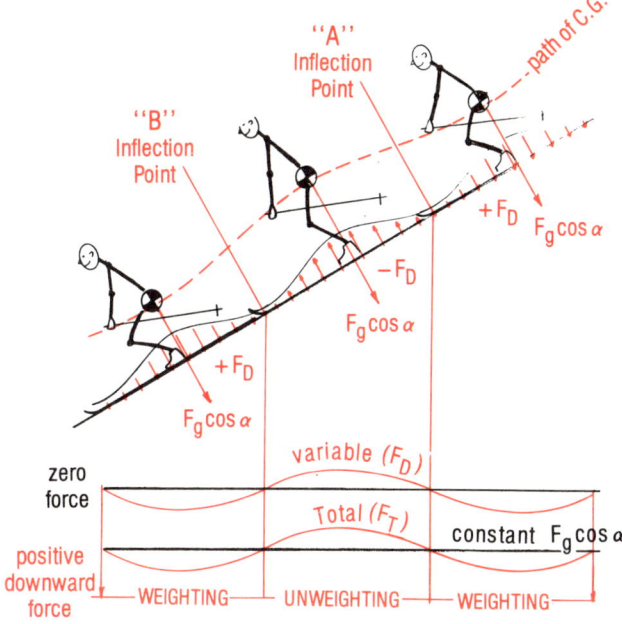

Figure 6—11
The temporary muscle-caused force (F_D) can be added or subtracted to the steady state gravitational force ($F_g \cos \alpha$). This results in upweighting as the skier pushes up or down unweighting when the skier relaxes the support of ($F_g \cos \alpha$) that is maintained by his leg muscles.

during the turn. The synchronization with the turn will be covered in detail in Chapter 11. However, we will continue the detailed analysis of weighting and unweighting in the present chapter since it is simpler to understand without the additional complexities of the turn. The temporary force (F_D) is by Newton's second law:

$$(6-14) \qquad F_D = \pm \frac{F_g}{g} \, a_v$$

The total force (F_T) against the slope is then:

$$(6-15) \qquad F_T = F_g \cos \alpha \pm \frac{F_g}{g} \, a_v$$

The acceleration (a_v) in this case represents the quickness with which the force (F_D) can be applied. For a positive (F_D) or upweighting, a quicker extension of the thigh muscles results in a higher (F_D), but for a shorter duration. In the case of negative (F_D) or down unweighting, the maximum acceleration possible is when (a_v) equals the component of the acceleration due to gravity ($g \cos \alpha$) which is colinear with (a_v) and (F_D) equals negative ($F_g \cos \alpha$); that is, they cancel and the net force against the ground is zero.

$$(6-15a) \qquad F_T = F_g \cos \alpha - \frac{F_g}{g} (g \cos \alpha) = 0$$

Any quicker retraction of the thigh muscles will only result in the skis leaving the snow. In other words, (F_T) cannot be less than zero.

It is important to understand the *exact* timing of the application of the temporary force (F_D). In figure 6—11, all three parallel forces ($F_g \cos \alpha$, F_D, F_T) are shown throughout a complete cycle of upweighting and down unweighting. The vertical raising and lowering of the skier's center of gravity is shown by the path of the C.G. The crux of this sketch is the location of the inflection points. As long as the C.G. is curving upwards, the temporary force (F_D) is positive. When the C.G. path is curving downwards, (F_D) is negative. When the C.G. path is changing most rapidly, (F_D) is highest (either positive or negative, as the case may be).

When the C.G. path is momentarily not curving up or curving down, as at the inflection points (or if the C.G. path is at a constant level above the ground), then the travel of the C.G. is in a straight line and the temporary force (F_D) is equal to zero. Per Newton's first law, a body tends to travel in a straight line at a uniform velocity if there is no external force acting upon it. The maximum (F_D) occurs at the instant there is the greatest change in direction of the C.G. path.

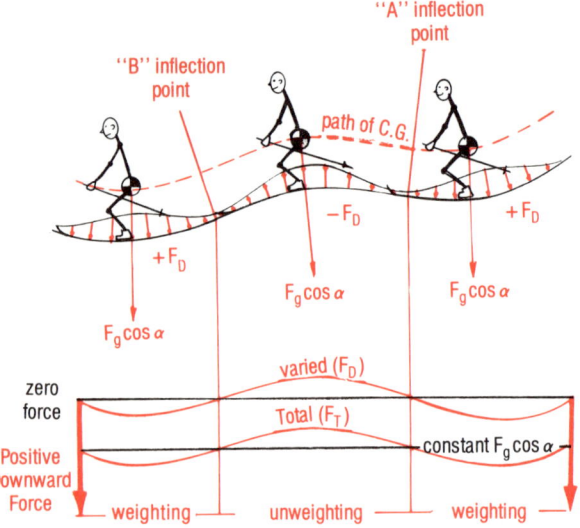

Figure 6—12
Terrain changes can also cause the temporary vertical force (F_D) to add or subtract from the steady state gravitational force $(F_g \cos \alpha)$.

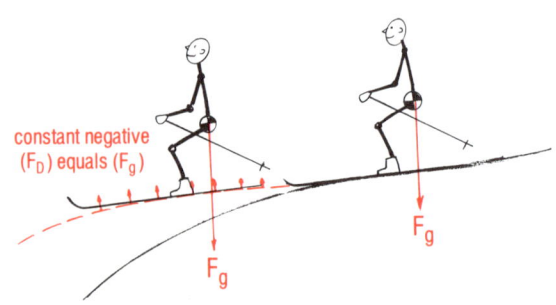

Figure 6—13
If the terrain falls away too rapidly with respect to the skier's speed, the skier will leave the ground and follow a trajectory determined by gravitational acceleration (g).

This discussion should help clarify the controversy of upweighting and upunweighting. In reality, as the skier begins deceleration of the upward motion of his CG at "A" in figure 6—11, down unweighting begins. The temporary force (F_D) goes negative and the total force against the slope (F_T) is reduced. Likewise, as the skier decelerates his down motion at "B", up-weighting begins even *before* the skier has reached his lowest position. Maximum up-weighting or down-unweighting occur when the skier, using his muscles, most rapidly accelerates his CG upwards or downwards.

Terrain Caused Temporary Forces

Vertical changes of the CG path can also be caused by terrain changes if the legs are kept concurrently rigid. Just as with the muscle-caused temporary force changes, there is a change in the total force (F_T) as the temporary force (F_D) either adds to or subtracts from the steady state gravitational force component $(F_g \cos \alpha)$. As the terrain ceases to thrust up (as at "A") or begins to fall away, the curvature of the CG path is downward; that is, the terrain is convex. While traveling over this terrain change, the downward acceleration of the skier's CG causes a negative temporary force (F_D) between the ski and the slope. The total force (F_T) between the inflection points "A" and "B" is therefore reduced. After point "B", the curvature of the terrain starts to become concave. The skier's CG path is altered in an upward direction and the temporary force (F_D) increases. Certainly every skier has felt the sudden very high loading on his body and skis as he skis into a concave slope transition. It is also readily obvious that the faster he does so, the greater the acceleration (a_v) on his body, and the higher the force (F_D) becomes.

Conversely, if a skier skis very rapidly over a drop-off in terrain, the negative temporary force (F_D) may equal the positive steady state, total gravitational force (F_g) and the skier will leave the ground on a downward trajectory determined only by the acceleration due to gravity (g).

By now it should be apparent that the skier can amplify or minimize terrain-caused temporary force changes with concurrent muscle-caused temporary force changes. Usually it is desirable to minimize the terrain caused forces with opposite muscle caused forces. As the terrain causes an upward or concave path of the CG, the skier can lower his body position to minimize the change. Conversely, as the terrain falls away, the skier can extend his legs to try and maintain a force against the ground. Remember, the final path of the skier's CG will determine the sign and magnitude of the temporary force (F_D) and the total force $(F_g \cos \alpha \pm F_D)$ against the slope surface.

In the concave zone in figure 6—14, the skier can extend his

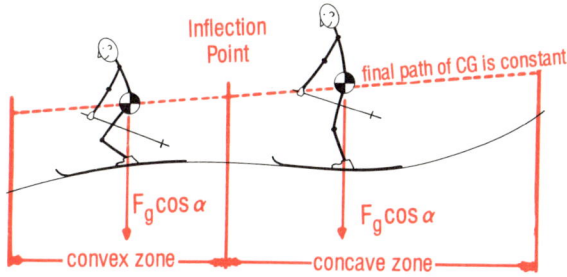

Figure 6—14
By adjusting the amount of leg flexion, the skier can "smooth out" varying terrain and keep the total force (F$_T$) against the ground nearly constant and equal to F$_g$cos α; in other words the skier is using varying muscle caused forces (F$_D$) to exactly counteract the varying terrain caused forces (F$_D$).

legs. In the convex zone, he can retract them. If the CG path is maintained constant, there can be no additional negative or positive temporary force (F$_D$) to be superimposed on the steady state gravitational force (F$_g$Cos α). As the skier covers the varying terrain his upper body is kept as constant as possible, while his legs absorb the terrain and keep a more uniform total force (F$_T$ = F$_g$cos α) against the snow. At least the corresponding muscle-induced forces can be used to minimize terrain-caused forces. This is the skier's suspension system at work to smooth out the ride.

chapter 7

THE MECHANICS OF THE TRAVERSE

TO TRAVERSE IS TO SKI in essentially a straight direction at some angle (β) across the fall line. This situation adds one new dimension of complexity to the preceeding chapter on straight gliding. In straight gliding, the gravitational force component parallel to the plane of the slope ($F \sin \alpha$) was parallel with the direction of the skis (and the skier's line of travel). In the traverse, this all important component parallel to the plane of the slope *is not* parallel to the direction of the skis and travel. Whereas in straight gliding we were primarily concerned with two forces ($F_g \sin \alpha$ and $F_g \cos \alpha$) that are components of the resultant (F_g), we are now interested in three forces (F_{TR}, F_{LA}, and $F_g \cos \alpha$) that are also mutual components of the same resultant (F_g). The following nomenclature is introduced for this chapter:

β = Traverse angle between direction of travel *and horizontal*; (eg., $\beta = 90°$ when skier is in the fall line).

F_{TR} = The force to accelerate the skier's mass in the direction of travel along the traverse.

F_{LA} = The force exerted *perpendicularly against the skis* and parallel to the slope.

Θ = The angle between the edged skis and the slope surface.

ϕ = The angle between the slope and a horizontal plane where the slope is viewed from a direction parallel with the skis and the direction of travel.

R = The reaction force from the skier's center of gravity acting through the skis. This is the total force exerted against the slope.

Figure 7—1
A skier traversing at an angle (β) to the slope is viewed here from above and perendicular to the plane of the slope. The forces illustrated are those acting in a plane perpendicular to our direction of view.

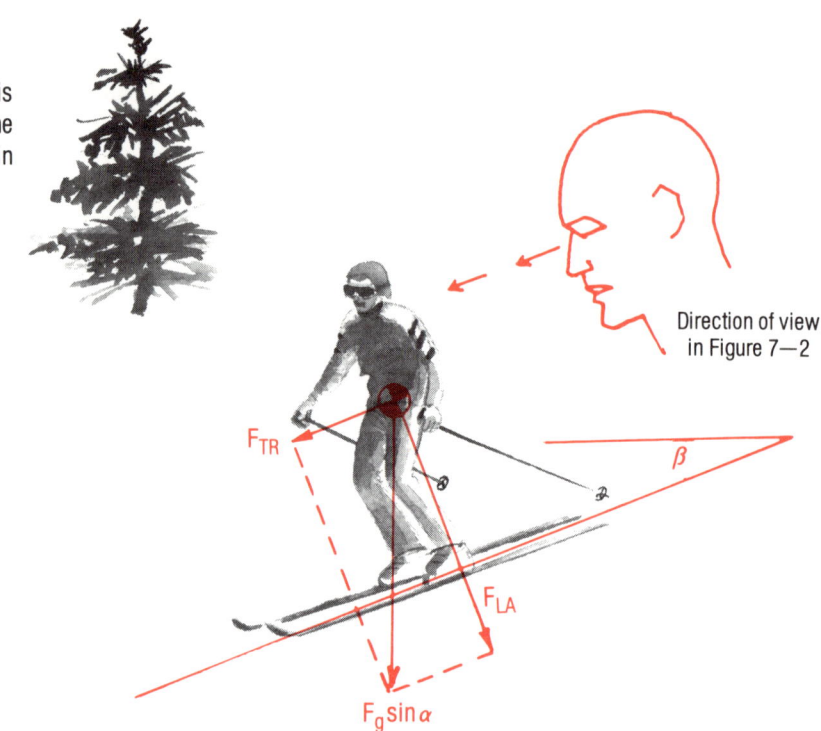

Direction of view in Figure 7—2

Figure 7—2
The same skier is shown as viewed from directly behind. The forces illustrated here are acting in a plane perpendicular to our direction of view.

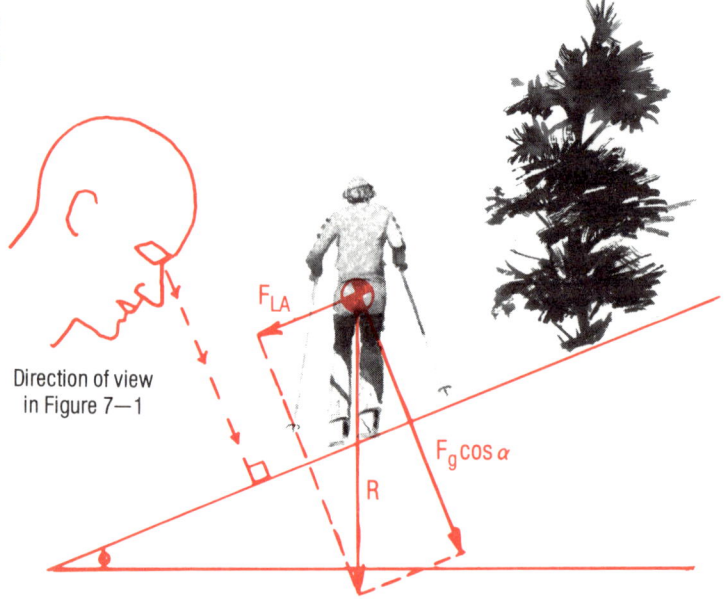

Direction of view in Figure 7—1

Let's begin with the force diagrams in figures 7—1 and 7—2 (the direction of view is very important). In figure 7—1, we observe a skier while looking perpendicular to the plane of the hill. The forces indicated in figure 7—1 are those situated *perpendicular to our direction of view.*

In figure 7—2, we observe the same skier while looking parallel with the plane of the slope *and parallel* to the skier's direction of travel. In both diagrams, we show *only* those forces that are *completely perpendicular* to the direction of view. To try to indicate other forces would require foreshortening them and this would misrepresent them. The directions of view (and appropriate diagrams) are *specifically selected* to place the important forces of interest perpendicular to the direction of view.

In the traverse, the force ($F_g \sin \alpha$), a component of gravitational pull (F_g) that is parallel to the slope, can be broken down into two components; one, in the direction of travel:

(7—1) $F_{TR} = F_g \sin \alpha \sin \beta$

and the other *perpendicular* to the direction of travel and

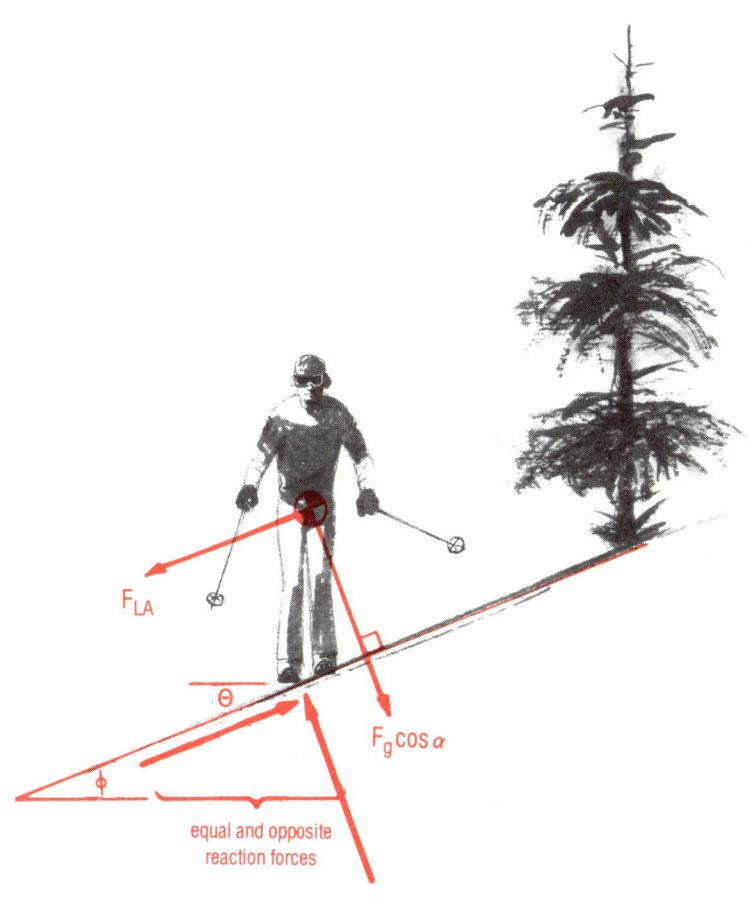

Figure 7—3
In a traverse, a lateral force (F_{LA}) is generated that acts perpendicular to the direction of travel and must be supported by placing the skis on edge at an angle (Θ) to the slope.

67

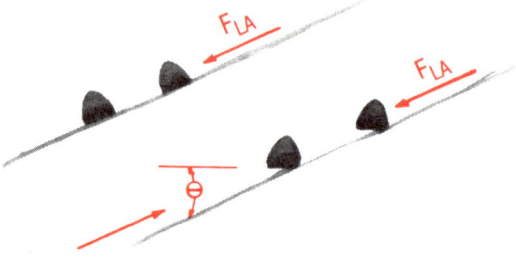

Figure 7—4
If the skis are flat on the snow, they cannot support the lateral force (F_{LA}) since they don't generate the necessary lateral adhesion as they would if they were edged.

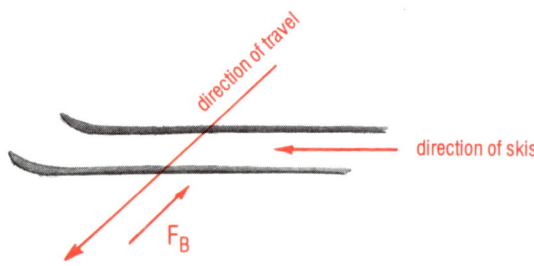

Figure 7—5
A skier can brake his speed by turning his skis so that they are directed at an angle to their line of travel, thereby generating greater friction (F_B).

supported by the edged skis on the snow (*parallel* to the slope):

$$(7—2) \qquad F_{LA} = F_g \sin \alpha \cos \beta$$

The force supported by the edged skis and *perpendicular* to the slope is still ($F_g \cos \alpha$) just as in straight gliding. For the first time, we have introduced a force perpendicular to the skis and parallel to the slope. This is the very important lateral force (F_{LA}).

If the skis are flat on the snow, they cannot support the force (F_{LA}) since they don't generate the necessary lateral adhesion that they would if they are edged by some angle (Θ). (Figure 7—4)

The all important concepts of edging and lateral adhesion of the snow surface are now introduced. The angle (Θ) that both skis are edged is very complex, and will be analyzed in considerable detail in the remaining chapters. The acceleration of the skier in the direction of travel is now due to the force in that direction ($F_g \sin \alpha \sin \beta$) plus any physical force (F_p) as added by the skier. Opposing these forces are the same friction forces (F_w) and (F_f) as in straight gliding, plus a very small to a very large force (F_B) depending upon how much the skier applies braking. Braking can be done by side slipping when the direction of the skis is at some angle from the direction of travel as shown in figure 7—5.

The total equation of motion, at maximum velocity, when the forces accelerating the skier are just equal to the opposing forces, is:

$$(7—3) \qquad F_g \sin \alpha \sin \beta + F_p = F_W + F_f + F_B$$

... or, disregarding the external forces of pushing or braking as supplied by the skier:

$$(7—3a) \qquad F_g \sin \alpha \sin \beta = F_w + F_f$$

The very important difference between this equation and the equation (6—2) is the term ($\sin \beta$), which can vary from zero, when $\beta = 0°$ (where the skier is standing perpendicular to the fall line), to unity, when $\beta = 90°$, and the skier is straight gliding directly down the fall line. Now by controlling (β), the skier has a perfect way to control his speed, rather than by introducing braking via some form of skidding. The only problem is that sooner or later, as the skier traverses across the slope, the edge of the slope will be reached and the skier must stop and kick turn or learn to turn down the hill at speed to reverse direction.

The Relationship Between Angles Θ and φ

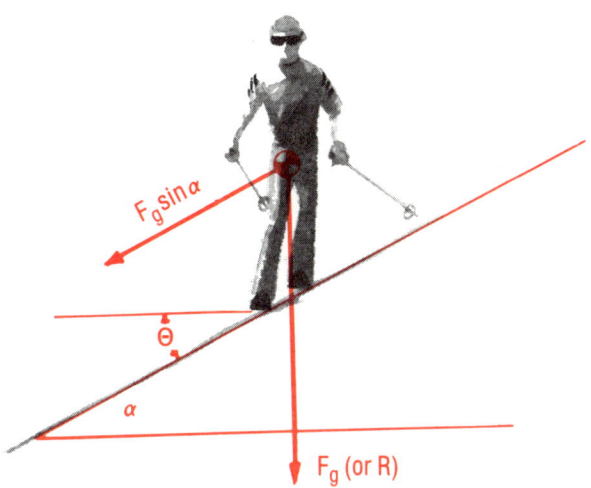

Figure 7—6
When a skier traverses perpendicular to the fall line (β = 0), then Θ = α. (Assuming no angulation)

The subject of traversing has introduced a lateral force (F_{LA}) acting perpendicular to the skis and parallel to the slope. We also still have the constant force perpendicular to the slope ($F_g \cos \alpha$).

For different traverse angles (β), the angle φ varies from a maximum of (α) when B = 0, to zero when β = 90°. The reason (φ) changes with (β) is because of the fact that we are viewing the skier directly parallel with his direction of travel and parallel with the slope. This is a difficult concept to comprehend at first, but it is necessary to see, in the figures, the real magnitude of the two force components acting upon the skis (F_{LA} and $F_g \cos \alpha$). By seeing these components, we can then understand how they combine to give the singular reaction (R) acting from the center of gravity through the skis against the snow. By trigonometry, we can now see from figure 7—2 that:

$$(7—4) \qquad \phi = \tan^{-1} \frac{F_{LA}}{F_g \cos \alpha} = \frac{F_g \sin \alpha \cos \beta}{F_g \cos \alpha} = \tan^{-1}(\tan \alpha \cos \beta)$$

and

$$(7—5) \qquad R = F_g (\cos^2 \alpha + \sin^2 \alpha \cos^2 \beta)^{1/2}$$

Now, what is the meaning of all this? the angle (φ) is important because (in the absence of knee or hip angulation to be discussed later) the angle (Θ) that the skis make with the plane of the slope is equal to φ. The force acting on the slope from the center of gravity through the skis is equal to (R). To make all this easier to visualize, consider the extreme cases of a skier perpendicular to the fall line (β = 0°) and a skier parallel to the fall line in a straight gliding position (β = 90°).
In the first case, as shown in figure 7—6:

$$(7—4a) \qquad \phi = \tan^{-1}(\tan \alpha \cos 0°)$$

... or φ = α, and therefore Θ = α.

also,

$$(7—4b) \qquad R = (\cos^2 \alpha + \sin^2 \alpha \cos^2 0)^{1/2} = F_g$$

and we are back where we started, standing still across the hill with F_g sending us nowhere because β = 0.

In the second case, as shown in figure 7—7:

$$(7—5a) \qquad \phi = \tan^{-1}(\tan \alpha \cos 90°)$$

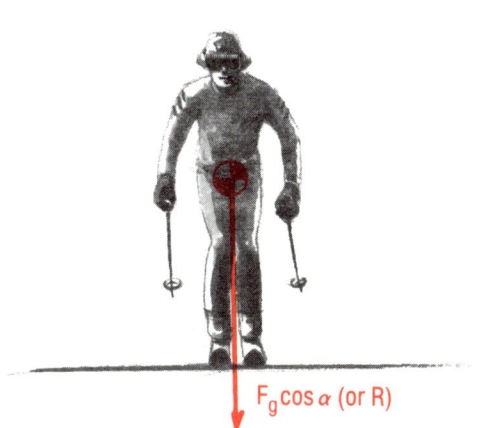

Figure 7—7
When a skier slides in a straight run down the fall line, Θ = 0. Here the skier is viewed from in front and parallel to the slope.

69

Figure 7—8
The skier in Figure 7—7 is shown from a side view.

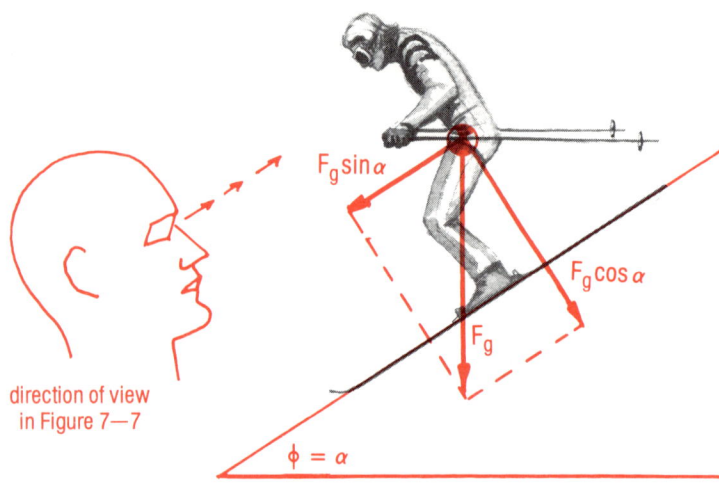

... or ϕ = zero, and therefore Θ = zero; and in this situation...

(7—5b) $R = F_g(\cos^2\alpha + \sin^2\alpha \cos^2 90°)^{1/2} = F_g\cos\alpha$

This is exactly the force acting through the skis *perpendicular* to the snow surface in the condition of straight gliding. The force diagram is exactly the same as in the beginning of Chapter 6. Remember the direction of view is *parallel* with the slope. This is why the horizon under the skier looks horizontal when β = 90° regardless of whether the slope is flat (α = 0) or steep.

This exhaustive discussion on reaction and angles during traversing may seem to be only of academic interest. A good understanding, however, is necessary for the later mechanics of the turn, as well as a better understanding of edging and lateral adhesion.

Lateral Adhesion And Skidding

We now have the exact expression for the force (F_{LA}) tending to push the skis sideways *parallel* to the slope and *perpendicular* to the direction of travel. If it were not for an equal and opposite reaction holding force, the skis would skid out sideways from the skier. This holding force is dependent on the second important force ($F_g\cos\alpha$) which pushes the skis perpendicularly into the snow surface. The edges (or the whole ski in soft snow) dig into the surface and provide a track to run on. This provides the equal and opposite force to counteract (F_{LA}). This counteracting force is sometimes called lateral adhesion.

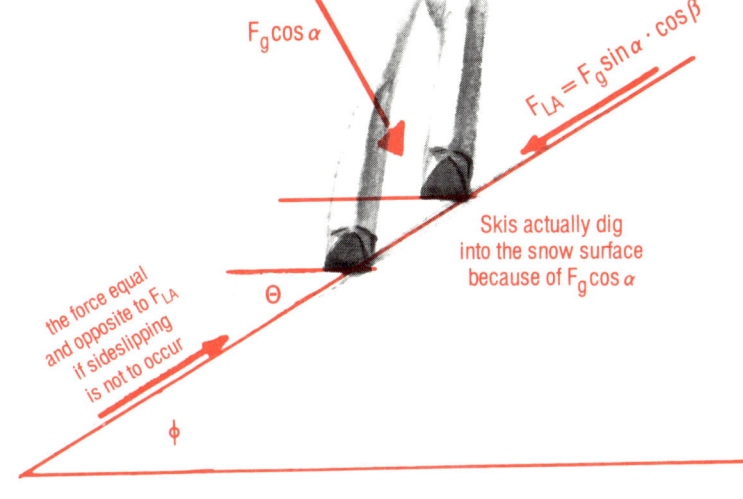

Figure 7—9
$F_g \cos \alpha$, a component of gravitational force, pushes the edged skis against the snow; thereby generating sufficient lateral adhesion to balance F_{LA} and prevent the skis from skidding sideways.

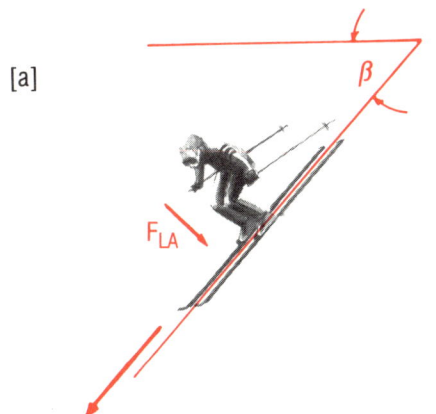

[a]

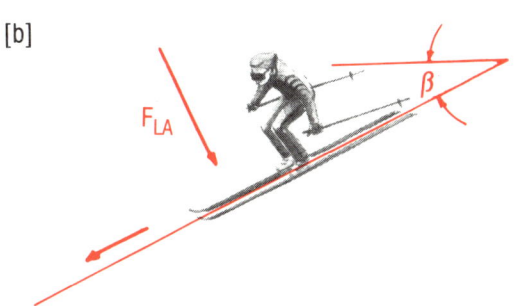

[b]

Figure 7—10
The skier in the upper illustration is on a steeper traverse. He consequently has a lesser (F_{LA}) to support and, therefore, is less prone to sliding sideways.

By analyzing the terms in both forces ($F_g \cos \alpha$ and $F_g \sin \alpha \cos \beta$), we see that:

1. For small hill angles (α), or large traverse angles (β), we don't have too much problem with lateral adhesion because ($F_g \cos \alpha$) is large or ($F_g \sin \alpha \cos \beta$) is small.

2. For steep hill angles (α), or shallow traverse angles (β), however, ($F_g \cos \alpha$) becomes small and ($F_g \sin \alpha \cos \beta$) becomes large. In other words, the ratio of the force tending to skid the ski (F_{LA}) is large compared to the force tending to make the ski bite into the snow and resist skidding ($F_g \cos \alpha$).

Note that the force tending to push the skis sideways (F_{LA}) is dependent only on the hill angle (α), traverse angle (β) and the skier's weight (F_g). The snow/ice surface needs only to provide an equal and opposite force to support (F_{LA}). The snow/ice surface may be such that it can support considerably more force than (F_{LA}) or it may be just borderline and skidding is imminent with only a slight increase, for some reason, in (F_{LA}). Every experienced skier knows that harder surfaces allow less edge to bite, even with a substantial perpendicular force component ($F_g \cos \alpha$). This, in turn, means that less (F_{LA}) can be supported and skidding occurs at less (β) or greater (α).

Also, it is interesting that (F_{LA}) increases as (β) decreases, whereas ($F_g \cos \alpha$) remains constant. This means that the more the skier assumes a direction across the fall line and (β) decreases, the greater chance that he will approach a critical point of snow/ice lateral adhesion.

The skier traversing in figure 7—10a generates less (F_{LA}) than the skier in 7—10b. On the other hand, the skier in [a] is also going to reach a higher terminal velocity because the force pulling in the direction of travel ($F_g \sin \alpha \sin \beta$) is greater and sooner or later the skier is going to have to cope with this velocity. The message here, very clearly, is that it is better to maintain a steep traverse (like [a] above) over an icy section if it looks like there is better snow or a flatter hill (less α) later. The racer can use this theory to his advantage in planning his line over varying degrees of steepness and hardness of surface. The skis should be allowed to run and not try to hold a shallow traverse (low value of β) over an icy section of hill. The experts do this by intuition, and the struggling intermediate without this confidence tries to hold a shallow traverse and ends up skidding sideways over the same terrain.

Two Types Of Traverses

A modern ski on its edge, as in a traverse, will not track a perfectly straight line because of its side camber. However, for the purposes of this chapter, the consideration of turning forces will be ignored. Keep in mind also that there can be varying degrees of turning force introduced depending upon the track and the snow surfaces; ie., is the ski truly on its edge and tending to carve, or is it really in a straight running situation only at a traversing angle? For example, in figure 7—11 the skis are edged on a very hard surface, and only the sidecut of the ski interacts with the snow/ice surface. In this case, the sidecut of the ski and the angle (Θ) will tend to make the skis carve uphill (see Chapter 9).

In figure 7—12, the traverse is in soft snow, and one of two things can happen. If it is a new traverse (in fresh, untracked, soft

In figure 7—11, the edges and side camber of the skis cause them to turn. In Figure 7—12, however, the situation is quite different. Here the entire running surface and the flexibility of the skis are used to create a turn.

Figure 7—11

Figure 7—12

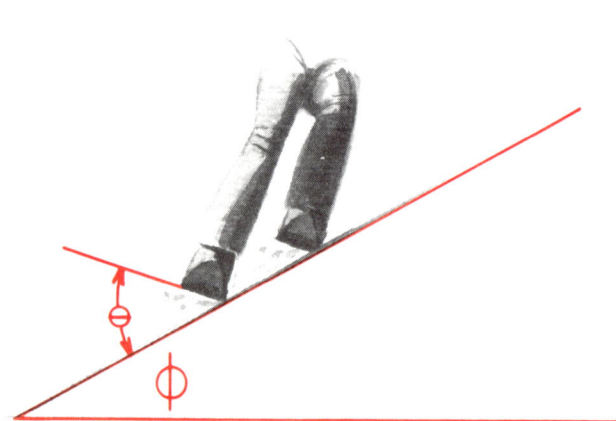

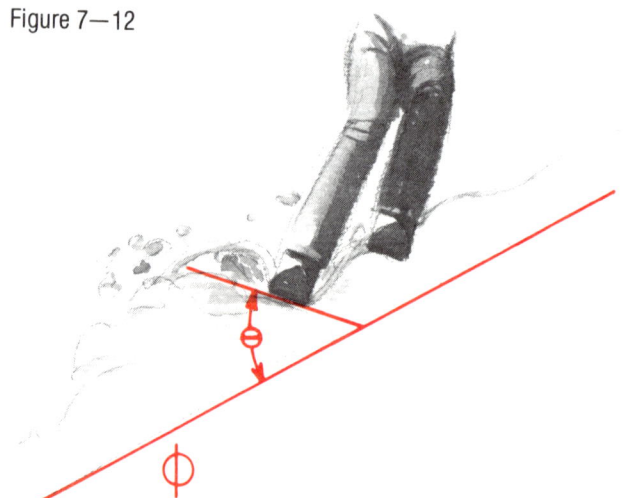

snow), the pressure of the skis against the compressing snow may force the skis into an arc (figure 7—13). If it is an old traverse, in harder packed tracks, then in reality the skis are following an artificial fall line. We consider the two hard tracks as a wider trail or road cut at a traverse to the fall line. In this case, (Θ) is effectively zero, although (α) and (β) are still very real and the force equations for traversing (F_{TR}, F_{LA}, and $F_g \cos \alpha$) still determine the forces on the skis and the velocity of the skier.

Figure 7—13
The flex of the skis will enhance their turning ability in soft, deep snow.

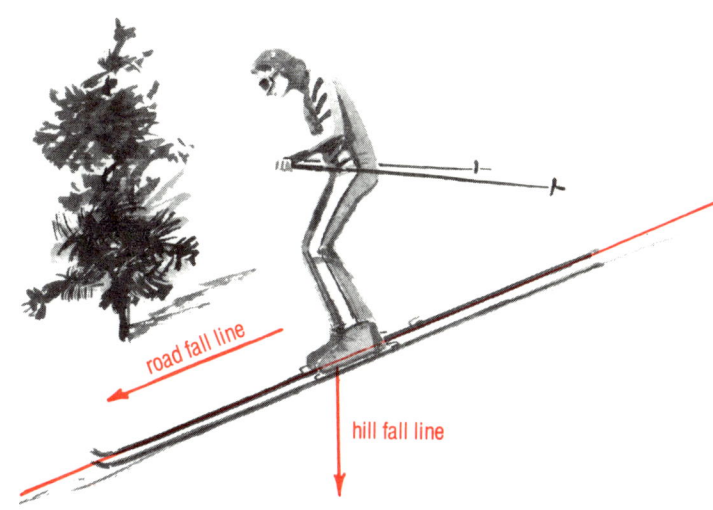

road fall line

hill fall line

Figure 7—14
When traversing a hard, packed track, the skis actually follow an artificial fall line. When viewed from the side, the skier appears to be skiing a normal traverse, but when viewed from directly in front it can be seen that he is actually in a straight glide with his skis running flat in the tracks in the snow.

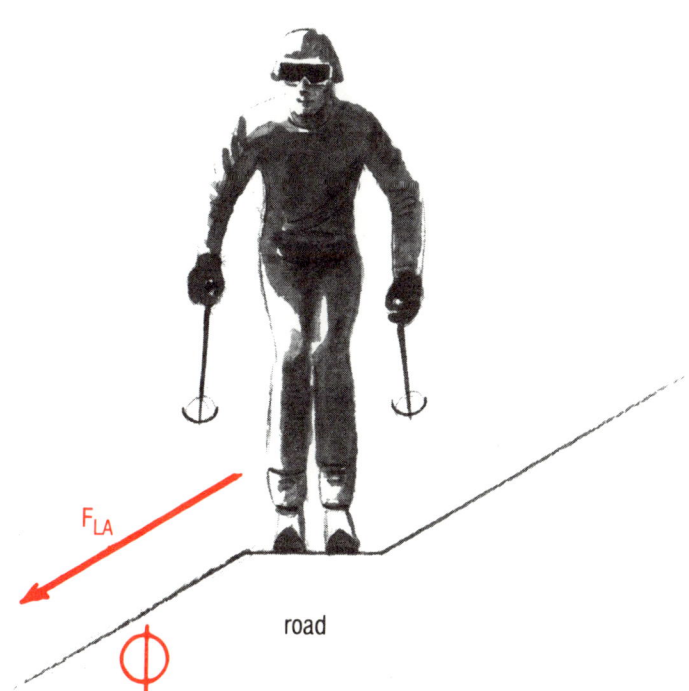

F_{LA}

road

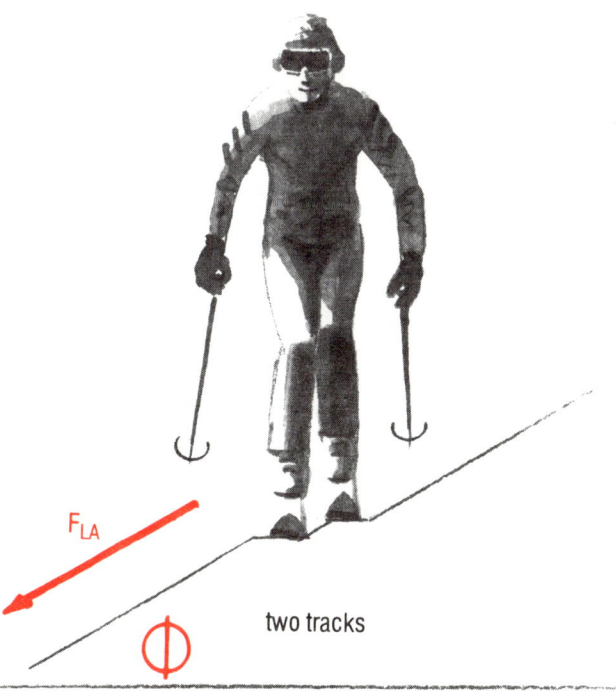

F_{LA}

two tracks

Angulation

Up to now, the skier appears to be totally at the mercy of the slope of the hill and the snow conditions; somewhat like a car with the steering locked in one position (practically straight) and no personal control over the direction of travel. Fortunately, the concept of angulation allows the skier to change (Θ) at will *regardless* of (α) or (ϕ) or (β). This personal control of (Θ) via angulation is probably the single most important mechanical principle that makes skiing what it is.

To digress for a moment; let us state that the unique thing about skiing is the phenomenon caused by the transition between edging (carving) and side-slipping (skidding). Skis running on snow allow both extremes (carving and skidding) and all variations in between. Skateboarding, for instance, allows only holding (edging) in a sideways direction. Subtle, lateral changes in position or dissipation of energy are not possible. By controlling (Θ), the skier can control the delicate balance between holding and skidding in the direction perpendicular to the skis. As the skier adds fore or aft pressure in addition to the control of (Θ), the tails can be made to skid sideways more than the shovel, and vice versa. There will be much more discussion of this later. First, we need to define the relationship between angulation and inclination. If the body is straight and aligned in the front and rear views, the body is said to be inclined without angulation. If the ankles, knees, and hips are bent to some angularity in the front and back views, then we have angulation. In actuality, most skiing is some combination of angulation and inclination, especially when the centrifugal force of turning is introduced in Chapter 8.

Figure 7—15
At all times, the skier must maintain (R) between the points where his ski edges contact the snow in order to remain in balance. With no angulation and a traverse angle (β) of zero, the edge angle (Θ) equals the hill angle (α).

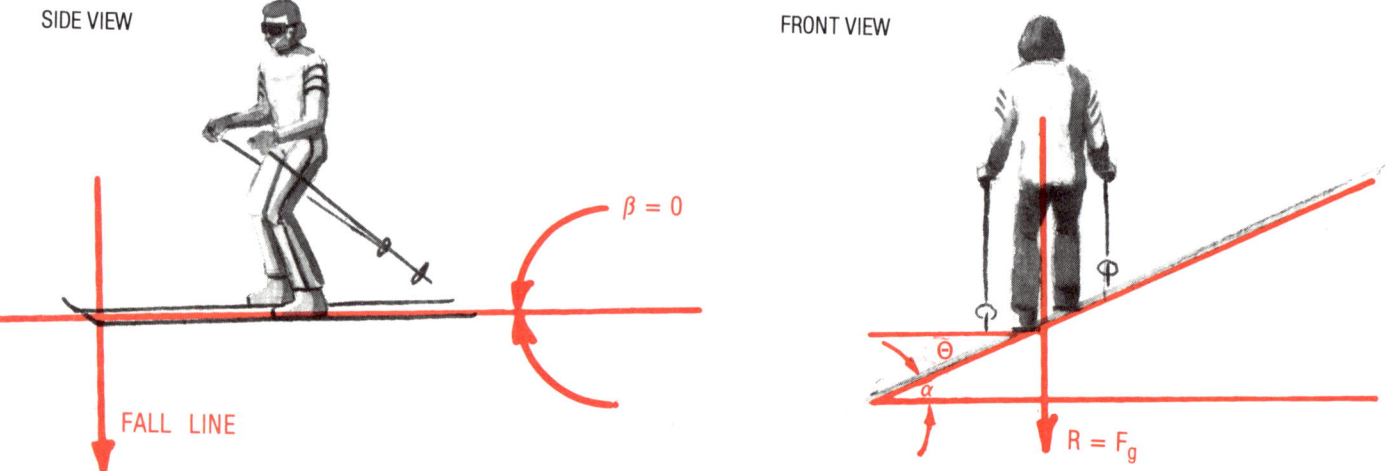

SIDE VIEW

$\beta = 0$

FALL LINE

FRONT VIEW

ϕ

Θ

α

$R = F_g$

[A]

[B]

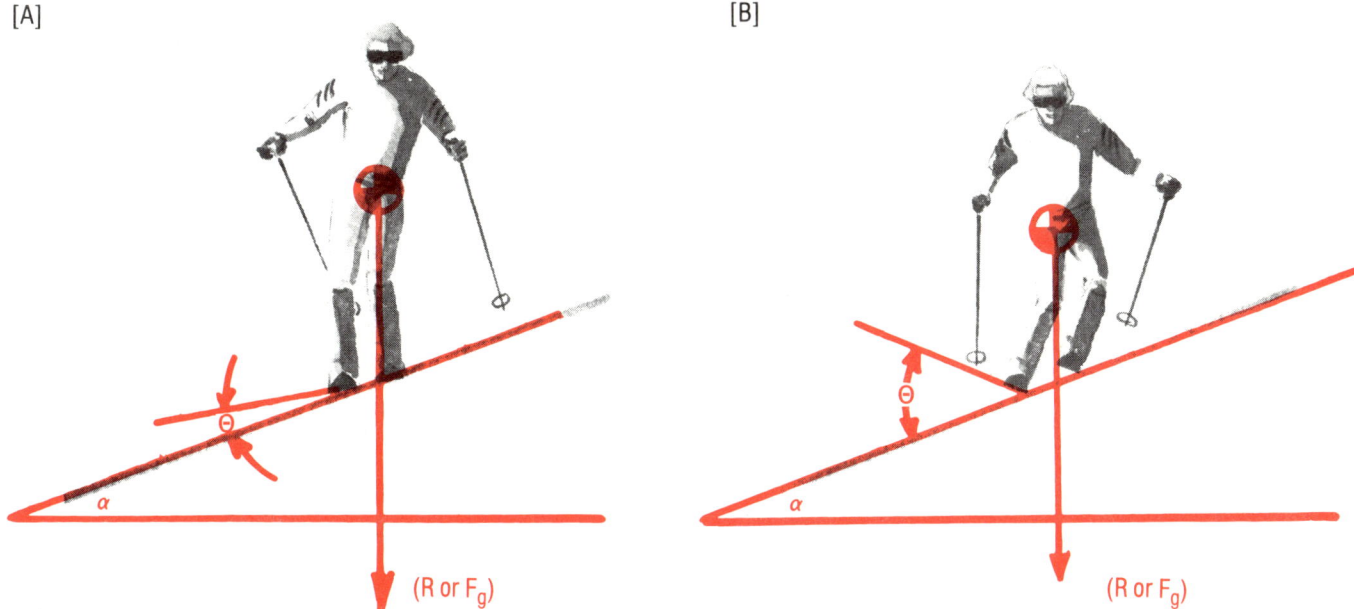

Figure 7—16
ANGULATION. A skier can move his body as a four-link system (head, torso, thighs, lower legs) to adjust edge angle (Θ) without moving his center of gravity.

The total force reaction by the body and skis against the slope is given in the earlier equation:

(7—5) $R = F_g (\cos^2 \alpha + \sin^2 \alpha \cos^2 \beta)^{1/2}$

In the simplest case, (R) becomes (F$_g$) when (β) equals zero and the skier is crossing the fall line at 90° (from trigonometry, $\cos^2 \alpha + \sin^2 \alpha = a$).

In figure 7—15, there is no angulation and the edge angle (Θ) equals the hill angle (α). If one is not to fall over, the skier must keep (R) acting between the points where the edges engage the snow (points A & B). If both skis are equally weighted, the line of action of (R) would be half way between the individual skis. By adding angulation, the skier can keep (R) in a constant line while at the same time varying (Θ) as desired. The body can be altered as a four-link system (head, torso, thighs, lower legs) without changing the relative positions of the CG and (R).

Clearly, the skier in figure 7—16a has decreased (Θ) by moving the head and upper body closer to the hill and the hips and knees away from the hill. Diagram (b) shows a greater (Θ) by just the opposite movements. (Remember, we are considering only straight traversing at this time, so there is no additional inclination of the body as will be required later when the centrifugal force of turning is introduced.) This adjustment of the vertical alignment of the upper and lower body to change (Θ) is called *angulation*. The inference is that angulation is a change of the entire body position, but it can be broken down further:

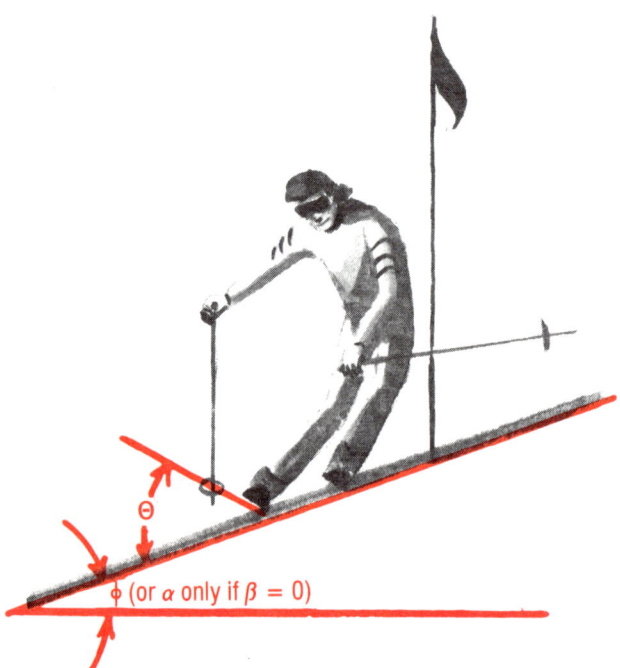

Figure 7—17
Ski racers use knee angulation for very rapid adjustment of edge angle (Θ).

Figure 7—18
Most skiing situations, and particularly higher speed turns, require the use of some degree of hip angulation.

Knee Angulation. This is the quickest way to effect angulation and change (Θ) since the knees have only a small amount of inertia and can be moved quickly from side to side. As the knees are thrust sideways, there may or may not be additional angulation of the upper body. Only a lowering of the upper body is necessary for pure knee angulation.

The major problem here is anatomical. Human knees just weren't meant to be flexed sideways. They will not bend sideways at all if the legs are nearly straight. However, if the knees are first flexed in the fore and aft direction and are reasonably supple, considerable knee angulation can be achieved. Long-time skiers develop a substantial amount of sideways flex in their knees; which is perplexing to beginners or stiff-jointed skiers. Modern ski racers even wear knee pads and assume very low positions at critical points in the turn in order to achieve extreme knee angulation. The knee pads help to protect the knees from the impact of possible contact with the slalom poles or from contact with the inner boot and binding.

Hip Angulation. The "comma" position taught by all reputable ski schools in the 1950's and 1960's more often meant hip angulation. The hips (lower back) are anatomically capable of bending sideways, and this is an easier concept to get across to the student who doesn't have laterally flexing knees and the thigh strength required to maintain a low body position.

Hip angulation is effective because it allows the skier to adjust (Θ); although not to the degree that is possible with knee angulation. Hip angulation is also not as quick as knee angulation since considerably more body mass must be moved sideways. The entire pelvic area is shifted and the upper body and shoulders move in the opposite direction. The knees may angulate slightly for anatomical harmony, but in this case the knee angulation is considerably deemphasized in favor of hip angulation.

True skiing is a continual adjustment of combined hip and knee angulation. The upper body reaction in the opposite direction is usually subconscious and natural. To achieve extreme angulation, it may help to consciously angulate the upper body. For instance, if an extreme edge angle (Θ) is needed, the skier might be sure that the outer shoulder and hand are extended out and down and that even the head is moved in the downhill direction.

Another way to achieve maximum angulation is through a conscious feeling of "ankle angulation." In other words, in spite of the lateral stiffness of the modern ski boot, it is possible to realize even more edge holding by pushing the sides of the ankles against the boot, toward the hill.

Because the skier can control (Θ) at will, the ability of the snow surface to resist the sideway pushing force (F_{LA}) can also be varied. In a traverse position, the edges can be "released" by a diminishing of angulation (de-angulation) and for a certain combination of (α), (β) and snow/ice surface the supporting force provided by the snow/ice surface is less than (F_{LA}). In this case, the skis will slide sideways. By subtle control of (Θ), the skier can make the skis track in a traverse, slide sideways, or assume any combination in between (figure 7—19).

Figure 7—19
By subtle control of (Θ), the skier can make his skis track in a traverse, slide sideways, or assume any combination in between

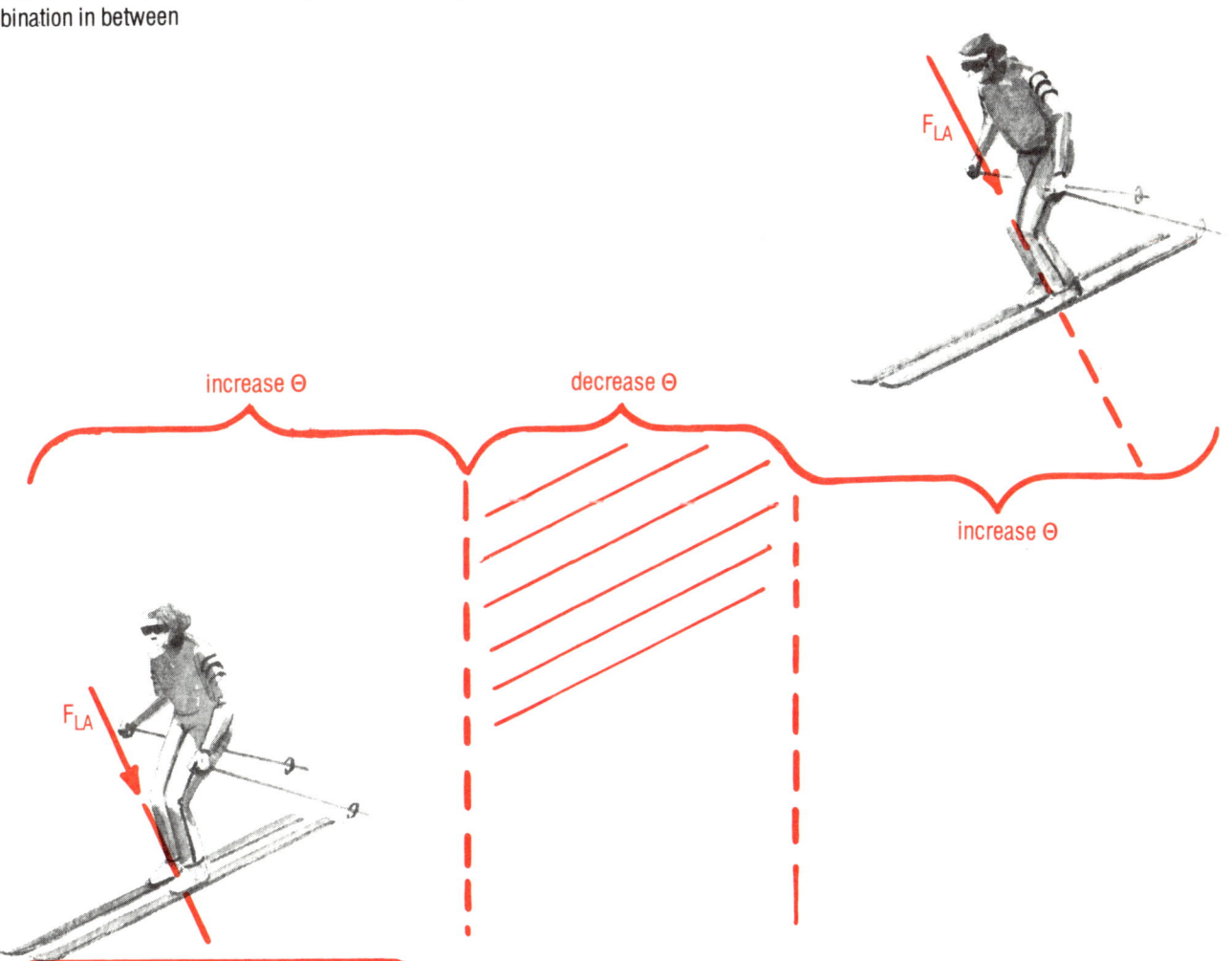

Weight Distribution Between Skis

In a traverse, the lateral force (F_{LA}) tends to push the skis sideways parallel with the slope and the perpendicular force ($F_g \cos \alpha$) pushes the edges into the snow/ice surface to provide sufficient equal and opposite force to resist (F_{LA}). The resultant force of the combined (F_{LA}) and ($F_g \cos \alpha$) acts from the skier's center of gravity, parallel with the plane of travel and through the ski's line of contact with the snow/ice surface. To this point, we have considered both skis as one; ie., assuming all the weight were on one ski, or the other, or balanced in between.

If all of the skier's weight is balanced on one or the other edged skis, it is not as stable a condition as with the weight balanced in some percentage between the two. In figure 7—20, condition (c) is shown to be more stable than condition (a), even though both are extreme (any condition beyond (a) and (c) will cause the skier to fall over). The reason it is more stable to have more weight on the uphill edge of the downhill ski is because, if the lateral adhesion of the snow/ice surface is suddenly less than required to support (F_{LA}), the skis will slip sideways in the downhill direction. If the weight is on the lower ski, the body will tend to fall inward, toward the slope, and the upper leg and ski are ready to support the transferred position of (R). If the weight is all

Figure 7—20
The skier is balanced on the uphill edges of his uphill ski in (a). (R) falls between the skis in (b) and is balanced on the uphill edge of the downhill ski in (c). Condition (c) is generally the most stable.

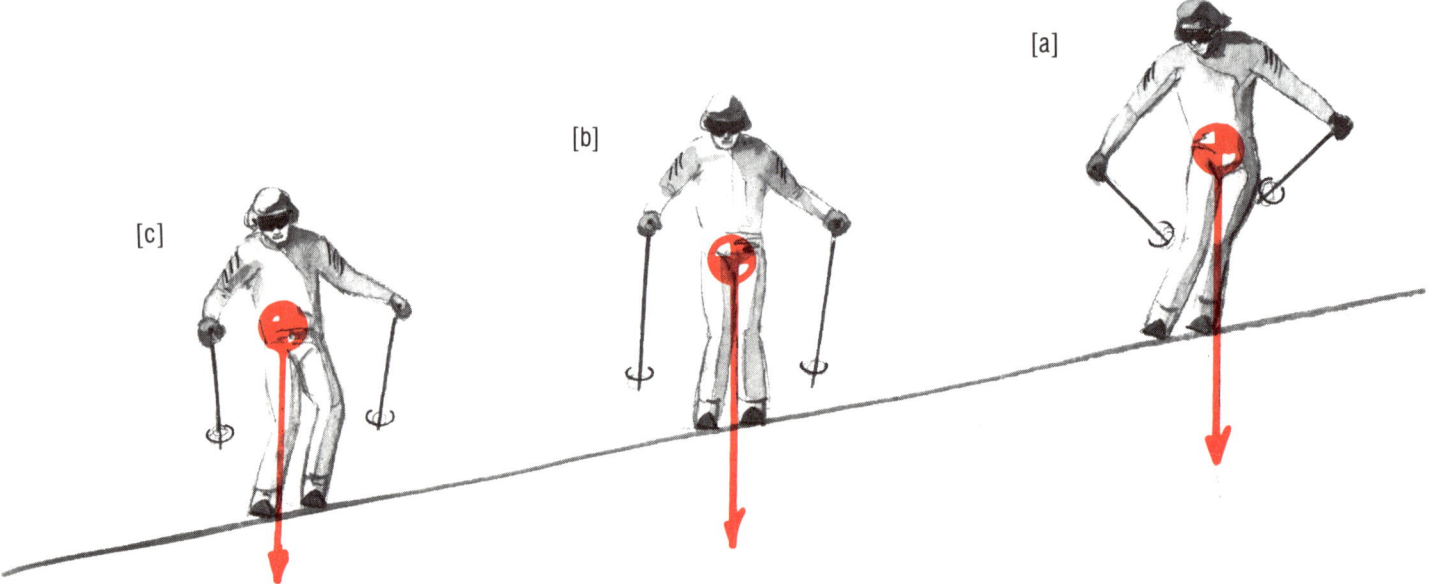

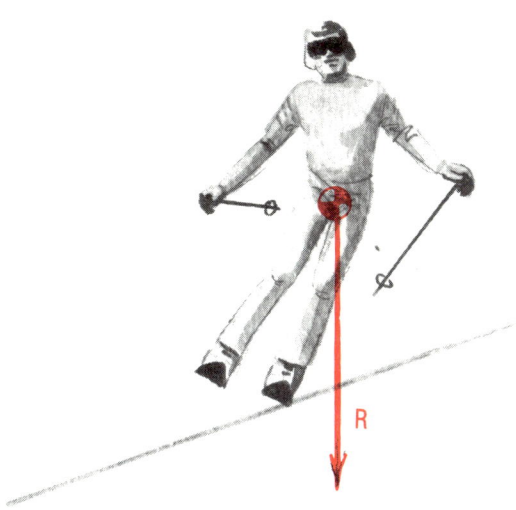

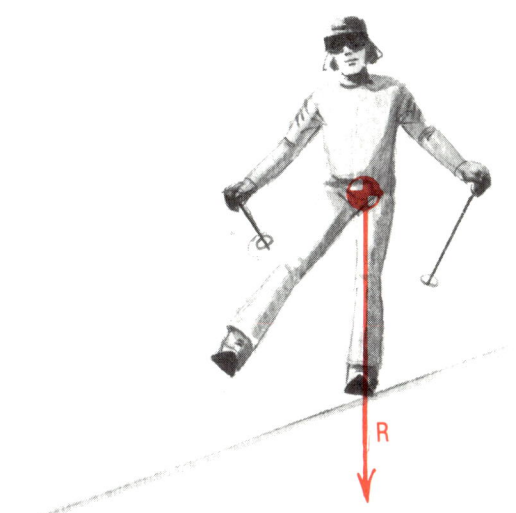

Figure 7—21
If the skis lack sufficient lateral adhesion and slide downhill, the skier risks falling into the slope (above). He can ''save'' himself by rapidly extending his downhill leg, thereby shifting his center of gravity out over his uphill ski (right).

on the upper ski, however, and the same thing happens, the line of action (R) and the slope will move uphill from the upper ski edge and the skier will fall into the slope (ie. ''catching an uphill edge'').

The only instant recovery for this situation is to retract the uphill ski so quickly that it leaves the snow and can be placed down again uphill from (R). A second possible ''save'' is by quickly extending the lower leg and ski so far out into space away from the hill that its weight and lever arm moves (R) back downhill from the uphill ski.

Either type of recovery is precarious at best. The safest thing to do is keep the weight balanced on both skis, or possibly more than half the weight biased on the downhill ski. In this way, some weight can be easily transferred to either ski if necessary. This also makes actual stepping or independent leg action easier. This all may seem obvious or elementary, but how many times do even advanced skiers fall into the trap of having all their weight on or above their uphill ski?

Fore And Aft Weight Distribution

Because of the sidecut of the ski, traversing on the edges of the skis is, in reality, turning in a long arc as carved by the skis. If the line of action of the weight is biased toward the tails, the skis will be discouraged from bending into a turn. In other words, it is easier to keep the skis in a straight, tracking traverse if the line of action of the weight is slightly toward the tail of the ski. This assumes there is adequate lateral adhesion and good edge angle (Θ).

In general, however, the normal reaction force (F_N) resisting the force due to gravity (F_g) and the usual wind resistance (F_w) and sliding friction (F_f) forces should be at a point near the center of the boot or slightly ahead for stability if the run is steep and bumpy.

The same comments for fore and aft balance and vertical terrain absorption hold true for traversing as for straight gliding in Chapter 6. A relaxed, neutral position with constant, fairly upright, upper body will let the legs and skis move with the terrain and provide freedom for quick adjustment of position if needed.

Figure 7—22
The skier's balance in the fore and aft plane is typically adjusted so that the normal reaction force is at a point near the center of the boot.

[A]

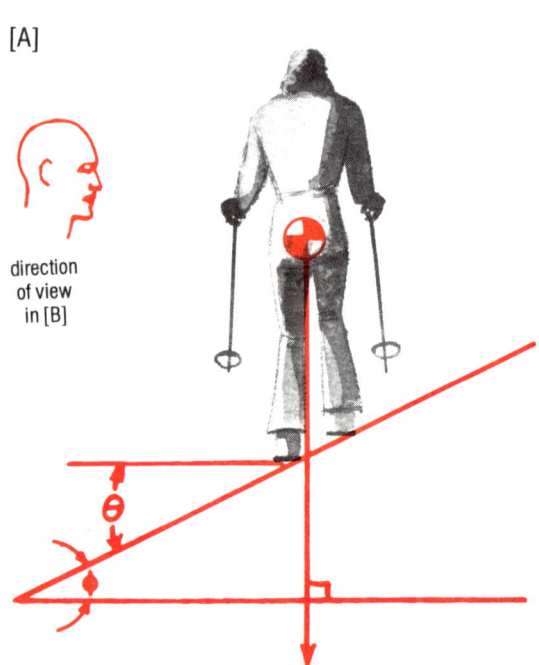

[B]

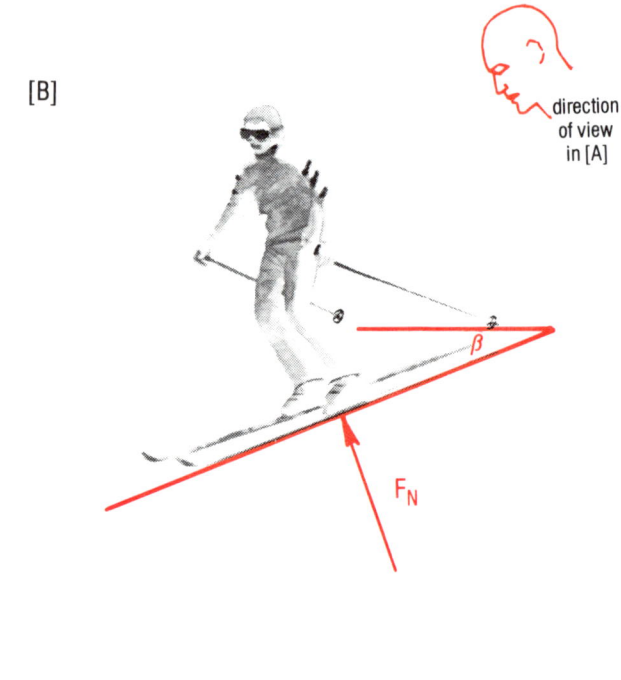

Shuffle And Upper Body Rotation

Top View

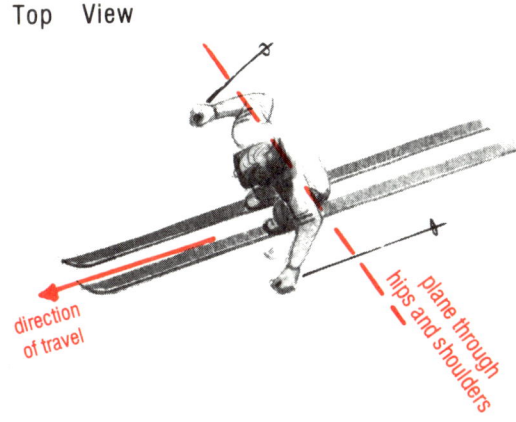

direction of travel

plane through hips and shoulders

Front View

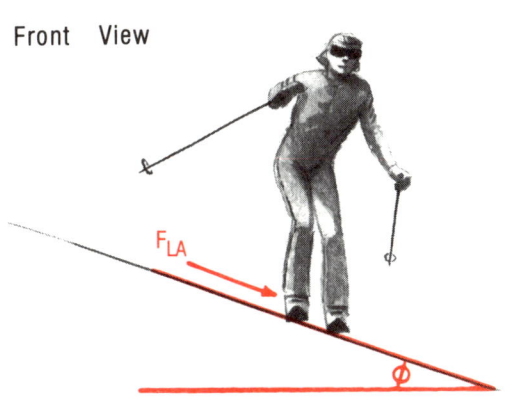

F_{LA}

ϕ

Side View

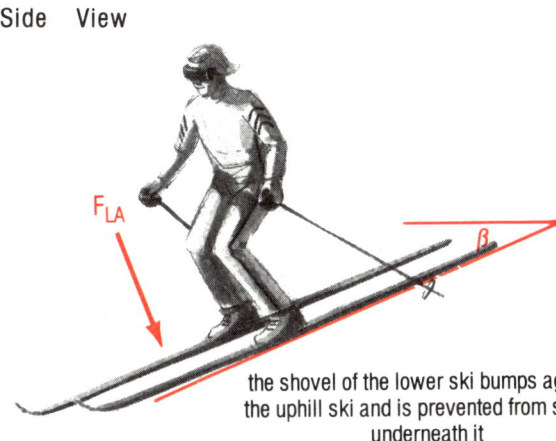

F_{LA}

β

the shovel of the lower ski bumps against the uphill ski and is prevented from sliding underneath it

The relative positions of the skis (shuffle) are different for traversing than for straight gliding. Since the upper leg is more flexed than the lower, it is anatomically more comfortable to have the upper body rotated and facing slightly downhill; especially for low traverse angles (β) and steep hill angles (α).

This hip and upper body rotation also makes it easier to achieve greater edge angle (Θ). This is because rotating the hips slightly makes it possible to move the butt closer to the hill and the upper body away from the hill — all of which allows a greater edge angle (Θ) and a better chance of achieving the lateral adhesion from the snow/ice surface necessary to counteract the sideways force on the skis (F_{LA}). In other words, the skier should be facing slightly downhill with the upper body as well as leaning slightly downhill — especially when (α) gets steep. (This slightly rotated position will also place the upper body in a better position to generate turning forces). The danger of having the body at too much of an angle from the skis is that body freedom and mobility will be lost, and it also becomes very difficult to keep the majority of the weight properly on the lower ski.

Since the outside, lower hip is slightly behind the uphill hip, it follows that the downhill knee and downhill boot should also be behind their uphill counterparts. This implies that the skis will normally be in a "shuffled" position when traversing; ie., the upper ski will be a few inches ahead of the lower ski. An advantage of shuffle is that by trailing slightly behind the upper ski, the shovel of the lower ski will be restricted from sliding underneath the upper ski ("crossed tips").

Excessive shuffle is undesirable, however, because the forces on the skis become too far apart. In this situation, it's likely that the force on the lower ski will be decreased as the ski lags further behind. If this happens on inconsistent snow surfaces, the skis are pulled even further apart and go their separate ways. The force on the lower ski should be the dominant, controlling force, and this can't happen if the lower ski and downhill body segments (knee, hip, shoulder) become rotated too far behind the uphill segments.

Figure 7—23
The concept of 'shuffle' is illustrated in these three views of a skier in a traverse.

Difference In Edge Angles (Θ)

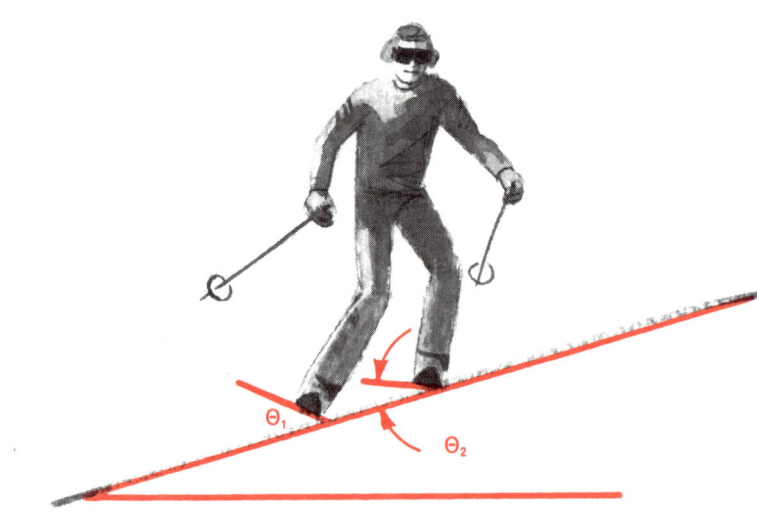

Figure 7—24
Anatomical and boot "geometry" factors can often result in one ski being edged more than the other.

Figure 7—25
The boot and leg geometry should be such that the edge angle is normally perpendicular to the plane of travel of the knee.

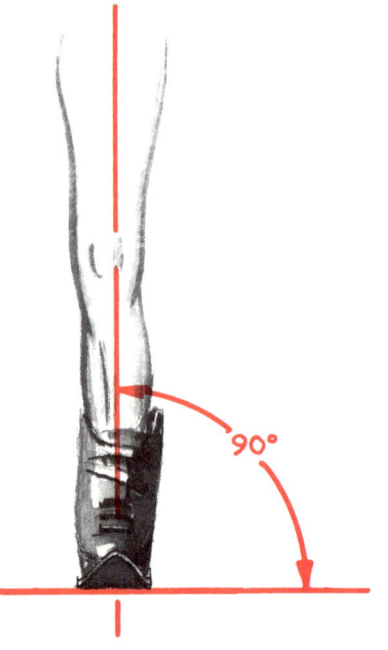

It is entirely possible to edge one ski more than the other. This may happen unintentionally if the skier has leg geometry or boot problems. The solution is to correct the boots or mount wedge-shaped "cants" between the boot and the ski.

It's desirable to have the boot and leg geometry such that the edge angle is normally perpendicular to the plane of knee travel without knee angulation. This relationship should remain constant as the knee is flexed forward.

The subject of canting, or otherwise achieving the proper alignment between the hip, knee, and flat ski, is extremely important and has been discussed extensively in other publications. Major ski shops have devices to determine canting for each leg, and various methods for achieving it after measurement.

Assuming that the leg geometry (as modified by canting, if necessary) is correct, it is rare that the skier will intentionally edge one ski more than the other during a simple traverse. The exception would be on a shallow traverse (small β) and steep hill, where the maximum (Θ) is desirable and better achieved by pressing the lower knee even further into the hill than the upper knee.

This lengthy chapter may seem like "overkill" of something as simple as traversing; but the principles discussed in this chapter are far more easily understood during a long and somewhat static traverse than during the brief instant of traverse between turns. Most of the mistakes of total skiing, ie. traversing, turning and covering all types of terrain, occur because of violations of the basic principles of body position, weight balance and angulation. All of these can be properly established and practiced during the traverse. The remainder of the mechanics of skiing is concerned

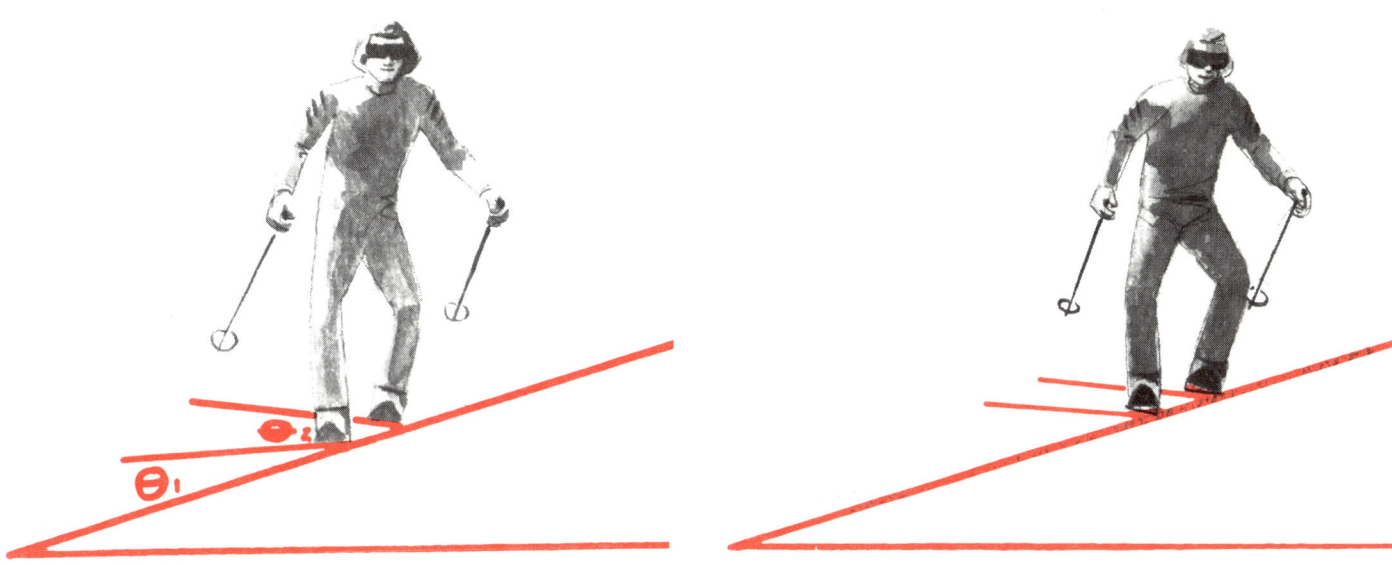

Figure 7—26
Uneven edging of the skis due to bowleggedness can be compensated for by using inside cants or wedges.

only with getting from one traverse to another. No matter how quick the turn is, it usually starts and ends with some type of traverse.

Straight gliding down the fall line, as presented in Chapter 6, is also not as common as one might think. A ski is much more stable if it is at a slight edge angle with the slope. Therefore, much of high performance skiing is likely to be a series of long, linked traverses (carved turns of large radii).

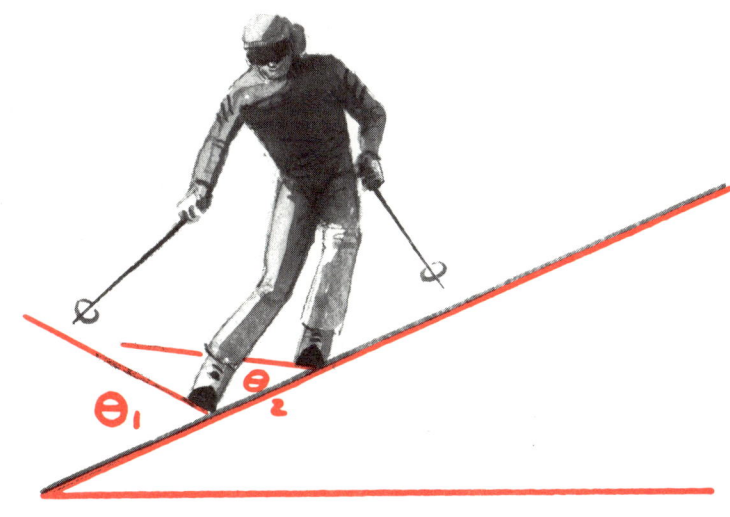

Figure 7—22
A skier can achieve maximum Θ on steeper slopes by pushing his lower knee further toward the slope than his upper knee.

chapter 8

THE MECHANICS OF THE TURN

Centrifugal Force

UP TO THIS POINT, we've only analyzed in detail four basic types of forces involved in skiing.

- Gravitational force (F_g) pulling the skier towards the center of the earth.

- Resistive forces (F_B, F_w, F_f) opposing the skier in the direction of travel.

- Body-generated forces (F_p) assisting in the direction of travel from poling or skating.

- Dynamic forces (F_D) added or subtracted for a short duration to the gravitational forces. These short time dynamic forces are due to the muscles accelerating the body mass upwards or downwards; or by insuring through their rigidness that terrain changes appear as dynamic forces.

The next force of concern, centrifugal force (F_c), may act with, or in opposition to, the four forces above. Newton's first law states that a body tends to continue in a straight line unless acted upon by an outside force. As soon as a skier decides to turn, centrifugal force tries to pull the body back to a straight path. An equal and opposite force called lateral adhesion is required from the snow/ice surface to counteract the centrifugal force and keep the skier turning through an arc without side-slipping. The direction of centrifugal force is radially outward from the instantaneous turning center of the arc on which the skier is traveling.

Usually, the path of the skier down the slope will be some type of curve; which may be a circular arc, elliptical, "fish hook" or

Figure 8—1 ▶
Two views are shown here of the same skier making a turn down the fall line. In "A", the skier is shown from above, with centrifugal force tending to pull him to the outside of the turn.

In "B", the skier is viewed from inside the turn, with centrifugal force tending to pull him away from the viewer.

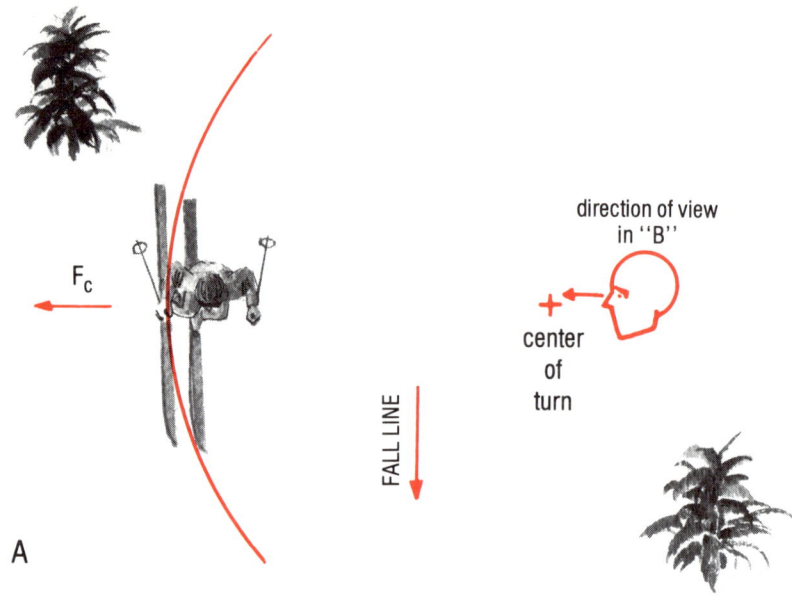

A

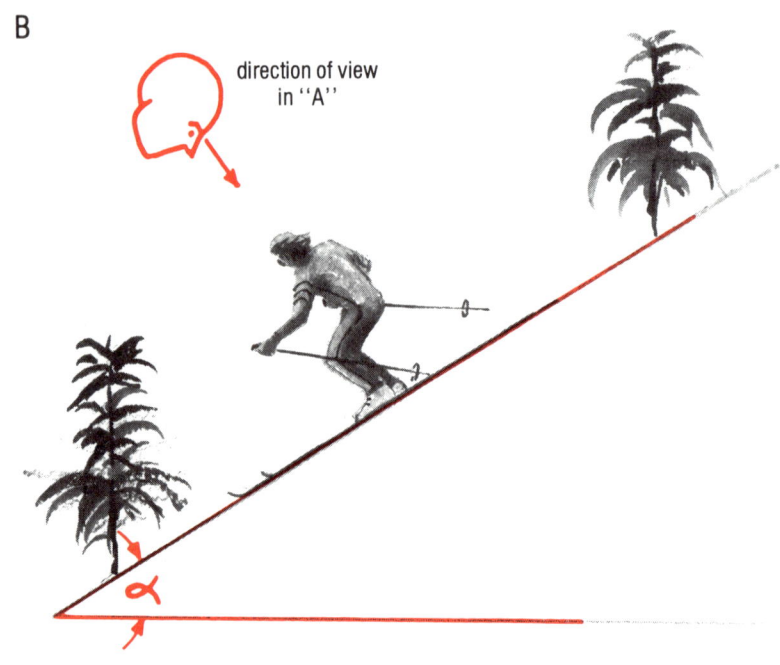

B

a more mixed form, depending on many variables. To investigate the details of turning mechanics, we shall examine the circular arc case, because the analysis is simpler and insight into the mechanics for all types of turns can be gained from such an investigation. To this end then, we show the turn as a circular arc and introduce centrifugal force (F_c) as shown in figure 8—1.

The following new nomenclature will be used in this chapter:

F_c = Centrifugal force

R = Force reacting through thighs, feet and skis against snow. (this is the same (R) as in Chapter 7 but with F_c as an additional component.)

r = Radius of turn being made.

F_{TL} = Total lateral force on the skis parallel to the snow surface

Θ_R = The edge angle *without angulation*; ie. the true angle between the slope and the perpendicular to the reaction R.

The magnitude of centrifugal force is dependent upon velocity, weight, radius of turn and the acceleration due to gravity (g).

(8—1) $$F_c = \frac{F_g}{g} \ \frac{V^2}{r}$$

Combined Forces Parallel To The Slope

In Chapter 7, we developed the expression (F_{LA}) to define the force perpendicular to the skis and parallel to the slope. Since this force is a component of gravitational pull (F_g), it can only act in a direction down the hill; ie. it cannot pull the skier up the hill.

Centrifugal force acts parallel with (F_{LA}) but centrifugal force can act in any direction with respect to the slope of the hill. Therefore, in the downhill quadrants centrifugal force is added to (F_{LA}) and in the uphill quadrants they are in opposition. This adding or subtracting of (F_c) and (F_{LA}) is an extremely important and interesting concept. A good understanding here will do much to explain the fine points of skiing.

The downhill lateral force (F_{LA}) is fixed by the skier's weight, the traverse angle, and the hill angle (a). The centrifugal force on the other hand, depends on a number of variables (equation 8—1)

Figure 8—2 ►
F_{LA} is a component of gravitational force and can only act in a direction down the hill. At [A], F_{LA} pulls the skier to the inside of the turn. When the skier slides straight down the fall line [B], F_{LA} is zero. But at [C], F_{LA} pulls the skier to the outside of the curve.

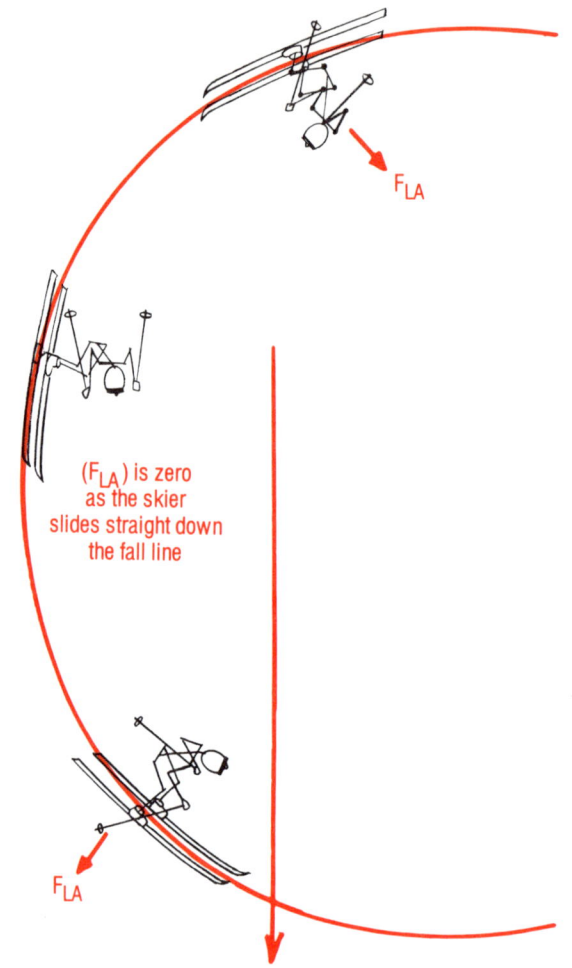

F_{LA}

(F_{LA}) is zero
as the skier
slides straight down
the fall line

F_{LA}

and can vary from zero to a very substantial force. It can be of more or less magnitude than (F_{LA}). If (F_c) is large and (F_{LA}) is small (for instance with a shallow hill angle (α) and high velocity (V)), then the sum of (F_c) and (F_{LA}) acts outward, and the skier can lean in toward the center of the turn as shown in figure 8—4. On the other hand, if (F_c) would be less than (F_{LA}), for instance while traveling slowly on a steep hill, the (F_c) would not be enough to counteract (F_{LA}) and the skier cannot lean into a long turn. The skier, therefore, must remain in a traverse position and effectively be turning up the hill. The skier cannot easily turn down the hill from this shallow traverse. This unstable situation is shown in figure 8—5.

This opposition of (F_{LA}) and (F_c) *in the uphill quadrants* means that the total force *parallel to the skis* and to be resisted by the lateral adhesion of the snow/ice surface is always quite small. In other words, if a turn can be made it is easier to maintain edge

A

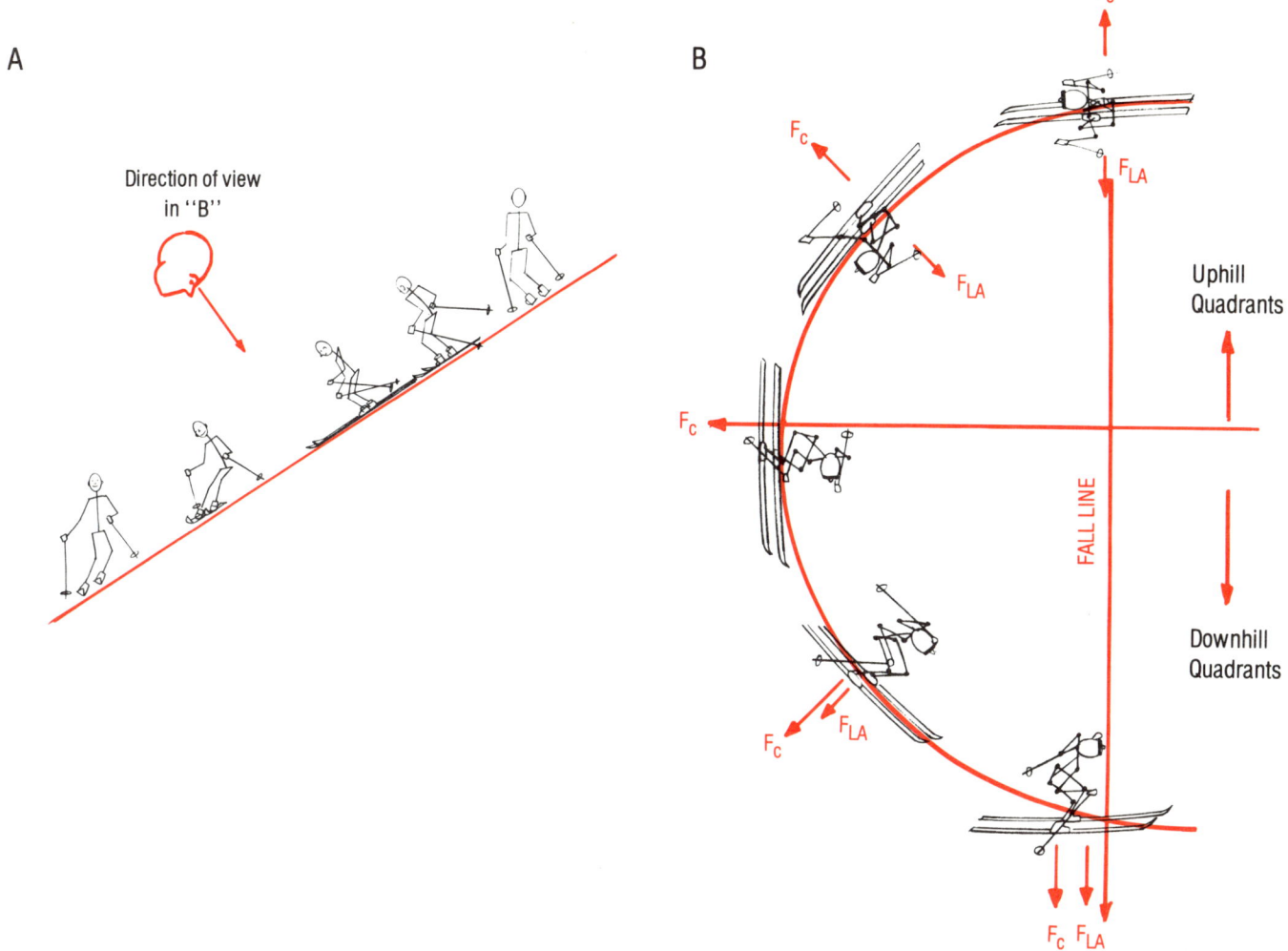

Figure 8—3
Centrifugal force acts parallel with (F_{LA}) but can either act in the same direction as (F_{LA}) or in the opposite direction. In the uphill quadrants, F_c and F_{LA} oppose each other, but in the downhill quadrants they add to each other.

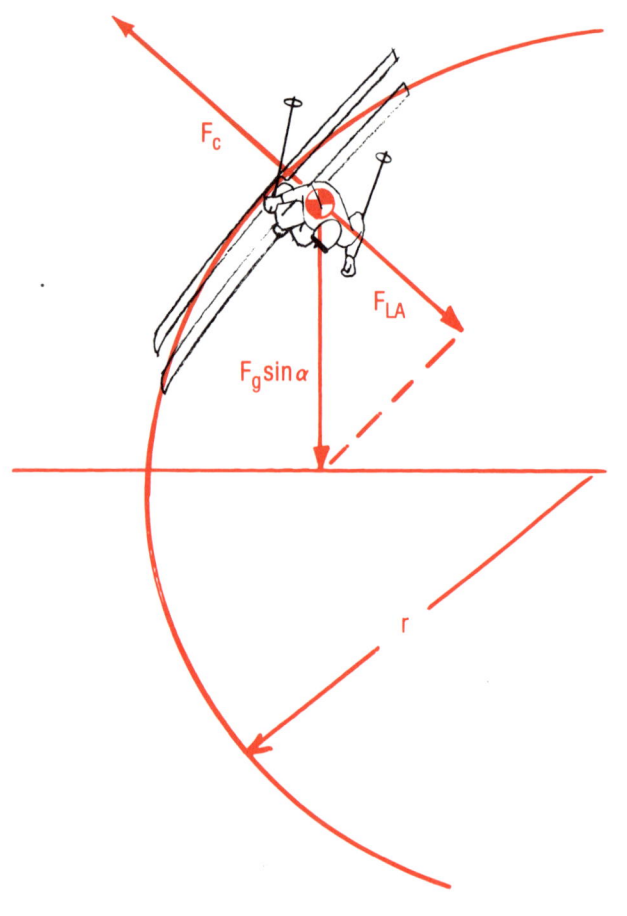

F_c

F_{LA}

$F_g \sin \alpha$

r

Figure 8—4
Centrifugal force (F_c) can vary from zero to a very substantial force, and can be of greater or lesser magnitude than (F_{LA}). If (F_c) is large and (F_{LA}) is small — for example; at high velocity (V) on a shallow hill angle (α) — the resultant of (F_c) and (F_{LA}) acts outward in the uphill quadrants of a turn and the skier can lean to the inside.

TOP VIEW

REAR VIEW (parallel with the skier's travel)

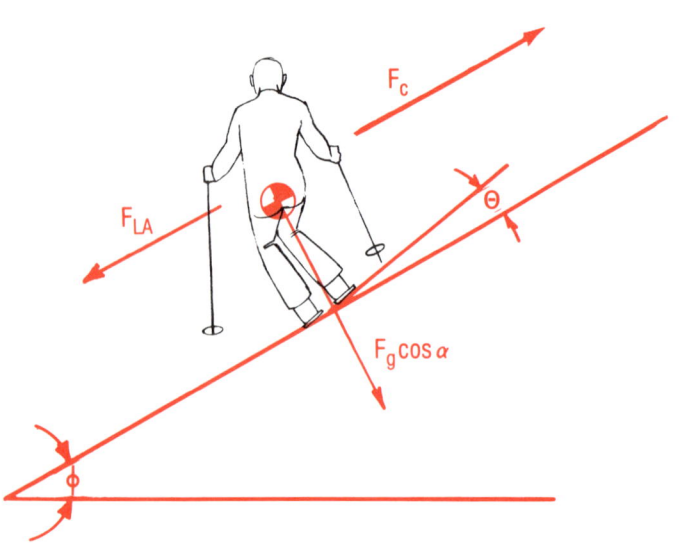

F_c

θ

F_{LA}

$F_g \cos \alpha$

ϕ

Figure 8—5
If (F_c) is less than (F_{LA}) — for example; while traveling slowly on a steep hill — then the skier cannot lean into a long turn. He is in danger of literally falling sideways down the hill.

TOP VIEW

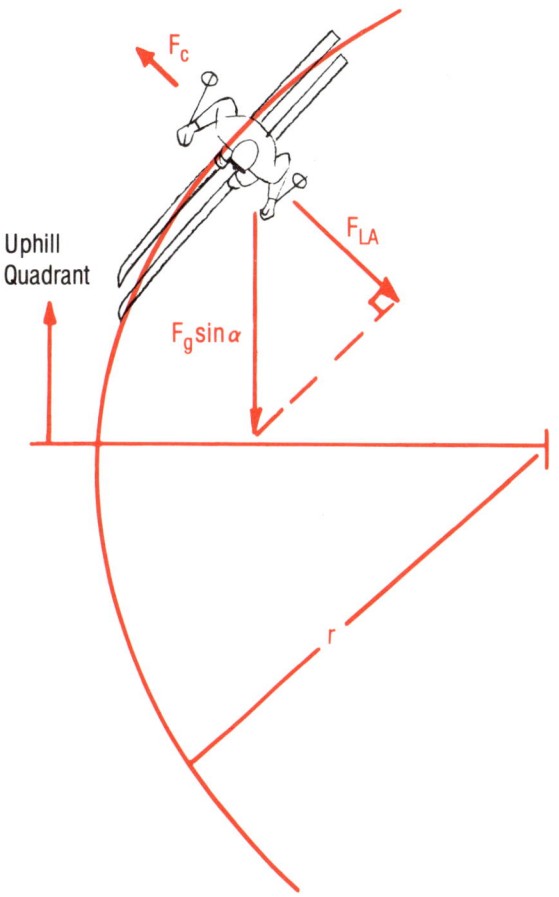

REAR VIEW

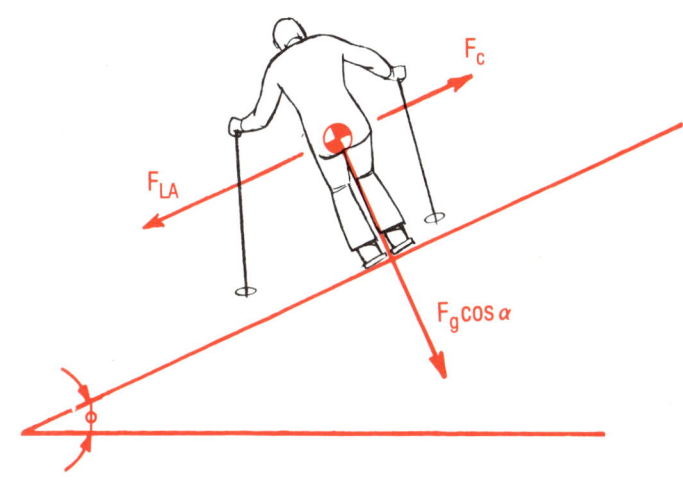

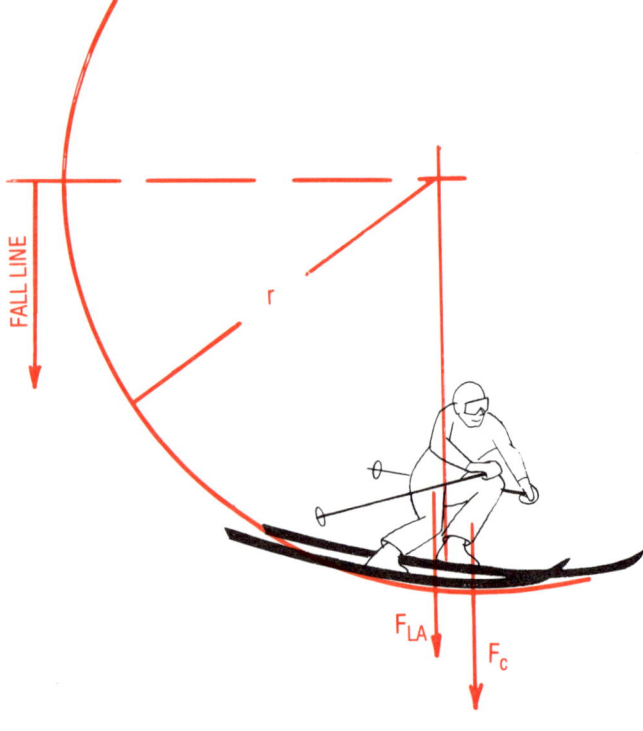

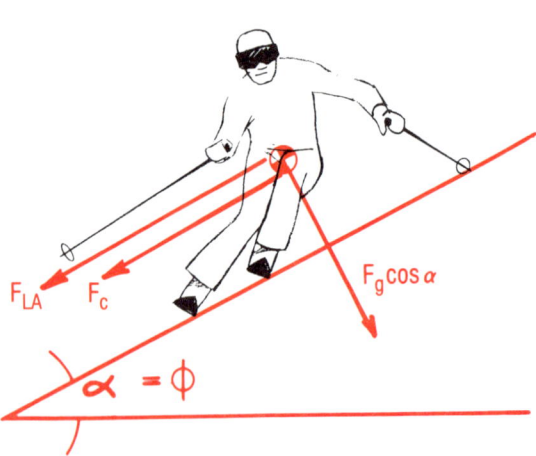

Figure 8—6
At the bottom of the downhill quadrant (F_{LA}) is at its greatest, resulting in a maximum value of ($F_{LA} + F_c$) to be resisted by the lateral adhesion of the snow/ice surface.

adhesion when turning in the uphill quadrants. The principle is exactly the same as turning against a bank.

At the bottom of the downhill quadrant, (F_{LA}) is at its maximum value and is acting in the same direction as (F_c). This results in a maximum value of ($F_c + F_{LA}$) to be resisted by the lateral adhesion of the snow/ice surface. It is difficult to hold an edge at this maximum point of a "fall away" turn.

In real life, very little turning is actually done downhill from a very shallow traverse. The skier is usually already closer to the direction of the fall line or must make some deliberate skidding or stepping movement to get into a steeper traverse. A further analysis of the complete spectrum of turns will be presented next — but first we must establish a convention for plus and minus forces for both left and right turns.

The total force (F_{TL}) perpendicular to the skis and parallel to the snow surface can now be expressed as:

$$(8—2) \qquad F_{TL} = F_c \pm F_{LA}$$

Or, substituting values for (F_c) and (F_{LA}) in equation (8—2) we find:

$$(8—2a) \qquad F_{TL} = \frac{F_g}{g} \frac{V^2}{r} \pm F_g \sin\alpha \cos\beta$$

The force perpendicular to the skis and perpendicular to the snow surface is still, from Chapter 6, ($F_g \cos\alpha$). Figure (8—8) shows (F_{TL}) and ($F_g \cos\alpha$) combining to give the total reaction (R) felt through the thighs and pressing the skis against the snow.

The total force (R) acting against the slope is given by vector addition of (F_{TL}) and ($F_g \cos\alpha$):

$$(8—3) \qquad R = [(F_c \pm F_g \sin\alpha \cos\beta)^2 + (F_g \cos\alpha)^2]^{1/2}$$

(for right angle vector addition, we can use the sum of the squares equation; $R^2 = X^2 + Y^2$)

The angle (without angulation) that the skis make against the slope is:

$$(8—4) \qquad \Theta_R = \cos^{-1} \frac{F_g \cos\alpha}{[(F_c \pm F_g \sin\alpha \cos\beta)^2 + (F_g \cos\alpha)^2]^{1/2}}$$

These two equations really represent the crux of the mechanics of skiing. They give the total force and edge angle for any combination of conditions *excluding* additional muscular forces (F_p) added by the skier, and

Figure 8—7
By convention, forces directed away from the center of rotation are positive whereas those directed toward the center of rotation are negative. Consequently, centrifugal force (F_c) is always positive. (F_{LA}) is negative in the uphill quadrants, positive in the downhill quadrants, and zero when the skier is on the fall line ($\beta = 90°$).

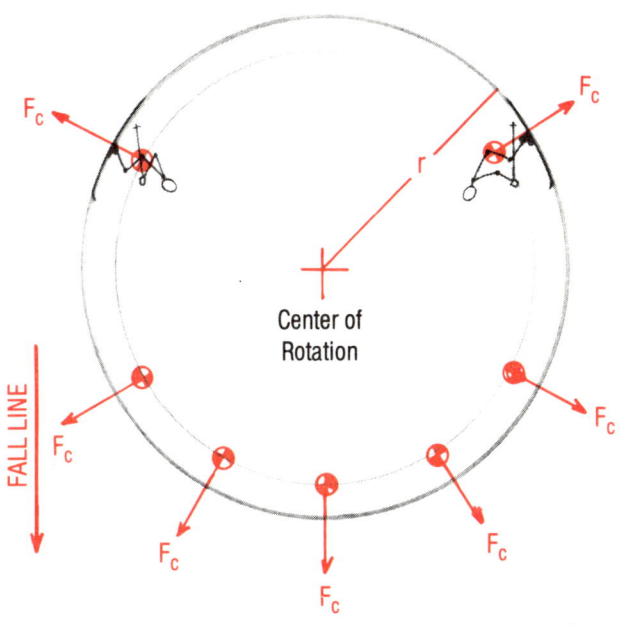

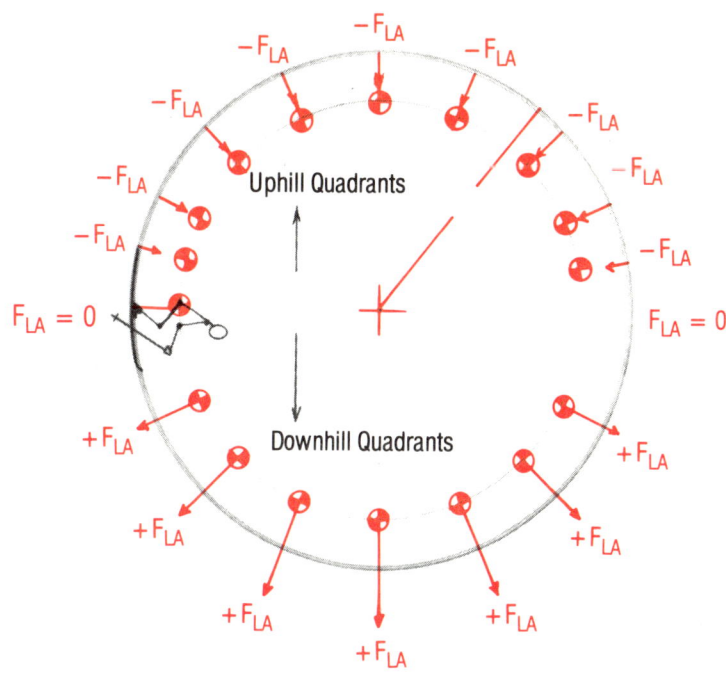

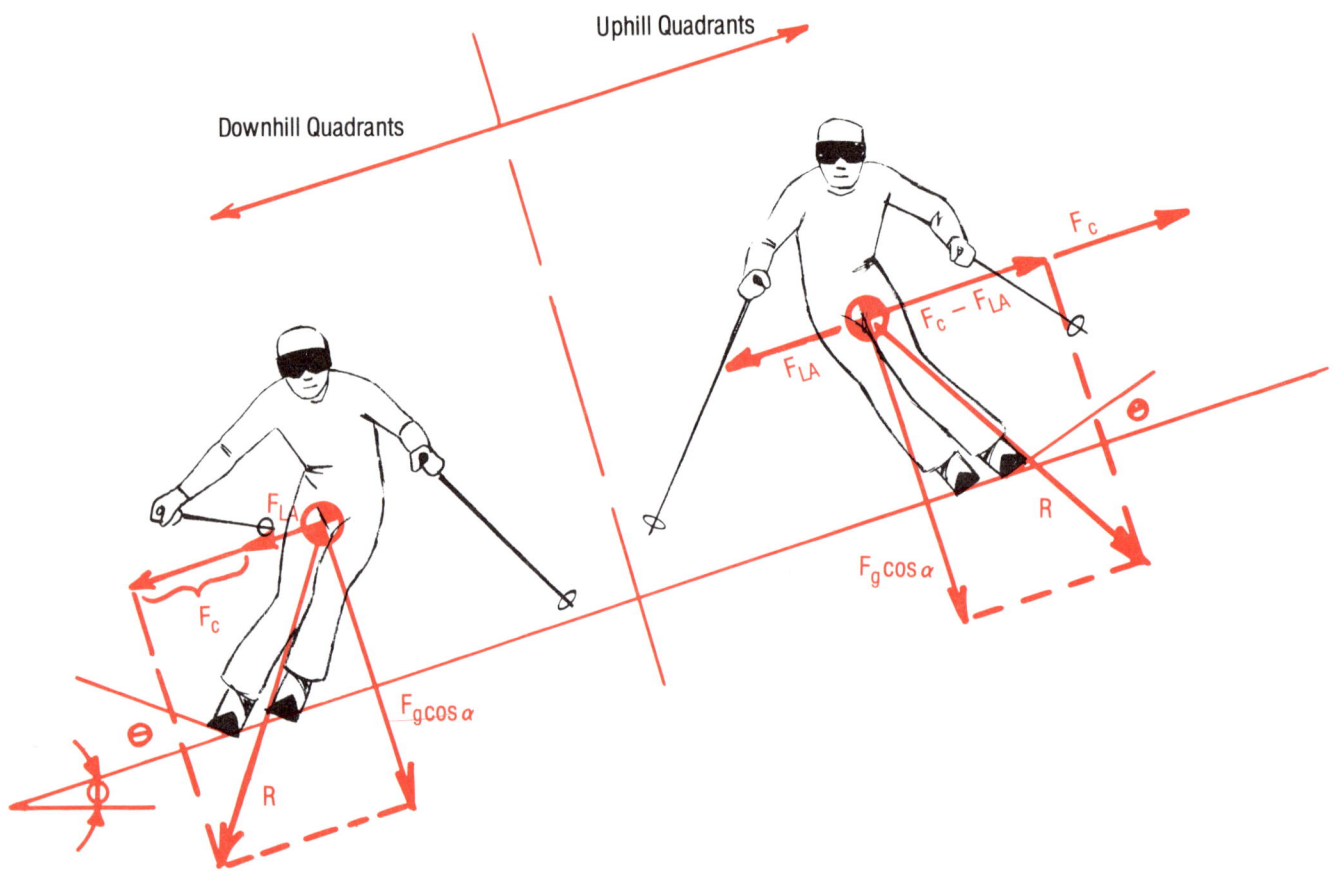

Figure 8—8
The total reaction force (R) that presses the skis against the snow and must be supported by the skier's legs is the resultant of ($F_c \pm F_{LA}$) and the force perpendicular to the snow surface and the skis ($F_g \cos \alpha$).

dynamic forces (F_D) caused by momentary muscular or terrain changes. By better understanding what these two equations really represent, we can now develop a feel for the interaction of speed, turn radius, skier's weight, hill angle, and especially, the position in the turn as specified by the traverse angle (β).

Don't be intimidated by the complexity of these equations at this point. They will be more meaningful and useful as the later chapters evolve into real life situations.

The Meaning Of The Edge Angle (Θ and Θ_R)

It is important at this point to have a clear understanding of the edge angle (Θ) as it relates to turning. When we discussed traversing in Chapter 7, the edge angle (Θ) was defined as the angle between the slope and the bottom surface of the skis. Without angulation, this angle (Θ) is defined by intersection of the perpendicular to the force equation (R) and the slope. This special case of edge angle (Θ) is now defined as (Θ_R) to distinguish it from any other edge angle (Θ) which can be achieved with angulation.

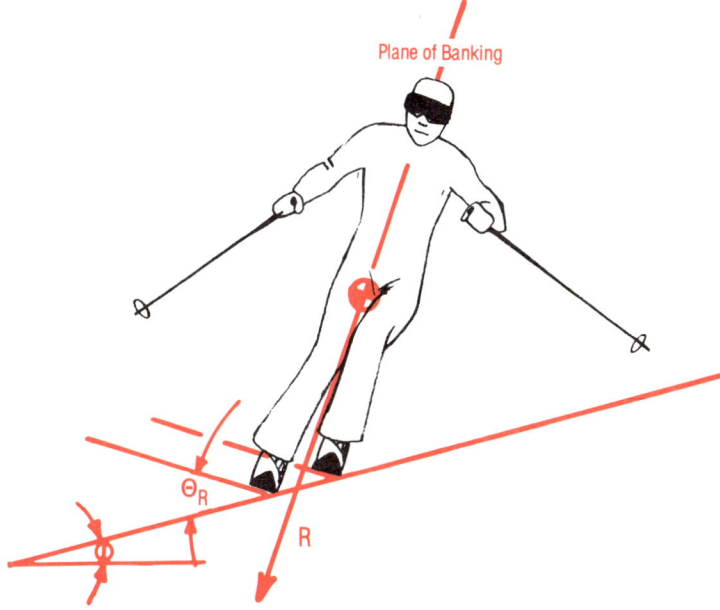

Figure 8—9

As centrifugal force is generated, the skier intuitively leans to the inside of the turn. If he does so wihout angulating, he is said to be "banking" or "inclining" into the turn and the bottom surface of his ski is at a 90° angle (Θ_R) to the resultant of all forces (R). If the skier angulates, as in "B", his ski edge angle (Θ) can be made to be greater than (Θ_R).

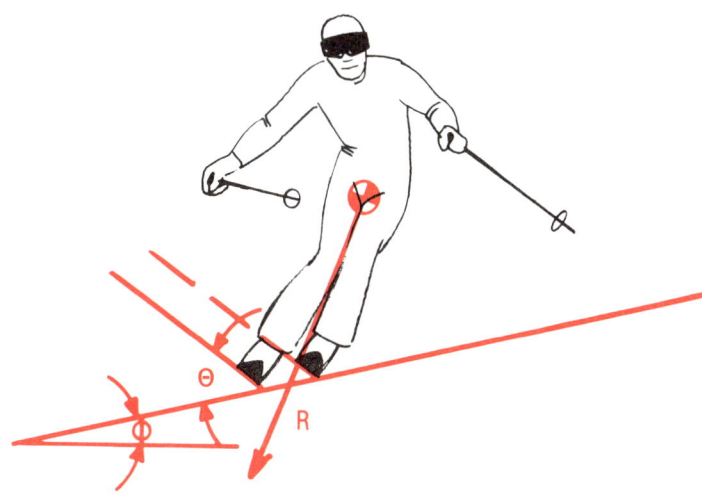

This special edge angle (Θ_R) will later be used as the key to combine the turn the skier is making with the turn the ski wants to make.

When centrifugal force is introduced, the skier (or runner, or bicyclist) naturally has to lean or bank into the turn. He intuitively does this and leans less or further, depending upon his speed and the radius of the turn. If he leans in a plane without any angulation, this is called "banking" or inclining into a turn.

Assuming the surfaces of the skis are perpendicular to the resultant (R) of all the forces, the surfaces of the skis then make the angle (Θ_R) with the slope. With angulation, the angle (Θ_R) can be changed to some other angle (Θ).

This is exactly the same situation as described in Chapter 7 on traversing, although it becomes even more important during turning because the lateral force (F_{LA}) against the ski can be greatly increased to (F_{TL}). By varying the edge angle (Θ), the skier can better achieve the lateral adhesion by the snow/ice surface to counteract (F_{TL}). Also, by varying the edge angle (Θ), the skier can actually help control the radius of the turn. This point will be developed in the next chapters. The conclusion at this point is that equation 8—4 for (Θ_R) at least gives the natural banking turn edge angle (Θ_R) around which variations are effected by the skier.

The Balance Of (F_{LA}) And (F_c)

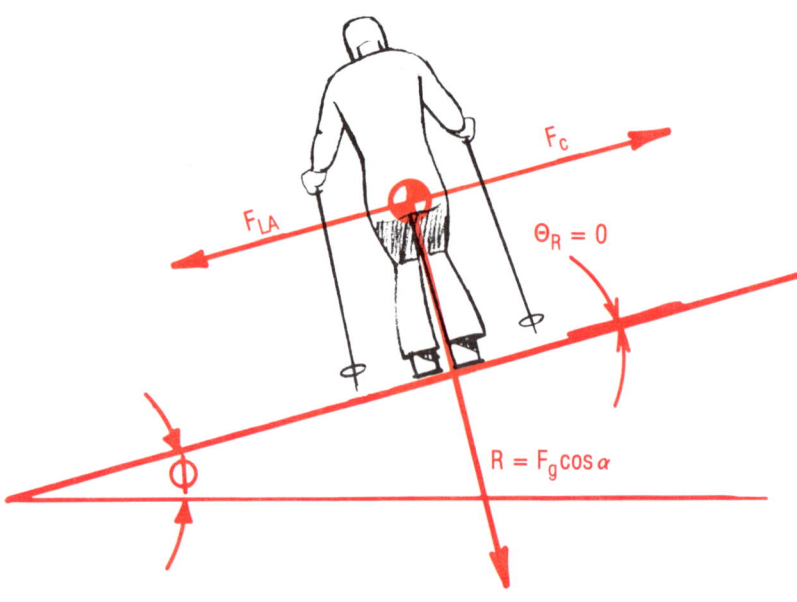

In equations 8—2 and 8—2a, the term (F_{TL}) is made up of a positive term (F_c) and a term (F_{LA}) which could be made negative or positive. Mathematically, there are an infinite number of combinations of (V), (r), (α) and (β) which can result in (F_{TL}) equalling zero. With these combinations, the centrifugal force is balanced exactly by the pull of gravity. This is a nebulous situation where (Θ_R) is equal to zero and the skier is gliding on flat skis.

◄ Figure 8—10
If (F_c) is equal in magnitude, but opposite in sign, to (F_{LA}); then $F_{TL} = 0$, $\Theta_R = 0°$, and the skier is gliding on flat skis.

THE MECHANICS OF THE TURN

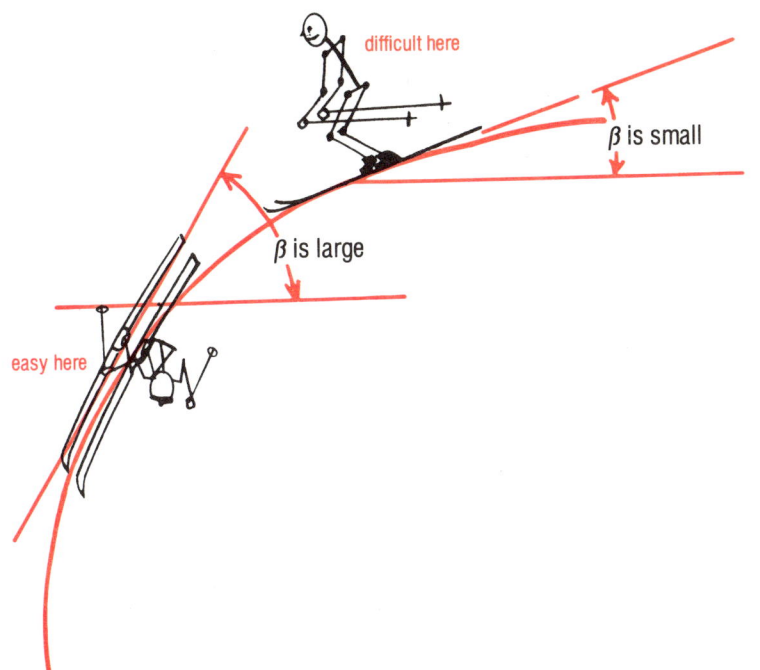

difficult here

β is small

β is large

easy here

Since (β) is constantly changing as the skier turns, this theoretical balance point can only occur once for a given set of (V), (r) and (α). The message here is that there is a balanced combination of forces to consider and the conclusion is offered that, on one side of this balance, when (F_{LA}) is greater than (F_c), it is very difficult to start and maintain a turn. When (F_c) becomes greater than (F_{LA}), usually because of greater (V) or increasing traverse angle (β), it becomes much easier to start and maintain a turn.

◀ Figure 8—11
At any given velocity (V), turn radius (r) and slope (α), there is only one point where $F_{TL} = 0$ since (β) changes constantly as the skier continues through the turn. When (F_{LA}) is greater than (F_c), it's very difficult to start and maintain a turn. But when (F_c) is greater than (F_{LA}) — because of higher velocity (V) or increasing traverse angle (β) — it becomes easier to start and maintain a turn.

Some Examples Of (F_{TL}), (R), And ($Θ_R$)

Several typical combinations of variables will be quantitatively analyzed to give a better meaning to the equations. Consider first a skier of 170 pounds (F_g) traveling at thirty miles per hour (V is 44 feet per second) on a hill of 20° slope (α) and making a turn of 150 feet radius (r). In no case yet, have we said that this is a carved turn. Chances are it is not. If it was, it could only be carved over a certain range of (β) for reasons to be explained later. In other words, it is assumed that the skier maintains (V) and (r) constant by various means; such as a choice of angulation and/or controlled skidding at the tips or tails of the skis. With shallower slope angles, the velocity would not change appreciably through the turn; but on a steeper slope (such as 20°), the skier would, in real life, probably accelerate slightly through the turn.

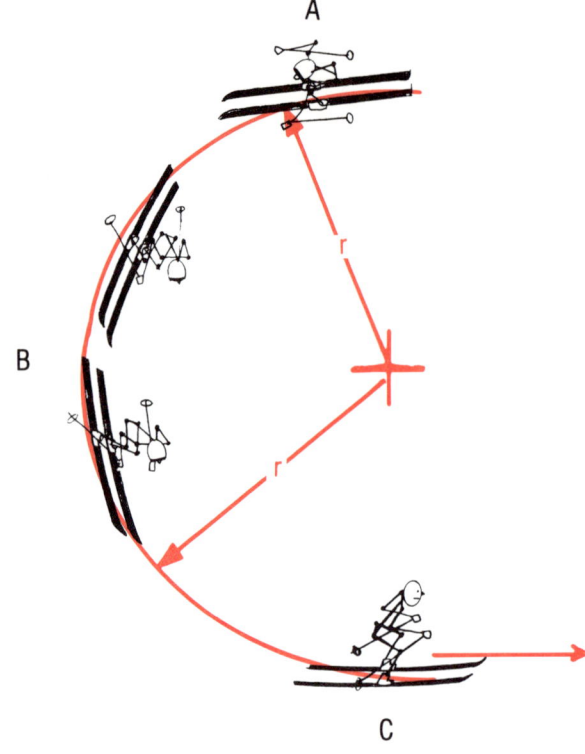

Figure 8—12►
The skier at [A] is in a zone where (F_c) may be less than (F_{LA}). In such a case, a turn is impossible without stemming, steering or stepping into a turn closer to the fall line.

Between [A] and [B], skidding the tails of the skis may be required. Pure carving is most likely achieved at [B], but the skis may skid or chatter at [C], especially if the velocity (V) is too high, the turn radius (r) is too short, or the slope (α) is too steep.

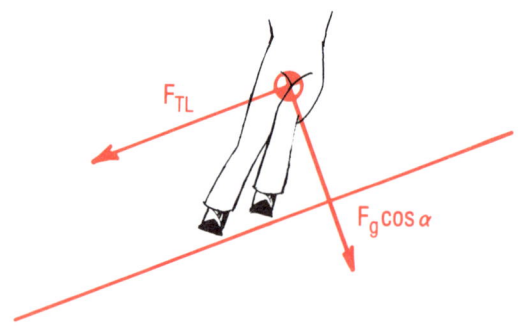

Figure 8—13
As the skier executes a turn, the perpendicular force component ($F_g \cos \alpha$) that forces the skis against the slope remains constant. In this example (where F_g = 170 pounds, V = 44 ft/sec, α = 20°, r = 150 feet), $F_g \cos \alpha$ is 160 pounds. But F_{TL} increases dramatically from 10 pounds to 126 pounds.

For the hypothetical case with (V) and (r) remaining constant, we can calculate (F_{TL}), (R) and (Θ_R) for various traverse angles (β) throughout the turn. Figure 8—14 shows these calculations in graphical form. It is apparent that all three resultant variables increase as the skier goes from (A) to (B) to (C) in Figure 8—12. The perpendicular force component ($F_g \cos \alpha$) that forces the skis against the slope remains constant at 160 pounds throughout the turn. However, the lateral force (F_{TL}) tending to skid the skis sideways increases dramatically from 10 pounds to 126 pounds. At some point in the turn, depending on the quality of the snow/ice surface and the sharpness of the ski edges, there may be a limit to the lateral adhesion the snow/ice can generate to resist (F_{TL}). For instance, assume the maximum lateral adhesion possible for the given ($F_g \cos \alpha$) and ski edge sharpness is 100 pounds. At this level of (F_{TL}) we find from Figure 8—14 that (β) = 60° in the downhill quadrant of the turn.

There is a real message here for serious skiers who frequently ski with combinations of (α), (r) and (V); or harder snow surfaces that give borderline lateral adhesion. The tightest part of the turn should be made early, before or at the fall line. This way, (r) can be increased as the traverse angle (β) comes around to zero on the downhill quadrant of the turn.

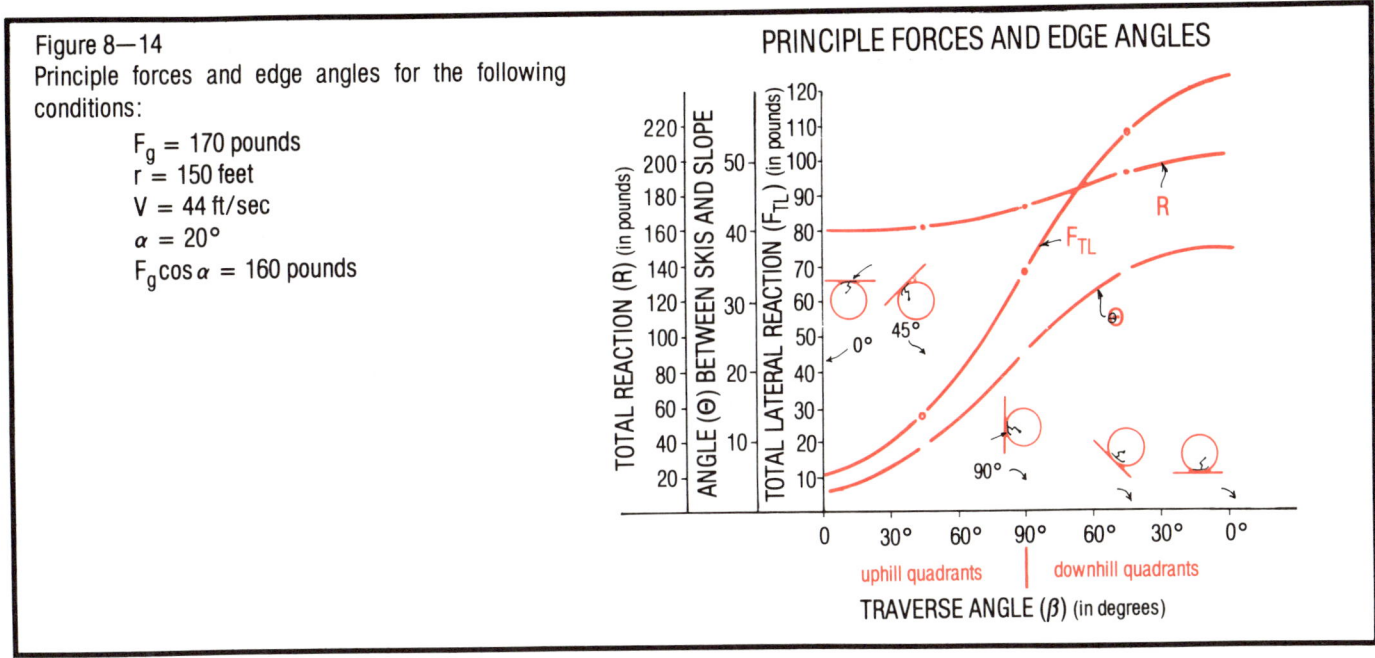

Figure 8—14
Principle forces and edge angles for the following conditions:

$F_g = 170$ pounds
$r = 150$ feet
$V = 44$ ft/sec
$\alpha = 20°$
$F_g \cos \alpha = 160$ pounds

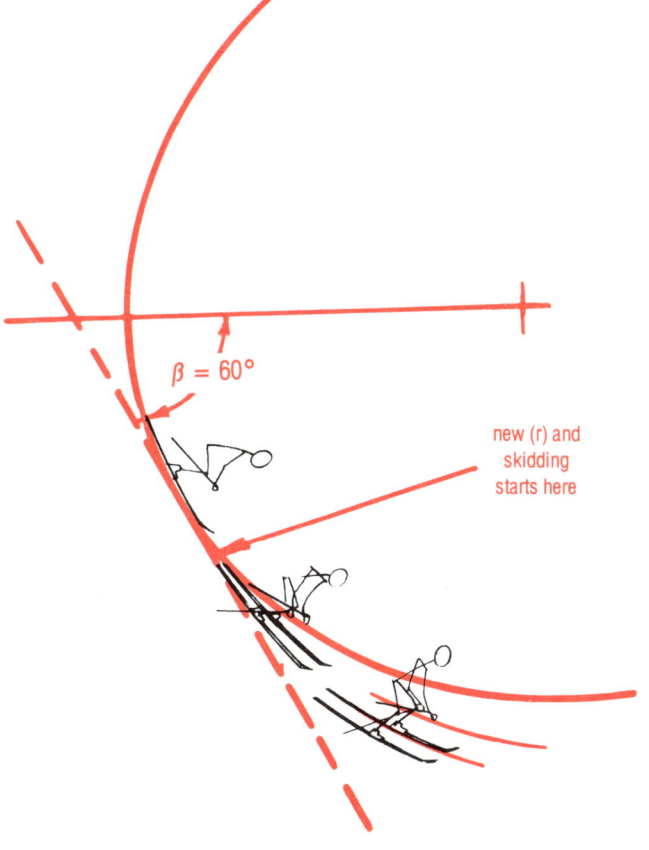

Figure 8—15
If the maximum lateral adhesion possible for a ($F_g \cos \alpha$) of 160 pounds with sharp ski edges is 100 pounds, then from Figure 8—14 $\beta \cong 60°$ in the downhill quadrant. If the skier attempts to continue the turn at the same velocity and radius, he will skid.

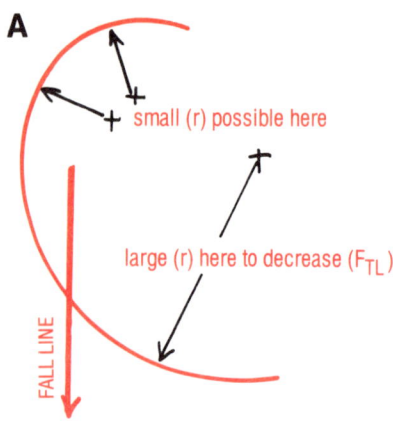

A

small (r) possible here

large (r) here to decrease (F_{TL})

FALL LINE

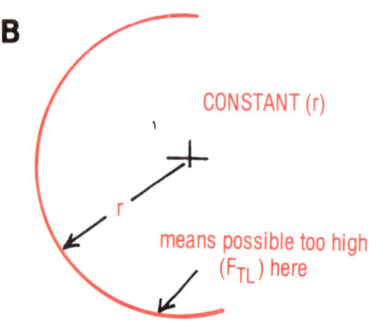

B

CONSTANT (r)

r

means possible too high
(F_{TL}) here

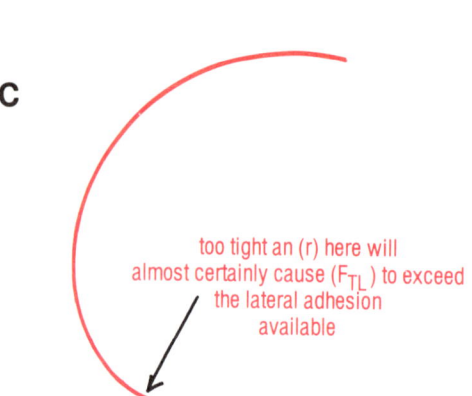

C

too tight an (r) here will
almost certainly cause (F_{TL}) to exceed
the lateral adhesion
available

There are also ways to improve in areas of instability by introducing short duration, dynamic forces via muscular action. This concept will be expanded further in the last chapter. At this point, we at least have the two primary external forces (gravity and centrifugal force) acting on the skier. How these forces are used for graceful, effective skiing depends on the understanding of them and how they can be synchronized with the skier's conscious intentions and other temporary forces. Carving, skidding, interacting with terrain, adjusting velocity and direction, the expert skier unconsciously blends all the internal and external forces with the speed of a computer while at the same time admiring the scenery and enjoying the fresh air. So much is happening, however, that frequently something goes wrong. Like a modern automobile, the results of the problem are usually much more easily observed than the cause. The serious student of skiing needs an understanding of the foundation and 'nuts and bolts' of the sport if one is to advance further or help others. So far, we have analyzed straight gliding, traversing, and turning as pure entities. It now remains to put them together and see how they interact with the ski.

Figure 8—16
In a situation where lateral adhesion is borderline, it is better to make a turn that is tighter in radius early in the turn (before reaching the fall line) as in [A] rather than a round, circular shaped turn as in [B], and far better than making a turn where the radius is tightest toward the end of the turn as in [C].

chapter 9

THE TURN
AS CARVED BY THE SKI

$\mathbf{E}$ARLY IN CHAPTER 2, the side cut of the ski was defined as the long arc formed by each side of the ski when viewed from above. Now we will go further and see how the ski, by virtue of its side cut, interacts with the slope to carve a turn. In Chapter 8, the radius of the turn (r) was as desired and controlled by the skier. This turn may have been skidded or partially carved. The edged ski tends to carve a specific radius (r_t). If the ski turn radius agrees with the skier's desired turn radius, things usually go very smoothly. This pure carved turn is the most efficient way of skiing, since the lack of skidding means virtually no energy is dissipated. A competitive racer must use primarily carved turns. A recreational skier will enjoy more precise, controlled skiing if the carved turn can be approximated as frequently as possible.

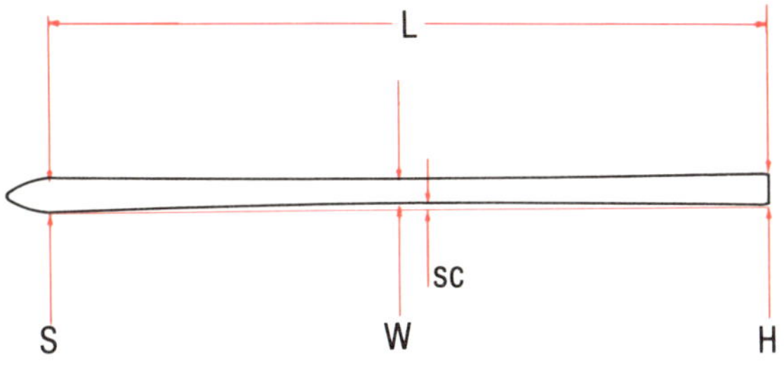

The Radius Of The Carved Turn

The side cut and geometry of the ski can be defined using the terms in figure 9—1. The intersection of the side cut arc and the plane of the *hard* snow/ice surface is defined by another arc. The radius of this semicircular second arc is the radius of the carved turn (r_t). The radius of turn depends on the angle (Θ) between the ski and the plane of the ski slope. If the ski is edged against the surface at a greater angle (Θ), the ski reverse bends deeper, resulting in a tighter turn radius.

Figure 9—2 is a little difficult to understand at first. The lower part of the diagram shows the shadow or projection of the ski in the upper part as it is pressed against the plane of the slope. If the edged angle (Θ) were zero, the ski would be flat and the upper and lower parts of the diagram would be mirror images. As (Θ) increases, the magnitude of the side camber, in the direction *parallel* to the slope, increases inversely proportional to the cosine

Figure 9—1
The side cut and geometry of a ski can be defined by the following terms:

S = widest point of the shovel
H = widest point in the heel
L = length between S and H
W = narrowest point in the waist
sc = side camber

Figure 9—2 ▶

The effective side camber, which defines the carved turn radius (r_t), is a function of the edge angle (Θ).

The silhouette of the ski in the upper part of the diagram is as seen from directly above the ski and perpendicular to the ski surface. The ski is edged and weighted to bend it into a reverse camber, but from our vantage point, the only distortion of the ski that we might likely notice in this 2-dimensional representation would be a shortening of the ski's length.

The lower part of the diagram is a view of the ski from below and perpendicular to the snow surface, just as if the snow surface were a plate of glass and you were viewing from below and at right angles to the glass surface. From this vantage point, we can see considerable distortion of the ski as it is edged and bent into reverse camber until the edge of the ski is in contact with the surface along its entire length. The effective side camber is now the ratio of the ski's side camber to the cosine of the edge angle (Θ) and the carved turn radius is now shorter. As the edge angle (Θ) increases, the carved turn radius (r_t) decreases.

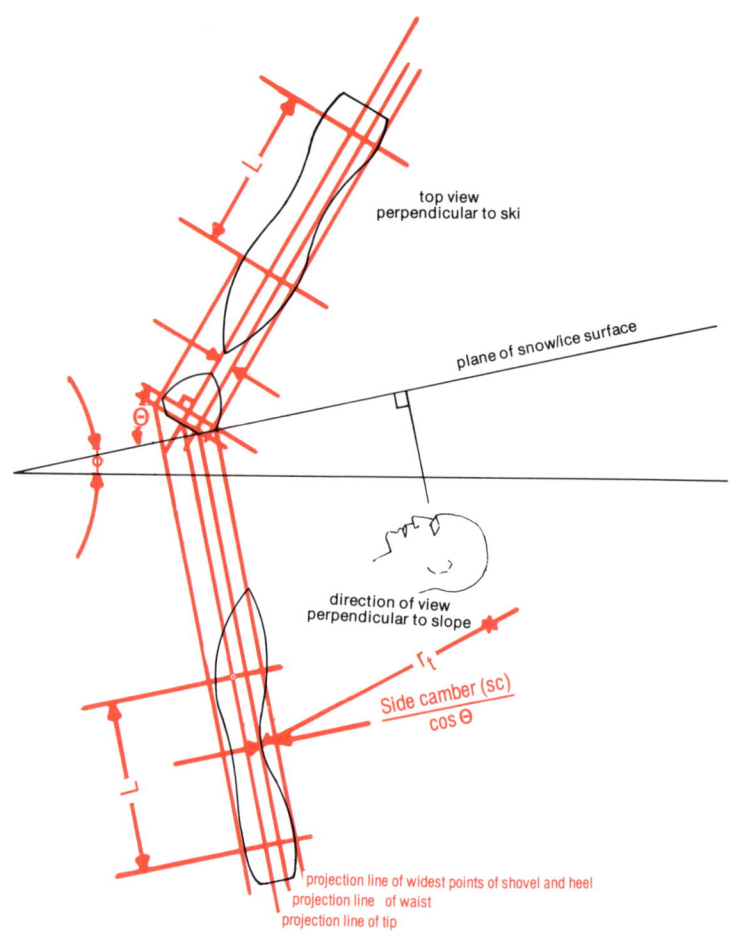

top view
perpendicular to ski

plane of snow/ice surface

direction of view
perpendicular to slope

r_t

Side camber (sc)
———————
$\cos \Theta$

projection line of widest points of shovel and heel
projection line of waist
projection line of tip

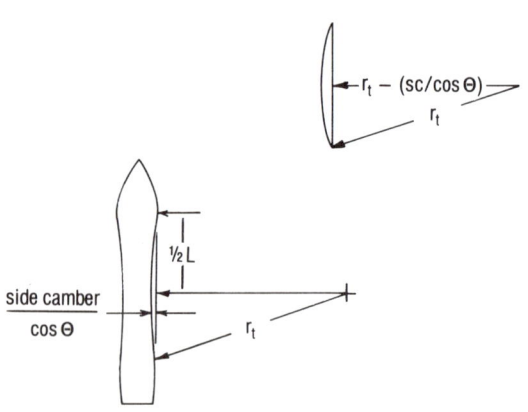

$r_t - (sc/\cos\Theta)$

r_t

side camber
—————
$\cos \Theta$

½ L

r_t

Figure 9—3

If the side cut of a ski approximates the arc of a circle, and the side camber is at ½ L, the radius of the turn (r_t) is found by the square of the hypotenuse equalling the sum of the squares of the two legs.

of the edge angle (Θ). It is this *side camber PARALLEL* to the plane of the slope which determines the radius of the carved turn.

Assuming the side cut of the ski does approximate the arc of a circle, and the side camber is at ½L, then the radius of the turn (r_t) is found by the square of the hypotenuse equalling the sum of the squares of the two legs (as shown in the right triangle of figure 9—3):

$$(9\text{—}1) \qquad (r_t - sc/\cos\Theta)^2 + (L/2)^2 = r_t^2$$

or, expanded:

$$(9\text{—}1a) \qquad r_t^2 - (2\,sc\,r_t/\cos\Theta) + (sc/\cos\Theta)^2 + (L^2/4) = r_t^2$$

This cumbersome equation can be simplified to:

$$(9\text{—}2) \qquad r_t = \frac{L^2 \cos\Theta}{8\,sc}$$

The term $(sc/\cos\Theta)^2$ was dropped out because its value is negligible compared to the other terms in the equation. The side camber magnitude (sc) can be represented by the three important ski widths:

$$9\text{--}3 \qquad sc = \frac{S + H - 2W}{4}$$

Substituting 9—3 into 9—2 gives the equation for turn radius in terms of five variables, three of which represent the side cut geometry of the ski.

$$(9\text{--}4) \qquad r_t = \frac{L^2 \cos\Theta}{2(S + H - 2W)}$$

This equation is among the several most important in this book, as it is fundamental to the carved turn. Some typical examples with three different types of HEAD skis are given in the following table:

Ski Dimensions	Long Turn (208 Cruiser)	Medium Turn (205 SL)	Short Turn (180 Yahoo)
sc	0.255''	0.300''	0.285''
S (width)	3.466''	3.500''	3.636''
W (width)	2.800''	2.705''	2.830''
H (width)	3.121''	3.110''	3.163''
L (length)	76''	75''	66''
edge angle Θ	CARVED TURN RADIUS		
0° *(ski is flat)*	236 ft.	195 ft.	160 ft.
30°	204 ft.	170 ft.	138 ft.
60°	118 ft.	97 ft.	80 ft.

The table shows:
• higher edge angles give shorter turn radii
• shorter skis of equal side cut give shorter turn radii
• greater side cut gives shorter turn radii

That's all! There is nothing more that can be calculated directly from equation 9—4 for the carved turn. However, there are several factors that need to be understood:

• The (r_t) given in equation (9—4) is only for a given (Θ). In real life, as the skier carves around a turn and the traverse angle (β) changes, the edge angle (Θ) will also probably increase. This means that there is no one constant (r_t) that the ski and skier will carve all the way around a turn. This will be explained further in Chapter 10 where the forces generated by the skier (R) are brought together with the radius of turn (r_t) that the ski desires to make geometrically.

• The slope is hard and planar. If it is concave or convex, the radius of concavity or convexity interacts with the turn radius. On a concave surface, the ski tends to carve a much tighter turn. On a convex surface, the ski tends to carve a less tight turn, or no turn at all if the convexity is such that contact is just under the foot. This subject is discussed further later in this chapter.

• The ski has good torsional stiffness. If the ski is torsionally soft, it will tend to generate poor lateral adhesion at the extremities and side slip at one or the other, or both, extremities. Even if the total side force (F_{TL}) is not sufficient to overcome the lateral adhesion provided by the snow/ice surface, the torsionally soft ski will still tend to carve a larger radius turn than if torsional flexibility were not present.

• The turn radius (r_t) that the ski desires to hold is the track it will make during a perfect carved turn. The above table indicates that, in most cases, the carved turn radius is a very long turn — longer than most recreational turns. Turns of shorter radius require some form of over-turning; ie. a subtle skidding of the tail. Until recent years, the beautiful sensation of a perfectly carved turn was only available to the giant slalom or downhill racer. This is because the radius of the carved turn coincided with the very long turns between gates. The high speed achieved by being so long on or near the fall line also required the skill of a racer and a cleared slope.

The advent of the shorter ski with a substantial side camber (like the HEAD YAHOO) has drastically reduced the radius of the carved turn, and brought it much closer to the realm of every day recreational speed and turn radii. This type of ski makes carved turn skiing more available to the average skier and slope angle (α).

The Meaning Of The Edge Angle (Θ)

It is quite clear now how the edge angle (Θ) influences the radius of the carved turn (ie. equation 9—4). In figure 9—4, for example, the skis in "A" will tend to carve a tighter turn; ie. (r_t) will be less than in case "B".

This is one of the most fundamental points in the mechanics of skiing — obvious in its simplicity, but extremely important. First, remember that (Θ) only approaches the value of the hill angle (α) for a slow traverse perpendicular to the fall line (where $\beta = 0$). As the traverse angle (β) changes, or as speed increases and centrifugal force starts to enter into the picture, the edge angle (Θ) will vary considerably. It can easily be zero for straight gliding; or as high as 50° to 60° as the skier approaches, at high speed, the critical perpendicular crossing of the fall line in the downhill turn

Figure 9—4 ►
From equation 9—4, the edge angle (Θ) influences the carved turn radius (r_t). As a consequence of this, the skis in "A" will tend to carve a tighter turn; ie. (r_t) will be less in "A" than in "B".

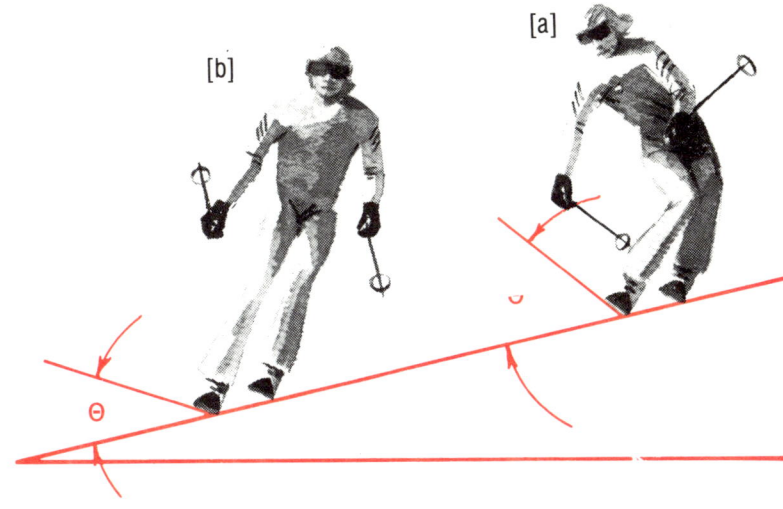

Figure 9—5 ►
The edge angle (Θ) only approaches the hill angle (α) for a slow traverse perpendicular to the fall line (where $\beta = 0°$).

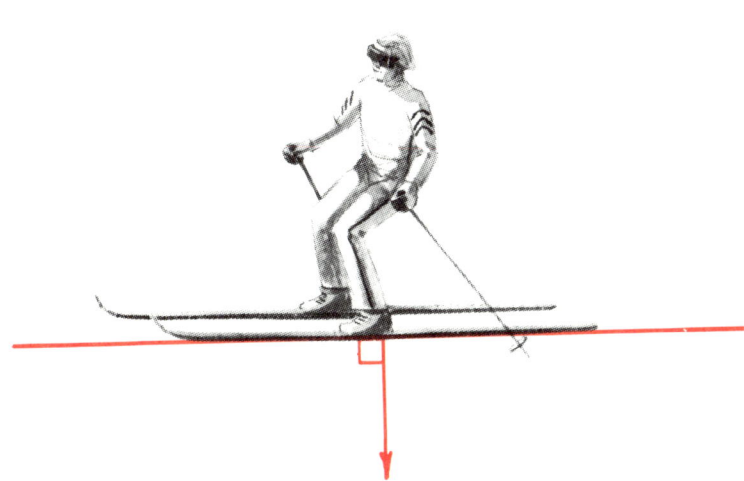

quadrants.

The point of the above is that there are many situations where (Θ) and the corresponding carved turn radius (r_t) are *considerably different* than the skier would like them to be. Most of ski design is a compromise. This is precisely why the side cut of the ski cannot be too great. If it were, the ski would automatically be trying to carve too tight a turn, especially if the slope is very steep or the centrifugal force is high. For instance, even in a traverse the radical side cut ski would be trying to carve uphill too sharply, trying to initiate a turn just when the skier wants to track straight.

An analogy would be that the side cut of the skis is like a steering wheel that is locked in one position and only changes of terrain and/or centrifugal force will affect the radius of turn.

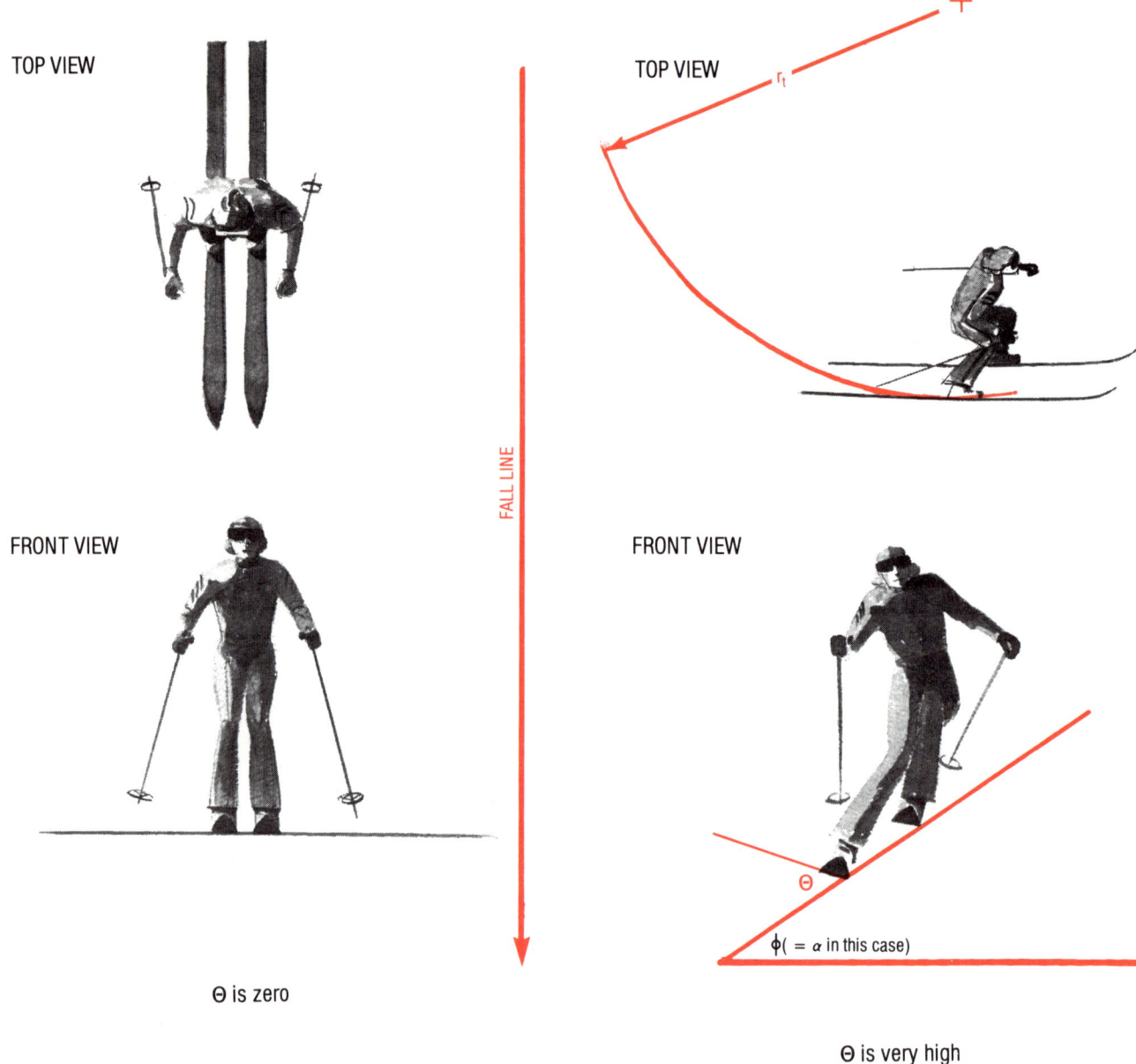

TOP VIEW

TOP VIEW

FALL LINE

FRONT VIEW

FRONT VIEW

Θ is zero

Θ is very high

Figure 9—6
The edge angle (Θ) can vary over a wide range, from 0° during straight gliding
to very high values as the skier approaches the critical perpendicular crossing
of the fall line in a high speed turn.

Changing Turn Radius Without Skidding

Fortunately for the skier, there are two convenient ways to change the radius of the carved turn *without* skidding.

• The actual value of the edge angle (Θ) can be quickly changed by changing the knee and hip angulation. For example, in figure 9—7 the skier can quickly change from the position shown in (A) to the position in (B) with a commensurate increase in (Θ) and decrease in (r_t).

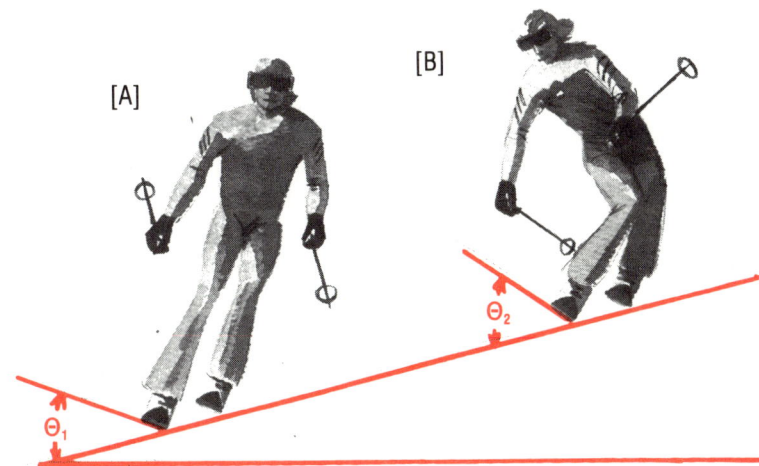

Figure 9—7 ▶
The edge angle (Θ) can be changed very rapidly by adjusting the degree of angulation. The resulting change in edge angle alters the carved turn radius.

• The skier can actually step (laterally project) from the path of one carved turn radius to another. The skier in figure 9—8 has lifted one ski (A) and stepped into a new path (B). This has the effect of drastically reducing the radius of the turn without skidding.

Figure 9—8
Ski racers routinely use a step or *lateral projection* in the bottom of their turns to achieve a higher line; thereby effectively diminishing the radius of their turn but without speed-robbing skidding. The carved turn radius (r_t) is the same after the step as before, but the center of the turn radius has been displaced up the hill, having the same effect as reducing (r_t).

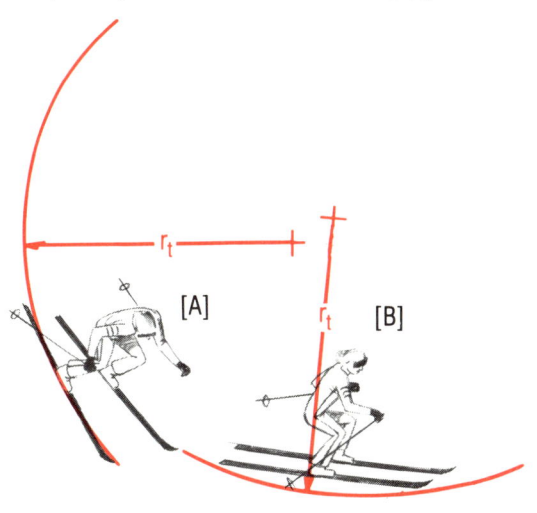

Certainly the above two techniques are common in high performance skiing and racing. Without them, the recreational skier is missing the essence of controlled, carved turn skiing.

As a final comment on the interrelationship of (Θ) and (r_t), it should now be clear that the expert skier who, as a matter of routine, skis with a higher velocity (generating more centrifugal force) on steeper hills, should normally achieve higher edge angles. Thus, the expert has a better chance of bringing the carved turn radius down into the range of every day skiing — say radii of one hundred to one hundred fifty feet on a full length ski. The slower skier on a flatter hill needs a shorter length ski with more sidecut to achieve carved turns in this range of radii.

The Effect
Of Longitudinal Bending Stiffness

Figure 9—9 ▶

From a practical standpoint, the longitudinal stiffness of the ski — on a hard, planar surface — has no effect on the edge angle (Θ) and, therefore, the carved turn radius, since even the stiffest of skis, when edged, are readily bent into a reverse arc only until the edge comes into contact with the snow surface. Here, a ski edged at an angle (Θ) to the snow surface and depressed into reverse camber is shown in three projections: (A) from a position directly above and perpendicular to the top surface of the ski; (B) from directly in front of the ski; and (C) a side view of the ski as seen parallel to the ski base. Since the ski can be depressed into reverse arc only until the waist of the ski contacts the snow, the magnitude of this bending deflection (B_D) is determined by the edge angle (Θ) and the side cut of the ski.

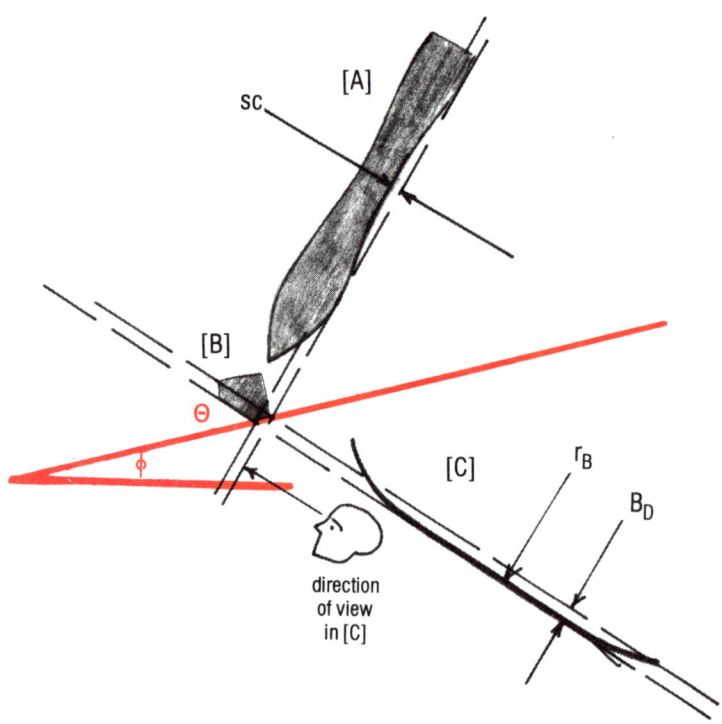

So far in this discussion on the natural carved turn radius (r_t), nothing has been said about longitudinal bending stiffness. Yet, we know intuitively that stiffness has some influence on the turn. Certainly skis for short radius turns need to be softer in longitudinal flex than skis for long radius turns. To answer this question, we first need to go back to the basic theory of a ski's side camber arc intersecting a planar surface (figure 9—9). Only this time, instead of looking at the intersection of the ski arc and the slope plane at a direction *perpendicular to the slope*, we will look at the same intersection at a direction *perpendicular to the side cut of the ski* and *parallel* with the ski base. This way, we see the ski bent into a reverse arc with the deflection called the bend deflection (B_D). If there is no weight on the ski, (B_D) would be negative and equal the ski camber. The magnitude of this deflection with the ski pressed against a hard, planar surface is:

$$(9\text{—}5) \qquad B_D = \tan\Theta\,(sc)$$

...or,

$$(9\text{—}5a) \qquad B_D = \tan\Theta \left[\frac{S + H - 2W}{4} \right]$$

and the radius of the ski bending curve (r_B) is:

$$(9\text{---}6) \qquad r_B = \frac{L^2}{2\tan\Theta(S + H - 2W)}$$

So far, there is still no term for longitudinal stiffness. The reason is; the ski will bend *only* as far as required to contact the slope, and no further (as long as the force available to bend the ski is equal to or greater than the stiffness of the ski). For instance, if we are standing with the ski flat against the ground ($a = 0, \Theta = 0$), we know intuitively that we still press the ski (skis) flat *and only flat* whether we weigh 150 pounds or 300 pounds. Figure 9—10 shows a range of force/deflection curves for typical skis ranging from soft (30N/cm) to stiff (60 N/cm) as measured by the standard test method (ASTM 498-77). From this figure, we can see that even the stiffest skis require less than 50 pounds to reverse bend them to a (B_D) of 1.0 inches. Now, for a typical slalom ski edged at an angle of 60°, we find from equation 9—5a that:

$$B_D = \tan\Theta\left[\frac{S + H - 2W}{4}\right] = \tan 60°\left[\frac{3.50'' + 3.11'' - 2(2.705'')}{4}\right]$$

$$= 0.519 \text{ inches}$$

Refering down to figure 9—10 for a stiff ski, a (B_D) of 0.519 inches requires only 30 pounds of force. This means that on a planar surface it takes quite a bit less force than is available to press even a stiff ski into its *full contact* reverse bend. From this, we can see that on a hard planar surface, the stiffness of the ski will not effect the natural radius of turn that the ski is carving.

Figure 9—10
The range of the ratio of bending force to deflection for typical skis is explored here. The longitudinal stiffness of modern racing skis ranges from a spring rate of 30 Newtons/cm to 60 Newtons/cm.

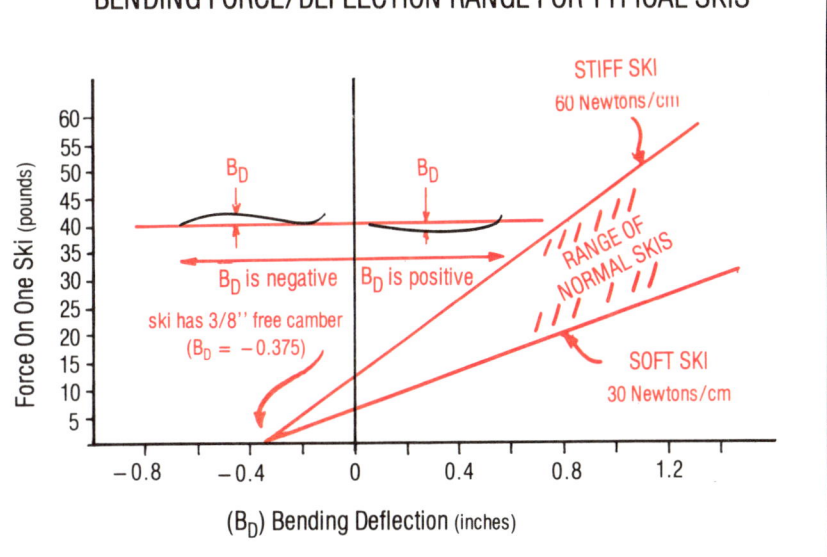

BENDING FORCE/DEFLECTION RANGE FOR TYPICAL SKIS

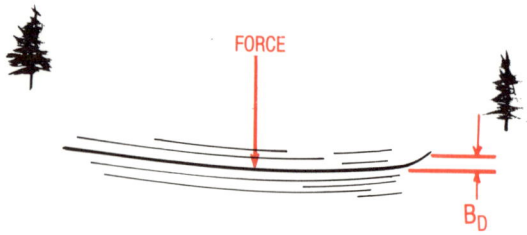

Figure 9—11
In practical terms, the magnitude of bending deflection possible (B_D) is also a function of terrain. A concave surface will allow a greater bending deflection than would be dictated by the edge angle and side cut of the ski.

This does not mean that stiffness is not important. A stiffer ski exerts much more force at the extremities and, therefore, is more likely to break loose at the tip or tail if the lateral adhesion of the snow/ice surface is borderline with respect to the total lateral force (F_{TL}) generated. Conversely, too soft a ski has not enough force at the extremities to maintain good stability — even when bent into a turn. This ski will feel like it is carving only under the foot and will tend to pivot easily. The proper ski flex is determined by the skier's weight and the type of terrain and snow conditions one will be skiing in. Obviously, as soon as the terrain is concave, this concavity must be considered in addition to the bending deflection (B_D) caused by pressing the edged ski into a reverse bend.

The Effect Of Soft Snow

A

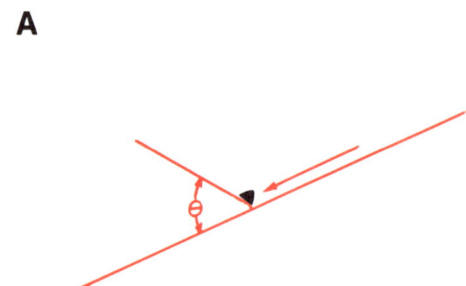

B

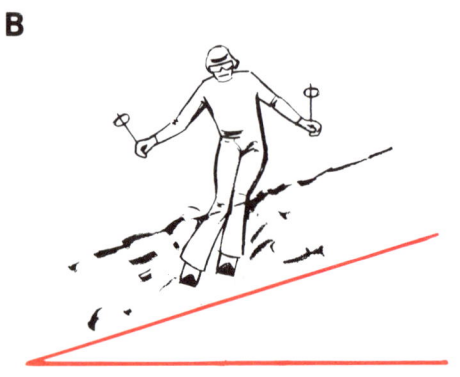

So far in this chapter, we have considered only a ski carving its natural arc on a planar, hard snow/ice surface. In this case, it is the intersection of the sharp edged arc of the ski and the hard surface that determines the radius of the turn.

If, however, the ski is submerged in deep snow, the theory presented thus far is not accurate. In deep, soft powder without an underlying base, the entire bottom surface of the ski is buoyed by the resistance of the snow (figure 9—13). In this case, the phenomenon of carving is not one of the ski side cut arc pressed against a hard, planar surface. Instead, the buoyancy of the powder interacts with the width and longitudinal flex distribution of the ski to reverse bend the ski and press it into a turn. The longitudinal flex of the ski becomes the major factor in determining how the ski will bend through a turn, although the skier generated forces and edge angles remain the same as developed in Chapter 8 for hard surfaces. It is not possible to

◄ Figure 9—12
On a very hard, planar surface (''A''), the carved turn radius of the ski is defined by the interaction of the sharp edge of the ski and the snow surface; which in turn is a function of the edge angle Θ) and the side cut of the ski.
But in soft or powder snow that is sufficiently deep that the underlying packed base doesn't effect the skis (''B''), the width and longitudinal flex distribution of the skis determine the amount of bending deflection and, thereby, the radius of turn. Most powder skiing situations fall somewhere between these two extremes.

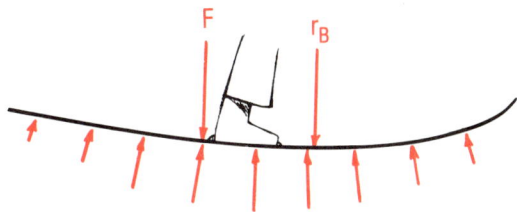

Figure 9—13
In deep, soft powder without an underlying base, the entire bottom surface of the ski is buoyed by the resistance of the snow.

calculate the radius of carved turn in deep powder since the density and bouyancy of the snow are extremely difficult to define.

The above discussion explains the general acceptance of the wide, thin profiled, very flexible metal ski as the best for deep powder skiing. Several ski companies have made specialized skis for this purpose. Unfortunately, for the "powder hounds," truly deep powder is rare, and when it does occur it doesn't last long. This means that the most practical ski also has to be acceptable in varying powder surfaces as well as on harder snow.

It is possible to determine the effect of *packed* powder on the theoretical carved turn radius. By starting with the analysis offered at the beginning of this chapter, we can build an argument for the theoretical carved turn radius when the ski is pressed further into packed powder.

The very edge of a ski is shown in figure 9—14. The shovel and tail are at the surface of the snow/ice plane. In case (A), the waist is pressed against a hard surface and the radius of the turn is determined by the depth of the ski waist (sc/cosΘ) parallel to the slope. This is the basis of the derivation leading to equation (9—2) for the carved turn radius (r_t). If the snow surface is soft (case B), the waist of the ski (assuming the longitudinal flex is reasonably soft) will sink into the snow an additional distance (X). This additional penetration appears parallel to the slope as (y) where:

$$(9—7) \qquad y = x \sin \Theta$$

Using the same approach as in the derivation of equations (9—1), (9—1a) and (9—2); we find the equation for the radius of carved turn on the softer surface to be:

Figure 9—14 ▶
The very edge of the ski at the shovel and waist is shown here. The edge of the shovel and tail of the ski are in contact with a planar snow/ice surface, though the tail of the ski isn't depicted in this illustration. In situation (A), the waist of the ski is pressed against a hard surface and the turn radius is determined by the depth of the ski waist, or effective side camber (sc/cos Θ), parallel with the slope. If the snow is soft, the waist of the ski will sink into the snow an additional distance (X).

In reality, of course, the shovel and tail of the ski will sink down through the surface of the soft snow as well as the waist, but the longitudinal flex distribution of the ski is such that the waist will sink down further, and the net bending deflection of the ski in soft snow is approximately (B_D + X).

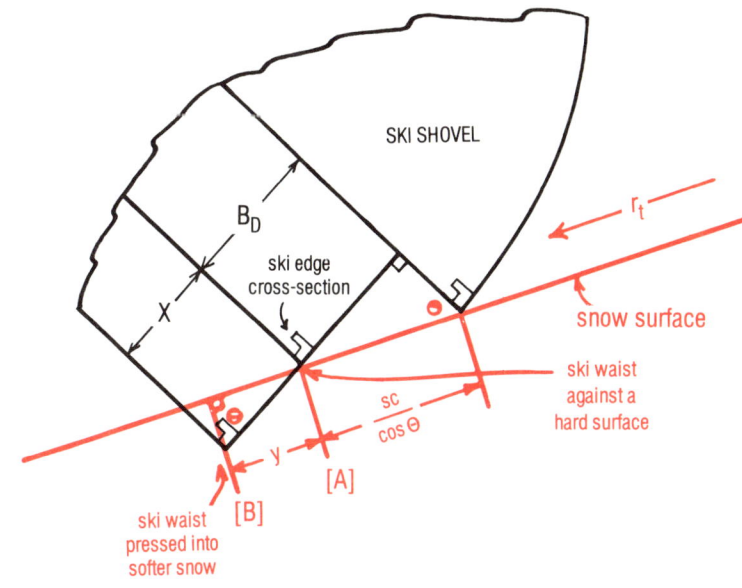

$$(9—8) \qquad r_t \text{ soft} = \frac{L^2}{8[(sc/\cos\Theta) + x\sin\Theta]}$$

By combining this equation with equation (9—2) for hard surfaces, we can derive the ratio of the soft surface carved turn radius to the hard surface turn radius.

$$(9—9) \qquad \frac{r_t(\text{soft})}{r_t} = \frac{sc/\cos\Theta}{[(sc/\cos\Theta) + x\sin\Theta]}$$

One might argue that it is impossible to have the shovel and tail at the surface of the softer snow concurrent with the waist penetrated into the snow. This argument is valid, but because of the longitudinal flex of the ski the pressure distribution of the reaction force (F_N) on the ski will be greatly biased toward the waist for small values of total bending deflection $(B_D + X)$. The depth of ski penetration (X) is added to the theoretical bending deflection (B_D) to find the total bending deflection. From figure 9—10, we see that additional values of (X) up to... say one inch will still not require a single ski force greater than fifty pounds with a stiff ski or thirty pounds with a soft ski. Even if the ski is stiff enough (or the snow soft enough) to cause the shovel and tail to sink slightly into the snow surface, the theory presented here is still valid. We only need to consider the additional penetration (X) as additive to the theoretical bending deflection (B_D) that would occur on a hard surface.

Figure 9—15 ▶
Here the effect of soft snow on the carved turn radius is explored. The side camber (sc) for all three skis is 0.300''.

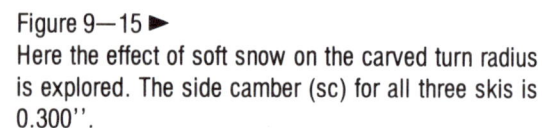

$$\frac{r_t(\text{soft snow})}{r_t(\text{hard snow})} = \frac{sc/\cos\Theta}{(sc/\cos\Theta + \sin\Theta x)}$$

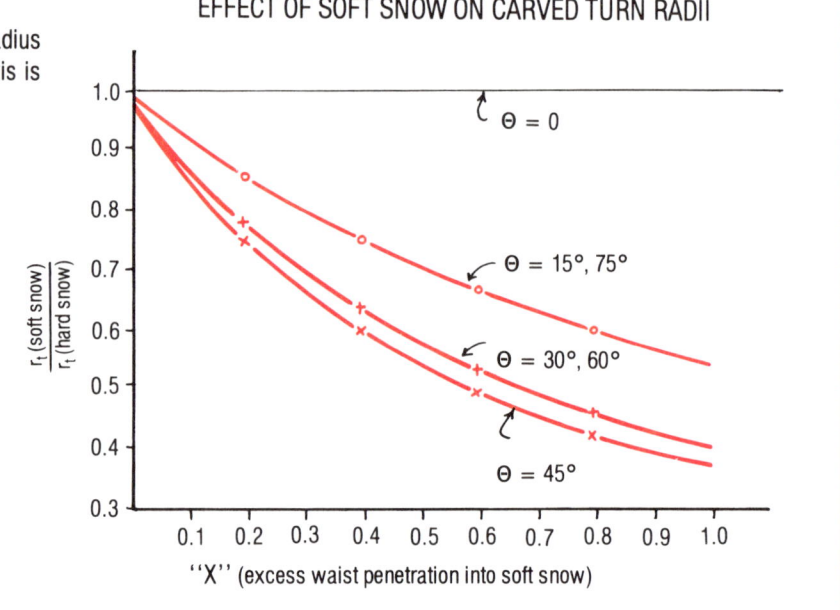

EFFECT OF SOFT SNOW ON CARVED TURN RADII

$\frac{r_t(\text{soft snow})}{r_t(\text{hard snow})}$

$\Theta = 0$

$\Theta = 15°, 75°$

$\Theta = 30°, 60°$

$\Theta = 45°$

"X" (excess waist penetration into soft snow)

Figure 9—15 shows typical reductions in the carved turn radius (r_t) as a function of the extra penetration of the ski waist *beyond* the penetration of the shovel and tail. The points on this figure were calculated using equation (9—9) and with a ski of side cut (sc) equalling 0.300''. It is very interesting to note the effect that the edge angle (Θ) has on the ratio (r_t soft snow/r_t). As the edge angle increases up to a maximum of 45°, the ratio decreases. Beyond 45°, the ratio starts to increase again; that is, the ratio is the same for an edge angle of 15° as for an angle of 75°. This anomaly requires some thought. The reason for it is that at higher edge angles, the side cut of the ski parallel to the slope (sc/cosΘ) becomes more of a factor than the additional penetration parallel to the slope (X sinΘ).

From figure 9—15, it can be seen that it is possible for a theoretical carved turn in soft packed powder to be as short as 50% of the same turn on the idealistic, very hard surface. This is why the skier can experience the feeling of a tighter carved turn if all the weight is pressed on one ski instead of balancing on two. It also explains the feeling of a tighter turn during the instant of upweighting on the carving ski.

Extra penetration (X) of the waist of the ski beyond one inch is unlikely because the longitudinal flex of the ski *does* start to become a significant factor. This prohibits the ski from bending further. If the ski were made very soft longitudinally, it would have a tendency to carve into extremely tight radii under circumstances of concave surfaces. It also would not have the required pressure distribution at the extremities for longer turn and straight line stability.

Hopefully, the foregoing discussion will shed additional light on the subject of ski flexibility and its interaction with the average radius of turn the ski is intended for, the skier's weight, and the type of snow surface on which the ski is to excel. In the next chapter, the theoretical argument will continue based on the true hard surface carved turn radius (r_t). The reader is reminded that a reduction in this radius due to extra penetration of the ski waist into soft snow is possible and should be kept in mind while considering the theoretical hard surface case.

The Effect Of Non Planar Surfaces

Natural skiing is done on essentially planar surfaces. The rolls and pitches of natural terrain are of long enough radius of curvature so they will have little interaction with the mechanics presented. The real problem created by skiers is the mogul. A mogul is a pile of hard snow. It was built by a repetitive series of skidded turns in the same place. These provide the energy to move the snow into a pile. A carved turn will make a rut if it is repeated, as in a race course, but it will not make a mogul. Race hills are not mogulled, they are rutted.

Once the checker-board nature of a mogul field is established, it is reinforced and amplified by the tendency for successive turns to be made in the same troughs. The radius of curvature of moguls can vary from several feet to 30 or 40 feet. Radii beyond this are rare because the turns between the moguls begin to approach carved turns.

Once a mogul field is established, smooth, pleasant skiing becomes impossible and carved turns, by their definition, become nearly impossible. The carved turn is an interaction between the arc of the ski side cut and a *planar* surface. If the snow surface is a random jumble of all radii of concave and convex surfaces, the ski cannot possibly carve a long, round turn. The only chance is for quick segments of carved turns on the planar parts of the moguls. Added to variations in the surface is the need for slower speed and tighter radii turns in the moguls. Both of these are contrary to the requirements for carving.

To summarize, everything adds up to a skidding style of skiing. A mogul field presents a real challenge to carving by a skier. The alternatives are:

1. To negotiate the field while trying to pick a path of quasi-planar surfaces suitable for segments of carved turns.

2. To revert to a skidding style of skiing; ie. to submit and join.

3. To ski fast enough to hit the high spots or clear successive moguls with longer, high speed turns. Only a very few exceptional skiers are capable of handling the problem in this way.

4. Avoid the mogul field.

chapter 10

THE RESULTANT TURN RADIUS

$\mathbf{I}$N THE PRECEEDING TWO CHAPTERS, we developed an equation for the reaction force for turns of any radius (not necessarily carved) and the finite radius turn as defined by a carving ski. In other words, on a hard planar surface, a carving ski (or pair of skis) at a certain edge angle (Θ) will tend to make a turn of a specific radius (r_t). This radius in turn, (depending also upon velocity and hill angle) determines a specific centrifugal force and resultant edge angle (Θ). We quickly get into a dilemma of which comes first; the edge angle determining the turn radius, or the turn radius determining the edge angle? Add to this the ever-changing traverse angle (β) and, in real life, we have an ever-changing, infinite combination of the basic principles presented so far. A good understanding of the basic steady state principle is a foundation. However, we must understand that nothing regarding skiing is constant. This chapter will combine everything presented so far to strive for a better mechanical understanding of what really happens on the ski slope. For instance, it would be nice to know the optimum ski geometry (length and side cut) to carve turns at the most frequently expected hill and traverse angles and, hence, calculate the radii of the resulting turns. Most turns are made between traverse angles of 60° to 90° and back to 60° (30° from fall line). With this premise, it should be possible to better design the ski geometry for the radii of carved turns expected for that particular ski.

The True Carved Turn

In Chapter 8, equation 8—4 was developed for the edge angle (Θ_R) for a turn of any radius. This turn need not be a carved turn. This equation also assumes no angulation so that the force resultant (R) is perpendicular to the ski surface as shown in Figure 10—1.

Figure 10—1
With sufficient speed, a skier can 'bank' through a
turn; ie. turn without angulating. The force resultant
(R) is then perpendicular to the bottom surface of the
ski.

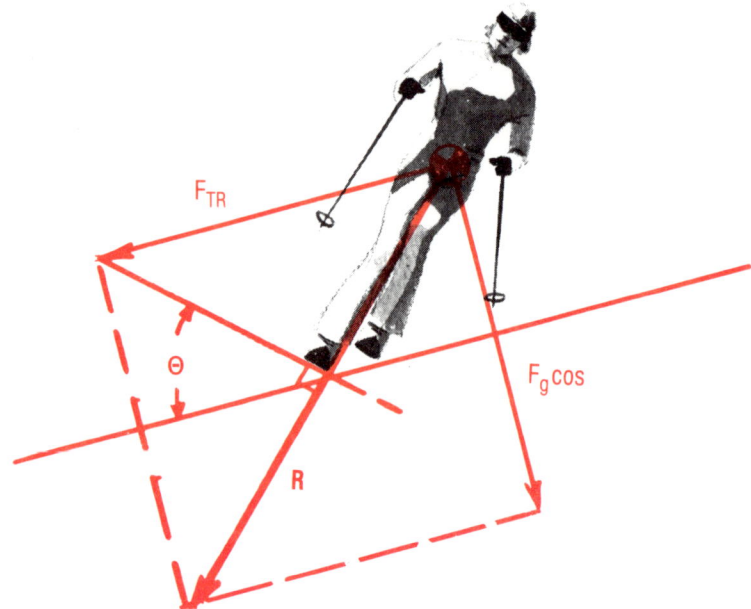

In Chapter 9, equation 9—4 gives the true carved turn radius
in terms of the ski geometry and the edge angle (Θ).

$$(9\text{—}4) \qquad r_t = \frac{L^2\cos\Theta}{2(s + H - 2w)}$$

If we let all the ski geometry terms be equal to one constant (K), the
above equation can be written as:

$$(9\text{—}4a) \qquad \cos\Theta = \frac{r_t}{K} \quad \left[\text{where } K = \frac{L^2}{2(s + H - 2w)}\right]$$

Another way of considering the ski geometry constant (K) is
that it represents the actual side cut radius of the ski (assuming the
total side cut of the ski is considered as one long radius arc). The
edge angle in equation 9—4a can be any edge angle, including the
special case where there is no angulation and (Θ) therefore equals
(Θ_R). If we equate equations 8—4 and 9—4a, we can begin this
chapter with the following expression:

$$(10\text{—}1) \qquad \frac{r_t}{K} = \frac{F_g\cos\alpha}{[(F_c \pm F_g\sin\alpha\cos\beta)^2 + (F_g\cos\alpha)^2]^{1/2}}$$

This combines *what the skier is doing* with *what the ski wants to do* to make a carved turn. In other words, it describes what the
skier will do during a complete carved turn with the reservation
that angulation is not yet present. If it were, the actual edge angle
(Θ) would *not* be the edge angle (Θ_R) established with no
angulation. From this complex equation, we desire to find the instantaneous radius of the carved turn (R_t) with respect to the ever-
changing traverse angle (β). This is difficult to do because the

radius of turn also appears in the terms (F_c) for centrifugal force. To find a solution, we will square both sides of the equation and multiply through by the denominators. Also, we will substitute the factors that make up (F_c) as given in equation 8—1.

(10—1a) $\qquad r_t^2 \ \dfrac{V^4}{g^2 r_t^2} \ \pm r_t^2 \ \dfrac{2V^2}{g r_t} \ \sin\alpha\cos\beta$

$$+ r_t^2(\sin^2\alpha\cos^2\beta + \cos^2\alpha) = K^2\cos^2\alpha$$

or, simplifying:

(10—1b) $\qquad \dfrac{V^4}{g^2} \pm r_t \ \dfrac{2V^2}{g} \ \sin\alpha\cos\beta + r_t^2(\sin^2\alpha\cos\beta + \cos^2\alpha) =$

$$K^2\cos^2\alpha$$

This might be considered the equation of skiing, because it combines everything that is happening except for temporary forces.

Equation 10—1b describes the basic situation of a skier carving a constant speed turn on a smooth, hard surface of moderate slope. Even though many assumptions have been made — such as neglect of varying speed, muscular-induced accelerations, undulating terrain effects, etc. — insight into the physics of turns and the interplay of the main influences of gravity, centrifugal force and ski-snow reactions may be gained from study of this simpler case. Unfortunately, even this equation is too cumbersome to solve algebraically without first substituting some values for the variables that remain constant for a given set of conditions. For instance, if a skier were skiing with the 205 SL ski described in Chapter 9, (K) is equal to 195 feet. Also, suppose this same skier were making a turn on a 20° slope (α) and is moving at a velocity (V) of 66 feet per second (45 miles per hour). The equation of skiing (10—1b) would then reduce to:

(10—1c) $\qquad 18{,}530 \pm 93.11\,r_t\cos\beta + r_t^2(0.117\cos^2\beta + 0.833) \ =$

$$33{,}576.9$$

We can now substitute various values for the traverse angle (β) and solve for the instantaneous radius of turn (r_t) at different points of the arc. For instance, at (β) equal to 30°, we have:

(10—1d) $\qquad 18{,}530 \pm 80.63\,r_t + 0.970\,r_t^2 = 33{,}576.9$

Equation (10—1d) is a quadratic equation in one variable; an equation of the form:

$$ax^2 + bx + c = 0$$

In this case, a = 0.970, b = 80.63, and c = 18,530 − 33,576.9 = −15,046.9. There are two solutions for r_t and they are defined by the expression:

$$r_t = \frac{-b \pm \sqrt{b^2 - 4ac}}{2a}$$

At this point, we can solve for (r_t) using the solution for a quadratic equation. For our problem, the "b" term is (± 80.63/0.970). The "plus or minus" means only that the turn is taking place in the uphill quadrants (in which case it is minus), or the downhill quadrants (where it is plus).

Solving equation 10—1d, we then find two real values for (r_t) at (β) = 30°:

(10—1e) r_t = 172.85 feet (in the uphill quadrant)

(10—1f) r_t = 89.74 feet (in the downhill quadrants)

Figure 10—3 shows various carved turn radii for V = 44 and 66 ft/sec (30 and 45 mph), and α = 20° and 40°. These points were all calculated using the technique given in the above text. It is very

Figure 10—2 ▶

There are two solutions to equation (10—1d). One of the values is negative and the other positive; with the sign of the value denoting in which quadrant the turn takes place. A negative value indicates that the turn is taking place in the uphill quadrants and a positive value indicates a turn in the downhill quadrants.

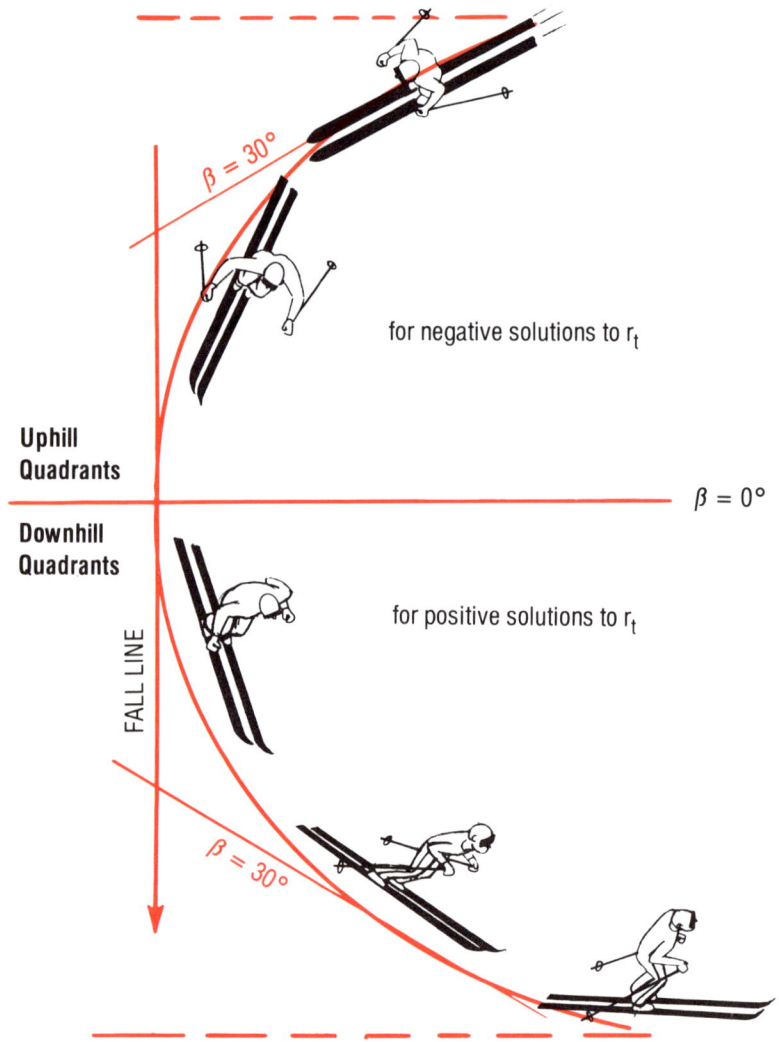

β = 30°

for negative solutions to r_t

Uphill Quadrants

β = 0°

Downhill Quadrants

for positive solutions to r_t

FALL LINE

β = 30°

Figure 10—3

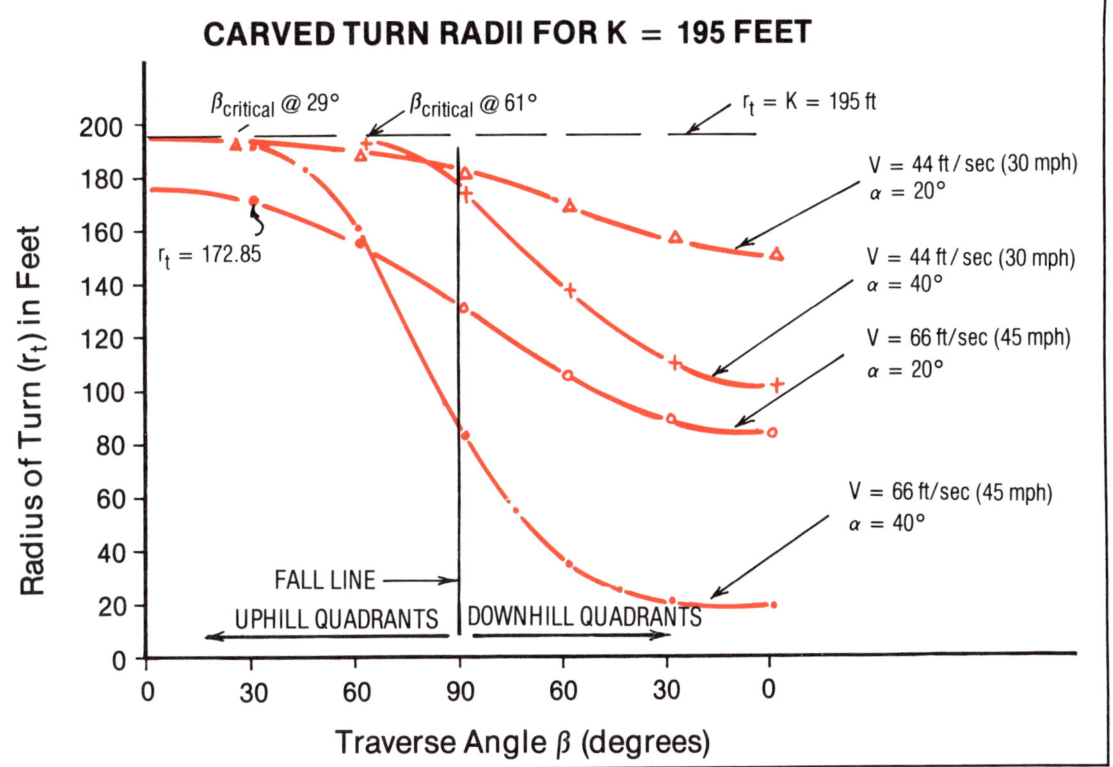

CARVED TURN RADII FOR K = 195 FEET
βcritical @ 29°
βcritical @ 61°
rt = K = 195 ft
V = 44 ft/sec (30 mph)
α = 20°
V = 44 ft/sec (30 mph)
α = 40°
V = 66 ft/sec (45 mph)
α = 20°
V = 66 ft/sec (45 mph)
α = 40°
rt = 172.85
FALL LINE
UPHILL QUADRANTS
DOWNHILL QUADRANTS
Radius of Turn (rt) in Feet
200
180
160
140
120
100
80
60
40
20
0
0
30
60
90
60
30
0
Traverse Angle β (degrees)

rt is large
β = 90°
rt becomes tighter
fall line
β = 0

clear from figure 10—3 that the radius of the carved turn tends to tighten as the skier continues around the turn.

There are also other interesting observations that can be made from figure 10—3; for instance:

- A higher constant velocity held thoughout the turn decreases (r_t) more effectively than increases in the hill anglc (α).
- At typical hill angles and velocities (say $V = 44$ ft/sec, $\alpha = 20°$) the carved turn radius stays quite long. It only decreases to 150 feet even as the skier crosses the fall line in the downhill quadrant. This would be typical of a traverse.
- Quite high velocities or hill angles are required to bring the carved turn radius of turn down to the range of everyday skiing radii and racing (more on this subject later).

◄ Figure 10—4. The radius of a carved turn tends to tighten as the skier continues around the turn.

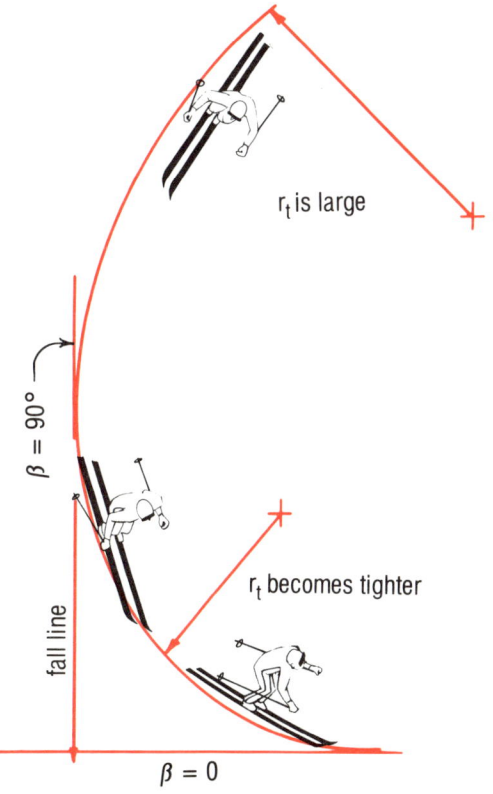

The Critical Traverse Angle

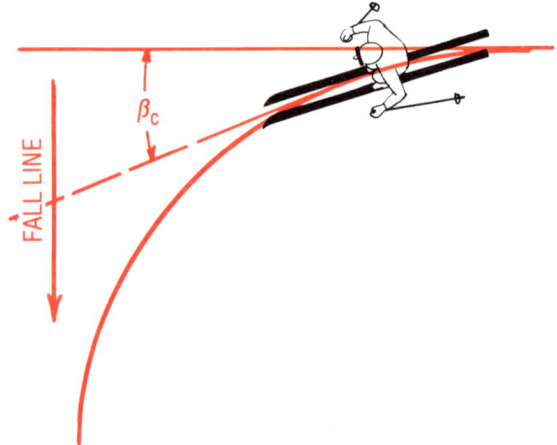

Figure 10—5
At values of β less than the critical traverse angle (β$_c$), centrifugal force is inadequate to overcome the downhill pull of gravity and a carved turn is impossible.

In figure 10—3, there are several combinations of conditions where a critical value of (β) is noted. This means that at lower values of (β) in the uphill quadrants, *a carved turn is just not possible.*

We now have a clearer insight into the balance of forces (F$_{TL}$) and (F$_c$) as was first presented in Chapter 8. The critical traverse angle (β$_c$) occurs when (F$_{TL}$) is equal to (F$_c$) and the skis are flat on the snow surface (Θ equals zero). Also, in this condition the carved turn radius (r$_t$) is equal to the ski geometry radius (K). One might question; "How can a turn be carved if (Θ) is zero?" In truth, it can't be done. The skis have to be edged slightly. At a traverse angle less than (β$_c$), the skier can only make a carved uphill turn of very long radius (traverse). At traverse angles greater than (β$_c$), the skier can carve either uphill or into a downhill turn. From figure 10—3, there are some combinations of (α) and (V) which allow a carved turn even at (β) equalling zero. Low values of (α) (eg. flatter hills) especially allow easy transitions into a turn providing high velocity is carried over from a preceeding schuss.

The values of the critical traverse angle (β$_c$) are shown for

Figure 10—6►

$$\beta_c = \cos^{-1}[V^2/(g\sin\alpha K)]$$

Θ = 0 in all cases

r$_t$ = K in all cases

K = 195 ft. (for the ski used in this example)

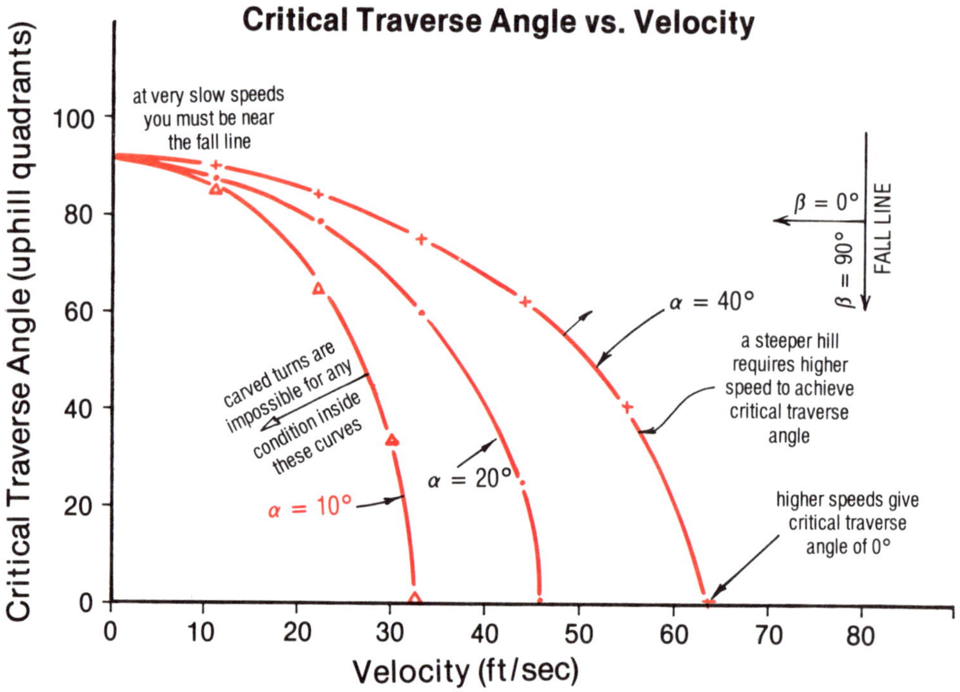

Critical Traverse Angle vs. Velocity

Critical Traverse Angle (uphill quadrants)

at very slow speeds you must be near the fall line

carved turns are impossible for any condition inside these curves

α = 10°

α = 20°

α = 40°

β = 0°

β = 90°

FALL LINE

a steeper hill requires higher speed to achieve critical traverse angle

higher speeds give critical traverse angle of 0°

Velocity (ft/sec)

various velocities and hill angles in Figure 10—6. Those angles are obtained from the equation:

$$(10\text{—}2) \qquad \beta_c = \cos^{-1} \left[\frac{V^2}{g \sin\alpha \, K} \right]$$

This equation is derived from the universal equation 10—1a with (K) substituted for (r_t). In Figure 10—6, for any combination of conditions (velocity and traverse angle) to the left of the curves, a carved turn is impossible. To the right of any of the curves, a carved turn is possible. Also from this figure, we see that a traverse angle approximating 90° (the skier must be close to the fall line direction) is necessary for a carved turn at low velocities and hill angles. This is an important point in everyday skiing. It means that good, carved turn skiing is easier if the skier stays closer to the fall line. Unfortunately, this type of skiing also means speed. The acceleration and higher velocities will quickly get any skier (except the racer on a prepared course) into a situation which is too fast and carving or skidding out of the fall line becomes necessary to control speed.

False Values From The Skiing Equation

It is possible to use values for the traverse angle in equation (10—1b) that are smaller than the critical traverse angle given in (10—2). The turn radii calculated in this manner are false, because it is impossible to carve a downhill turn at a traverse angle (in the uphill gradients) less than the critical angle. The best thing to do is calculate the critical angle first, using (10—2). Then, only use traverse angles greater than the critical angle (β_c) in equation (10—1b) for *uphill quadrant* calculations; eg., when the second term in (10—1b) is negative. In *downhill quadrants*, where the second term is positive, even the slowest speeds or flattest hills are sufficient for a carved turn and any value of traverse angle (β) can be used to determine the carved turn radius. A typical case is the zero degree traverse perpendicular to the fall line. For any zero degree traverse, the ski equation simplifies to:

$$(10\text{—}3) \qquad \frac{V^4}{g^2} \pm \frac{2V^2}{g} \, r_t \sin\alpha + r_t^2 = \cos^2\alpha \, K^2$$

— and (r_t) can easily be calculated using the quadratic solution and any combination of values for velocity (V), hill angle (α), and ski turn radius (K). This is described graphically in Figure 10—7. The

Figure 10—7
A skier traversing on his *uphill* edges (**A**) is actually carving a turn in the downhill quadrants. The second term of equation 10—1b is therefore *positive*. It is impossible to carve a turn between $\beta = 0$ and $\beta = \beta_c$ (ie. between **A** and **B**). Between $\beta = \beta_c$ and $\beta = 90°$, the second term in equation 10—1b is *negative*. Between $\beta = 90°$ and $\beta = 0$ in the downhill quadrants (**C**), the second term in 10—1b is *positive*.

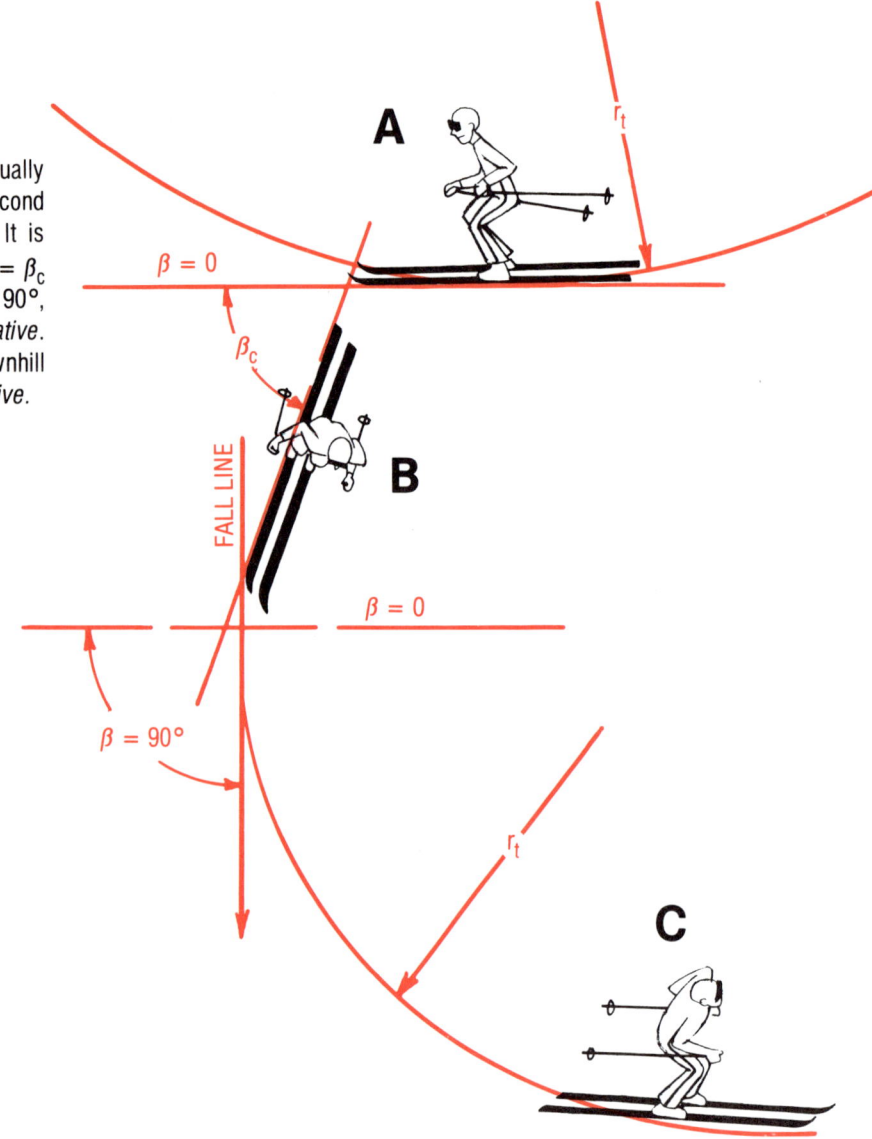

skier in position (A) and (C) is actually carving the same uphill turn. The problem is to get the downhill turn started *between* (A) and (B). If speeds are low, the skier must resort to extra muscular movements (rotation, unweighting, etc.). These subjects will be covered in greater detail in Chapter 11.

Limitations On The Radius Of Turn

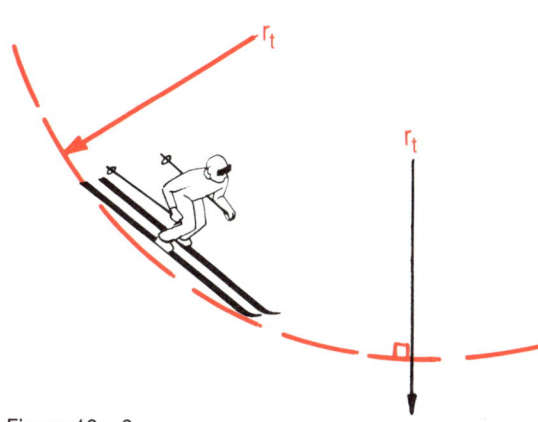

Figure 10—8
In a true carved turn, the radius of turn decreases as the skier approaches the perpendicular to the fall line in the downhill quadrants. This increases the likelihood that the skier's centrifugal force will exceed the lateral adhesion of the snow / ice surface.

In Chapter 8, it was shown that the total lateral force on the skis (F_{TL}) increased significantly as the skier advanced through the downhill quadrants and approached the fall line perpendicularly. In that chapter, a *constant* radius was assumed in equation 8—2a. This turn would not be carved throughout. Now, in Chapter 10, we see that for a true carved turn, the radius is *decreasing* as the skier approaches perpendicularity of the fall line. This makes the possibility of exceeding the maximum possible lateral support provided by the snow/ice surface even more important.

Figure 10—9 shows the edge angle (Θ_R) and total lateral force (F_{TL}) for various radii of turns. As the radius decreases, the edge angle increases as does the total lateral force which has to be supported by the snow/ice surface. In all cases, however, the force available to hold the skier perpendicularly against the snow ($F_g \cos \alpha$) remains constant for each value of hill angle (α). It now becomes quite obvious from Figure 10—3 that even with increasing values of edge angle (Θ), there is going to be some value of total lateral force (F_{TL}) that even a good quality snow/ice surface cannot support. The exact value is not known, as it would require many empirical

Figure 10—9 ▶

$K = 195$ ft.

$F_g = 170$ lbs

No Angulation

$\Theta_R = \cos^{-1}(r_t / K)$

$F_{TL} = F_g \cos \alpha \tan \Theta_R$

$F_g \cos \alpha_{20°} = 159.74$ lbs.

$F_g \cos \alpha_{40°} = 130.22$ lbs

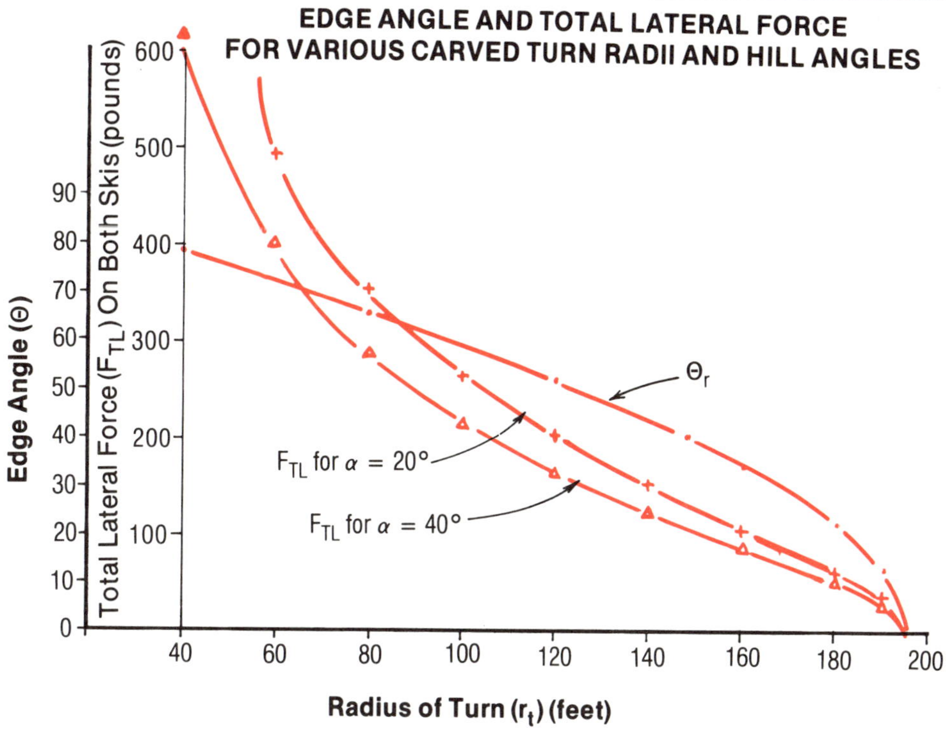

EDGE ANGLE AND TOTAL LATERAL FORCE FOR VARIOUS CARVED TURN RADII AND HILL ANGLES

Edge Angle (Θ)

Total Lateral Force (F_{TL}) On Both Skis (pounds)

Θ_r

F_{TL} for $\alpha = 20°$

F_{TL} for $\alpha = 40°$

Radius of Turn (r_t) (feet)

tests as well as a way to describe the quality of the snow/ice surface; but, at least the reader can see how sharply (F_{TL}) increases with decreasing radius.

Another way to consider the lower limitation on the radius of turn is to calculate the total reaction force (R) that has to be supported by two legs (or one leg if all the weight is carried on one ski). Figure 10—10 shows this force for various radii and hill angles. Certainly, no skier could support more than... say 300 pounds with one leg, except in the case of an exceptional athlete. An (R) value of 300 pounds converts to a minimum possible radius of 80 to 100 feet for values of hill angle (α) of 20° to 40°. If we refer back to Figure 10—3, with radii of this magnitude we see that for velocities of 44 ft/sec (30 MPH), it is quite possible to carry the carved turn throughout until the traverse angle (β) is zero and travel is again perpendicular to the fall line.

If, in Figures 10—3 and 10—10, we consider a velocity of 66 ft/sec (45 MPH), then as the skier crosses the fall line, the reaction force will approach 380 pounds for a hill angle of 20°. The reaction force would be as high as 310 pounds at the fall line (β = 90°) for a hill of 40°!

By referring back and forth between Figures 10—3 and 10—8 and 10—10, we can begin to appreciate the problems of excessive laterl force and total reaction as the turn is continued around beyond the fall line. In real life, the lateral adhesion of the snow/ice

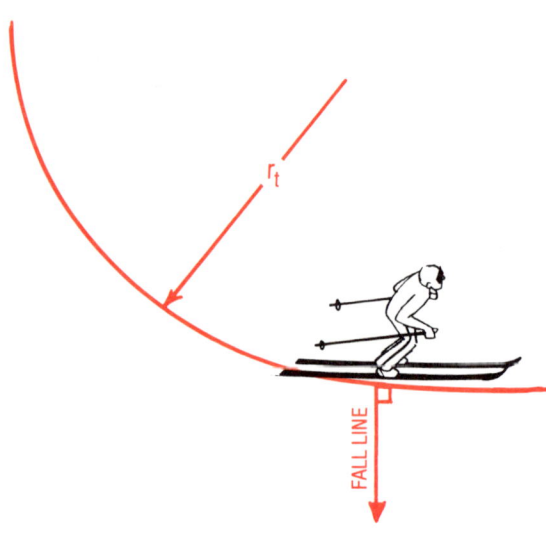

A carved turn is still possible perpendicular to the fall line for lower speeds and hill angles. This condition is, in actuality, a normal traverse.

Figure 10—10

K = 195 ft.

F_g = 170 lbs.

No Angulation

TOTAL REACTION FORCE FOR VARIOUS CARVED TURN RADII AND HILL ANGLES

Total Reaction Force (R) On Both Legs

Reaction Force ($R_{\frac{1}{2}}$) On Each Leg (If Distributed Equally)

$R = F_g \cos\alpha [K / r_t]$

Θ_R

$F_g \cos\alpha$

R

R for α = 20°

R for α = 40°

Radius of Turn (r_t) (feet)

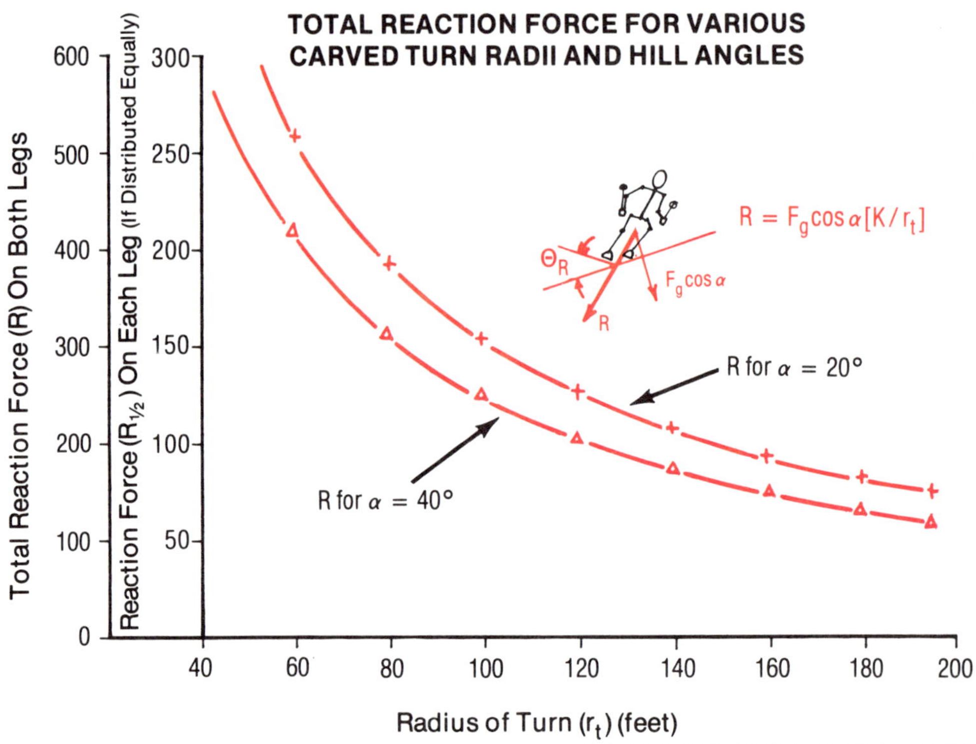

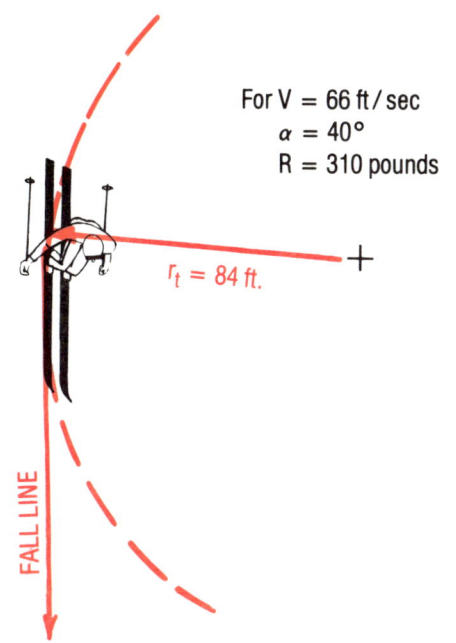

For V = 66 ft / sec
α = 40°
R = 310 pounds

r_t = 84 ft.

FALL LINE

surface will probably give way first as (F_{TL}) increases. On the other hand, the high total reaction force loads that have to be carried by the thigh muscles should be noted. If a skier intends to carve turns of fairly tight radii (say 80 to 120 feet), the skier must have very high thigh strength. That doesn't mean that lesser skiers cannot make turns of this short radii; obviously they do every day. But these are clearly skidded turns at lower values of edge angle and velocity. In this case, the equations 8—2a and 8—3 can be used to determine the forces.

◄ Figure 10—11
The reaction force would be as high as 310 pounds at the fall line (β = 90°) of a carved turn with a velocity of 66 ft / sec (45 mph) on a hill angle (α) of 40°. This reaction force would have to be absorbed by the skier's legs.

Deviations In Turn Radius Due To Knee Angulation

The skier is able to change the actual value of the edge angle (Θ) at any time by using various amounts of hip and/or knee angulation. Values of plus or minus 30° have actually been measured by the writer. In other words, it's theoretically possible to change the radius of a carved turn during the turn by moving the hips and/or knees to one side or the other. Using Figure 10—12, we might consider a skier carving a turn that at one point has a radius of 150 feet. This will be at a definite point in the turn as defined by the traverse angle in Figure 10—3. It might be very early in the turn for high velocities, or late in the turn after the fall line is passed for low velocities. At this radius of 150 feet, if carved (and K equals 195 feet), the corresponding edge angle equals 40°. If the skier were to suddenly increase the value of (Θ) to 70°, the skis would try to carve a new, tighter radius of 70 feet. If the skier were to decrease the value of (Θ) to 10°, the skis would begin to carve a new radius of 190 feet. This theory suggests a tremendous range of radii with carved turns is possible through the use of angulation. The real limitations, however, are;

• Usually a skier is already excessively angulated to increase (Θ) as much as possible, and also to gain the maximum possible lateral adhesion from the snow/ice surface. The chapter on traversing gave several good arguments for being angulated at most times.

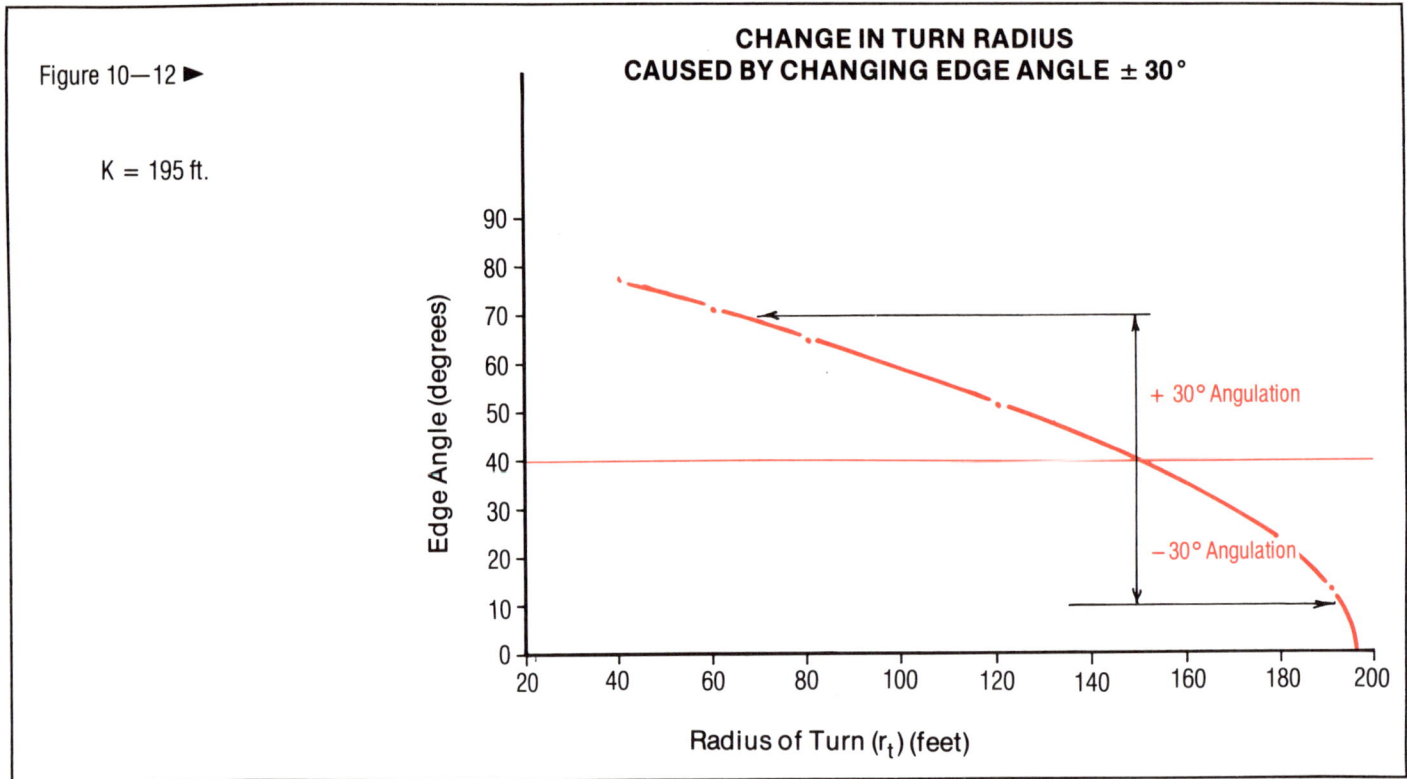

Figure 10—12 ▶

K = 195 ft.

**CHANGE IN TURN RADIUS
CAUSED BY CHANGING EDGE ANGLE ± 30°**

Edge Angle (degrees)

+ 30° Angulation

− 30° Angulation

Radius of Turn (r_t) (feet)

• Variations of plus or minus 30° are difficult to achieve, especially if the legs are extended.

    At least the theory presented suggests the possible effectiveness of angulation in controlling the radius of turn. The argument for angulation (especially knee angulation) as one of the keys to advanced skiing is clearly made.

Deviations In Turn Radius
Due To Lateral Projection

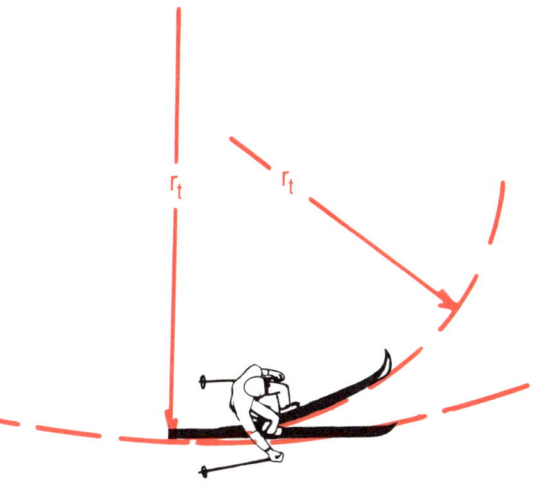

Figure 10—13
Lateral projection can be used to effectively tighten the turn radius. The skier projects (or steps) into a new turn.

In addition to changing (Θ) via angulation, the skier has a second, extremely powerful way to instantly change the radius of a turn without skidding. This may be done by projecting laterally from the outside, carving ski into a new radius defined by the physically displaced uphill ski.

Actually, the new radius is no different than as defined by the equations developed in this chapter. It just follows a discontinuity from the old radius and the overall effect is to tighten the turn considerably. By pushing off the lower ski with a powerful muscular force, the skier also adds to the kinetic energy of his velocity. This type of skiing is universal in modern racing for all except the longest radius, high speed turns. A racer who is not laterally projecting will not be competitive in a contemporary ski race. Consider, for instance, the concept of skating; where gravitational pull is not available and the skater must rely totally on muscular energy. If this analogy can be carried over into ski racing, the racer can readily visualize how he can add to his velocity down the mountain. In some situations, on flatter hills, he may actually step off the outer ski before the fall line is reached. The racer literally *skates* down the hill and only rarely weights both skis simultaneously.

These concepts of stepping for lateral projection — plus the judicious use of angulation — are the reasons why racers are able to effect turns of radii considerably shorter than the true carved turn radius without skidding. The recreational skier has all of the following alternative methods to make turns of desired radii other than the carved turn radius.

• Introduce skidding.

• Use shorter skis with less natural radius (K).

• Adopt the techniques of lateral projection and angulation.

A good recreational skier will understand which of the above should be used in each particular circumstance.

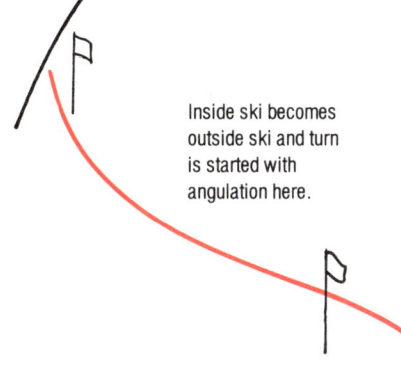

Inside ski becomes outside ski and turn is started with angulation here.

◄ Figure 10—14
By pushing powerfully off his outer ski, the skier can use muscular force to increase his velocity. On flatter sections of a course, racers literally *skate* down the hill.

chapter 11

THE SYNCHRONIZATION
OF ALL FORCES
THROUGHOUT THE TURN

IN THE PRECEEDING CHAPTERS, equations have been developed to define the radius of a carved turn and the basic forces involved in any turn, carved or not. However, these basic forces considered for turning were only those caused by gravitational pull and centrifugal force. In the earlier chapters, other forces involved with skiing were presented only as definitions or as in their relationship to simple straight gliding or traversing. Now we have come to a point where we need to add these other forces to the basic two forces involved in turning. Obviously, in real life, the complexity and beauty of skiing is the interplay of all these forces and how the expert skier uses them to enhance his efficiency and pleasure. To summarize then, we have built a foundation of understanding for:

- The basic and constant force due to gravitational pull (F_g)

- The basic force due to centrifugal force which is only present during turning (F_c)

To these two forces we now should be able to better understand when and how to best use the following secondary forces:

- The braking force caused by skidding or deviating from a carved turn (F_B)

- The muscular force induced by skating or stepping (F_p)

- The rotational forces (torque) caused by some form of twisting of the feet or body about a vertical axis (F_R)

- The temporary force on the skier's legs and skis caused by instantaneous vertical acceleration or deceleration of the skier's mass (F_D). This force arises either from a change in thigh muscle support or a terrain change.

• The force provided by the ski during the time it is flexed has stored energy (F_S)

• We will not reintroduce the drag forces such as wind friction (F_w) or sliding friction (F_f) in the direction of travel because these are minor forces when turning is involved and are of more importance when high speed and straight gliding are concerned.

At this point in the text, the train of presentation will deviate from a step-by-step building of a theoretical argument. The algebra and mathematics have already become quite complicated and from now on, as we add secondary forces, the strict analytical approach would be too complex to be useful. Instead, hopefully we have a foundation of understanding regarding turn radius and the steady forces involved. To this, we will add more subjective premises as to how the secondary forces are best superimposed during the turn. The smoothest, safest skiing (and fastest in the case of the racer) should be possible if we have a better understanding of the optimum synchronization or timing of all the forces.

Synchronization of the Up and Down Motion Caused by the Legs

In Chapter 6, the concept of temporary force changes against the snow surface was introduced. In other words, as the skier pushes his upper body up with his thigh muscles he concurrently adds this force required to accelerate his body upwards (up-weighting) to the steady state pull of gravity acting through his thighs and skis. Conversely, if he suddenly relaxes the support provided by his thighs, he subtracts this force opposing the steady state force due to gravity (down unweighting). His body suddenly moves lower and the force on the thighs and snow is reduced. It is during turning that it is highly desirable to utilize and synchronize this ability to suddenly decrease or increase the total force against the snow surface.

For instance, at the early stage of the turn, where it is difficult to get the turn started, it is desirable to have the force between the skis and snow surface minimized — even zero in some cases. Later, as the critical holding part of the turn is approached, it is desirable to be able to add instantaneous extra force against the ground.

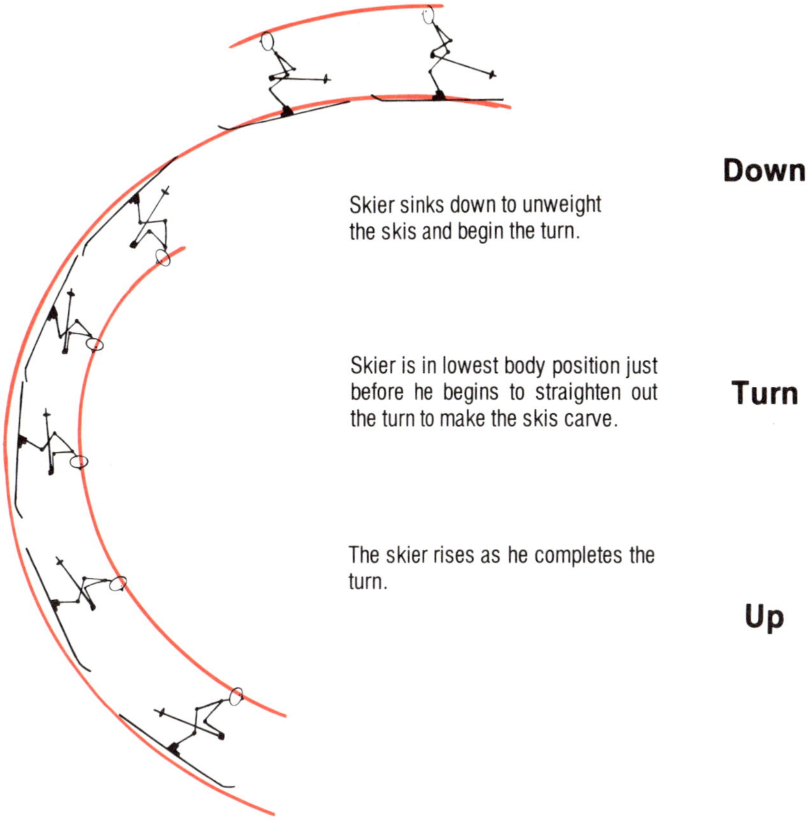

Figure 11—1 ▶

In modern skiing, it is generally most effective to use a skiing style that utilizes a "down motion — turn — up motion" sequence. This allows the skier to exert less force against the slope at the beginning of the turn and more toward the end of the turn.

Down

Skier sinks down to unweight the skis and begin the turn.

Turn

Skier is in lowest body position just before he begins to straighten out the turn to make the skis carve.

The skier rises as he completes the turn.

Up

Let us start, then, with the following premise: *it is generally desirable to exert less force against the slope at the beginning of the turn, and more near the end of the turn.* We also know from our discussion of angulation that the best control of the edge angle (Θ) via changes in angulation is possible if the legs are flexed to a low body position. Also, for independent leg action, much more power and movement are possible from a compressed leg. All of these factors add up to a strong case for a basic style of skiing that utilizes a *"down motion — turn — up motion"* sequence.

As turns are linked, the *end* of the up-motion from the preceeding turn enhances the lightness of force against the snow required for the beginning of the next turn. However, this up-motion *should not* be confused with the necessity to move lower at the beginning of the next turn. If the termination of up-motion from the preceeding turn provides adequate unweighting for the next turn, and the skier does not sink down into the next turn, he will lose the ability to angulate and apply additional upweighting at the critical points in the next turn.

In the 'old days,' skiers were taught to extend or "up-unweight" to begin a turn. At the end of the upward motion, the force against the skis becomes very light and the skier could almost float as in a jump off the ground. At this point, it is very

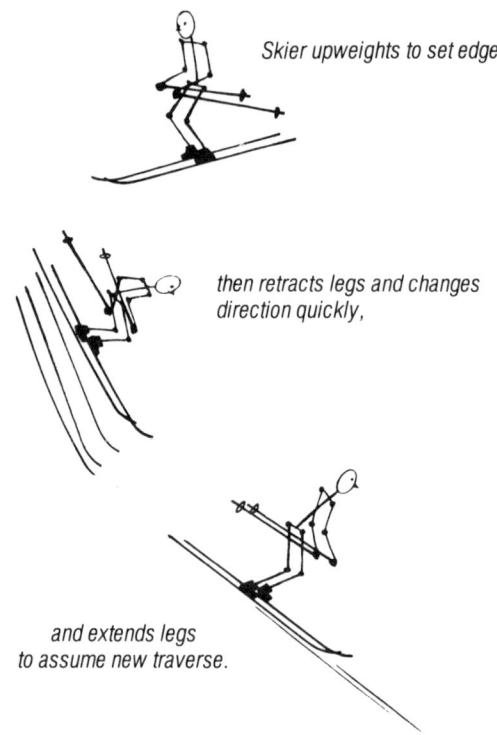

Skier upweights to set edge,

then retracts legs and changes direction quickly,

and extends legs to assume new traverse.

Figure 11—2
The use of longer, stiffer skis a number of years ago required excessive unweighting to change direction. Skiers were taught to extend or "up-unweight" to initiate a turn. This style of skiing, using an "up-motion—turn—down-motion" movement sequence, is only applicable in modern skiing in extremely heavy powder, 'crud' or crust, where the skis have to be released from the snow surface in order to start a turn, or on very steep slopes as shown above.

easy to change the direction of the skis. This was especially necessary in the days of longer, stiffer skis which required excessive unweighting to change direction. Also, the subsequent down unweighting at the critical part of the turn allowed the skis to skid easier. This style of skiing is an *"up-motion — turn — down-motion"* sequence which is *exactly the opposite* of the preferred method presented first. The only place in modern skiing for this style is in extremely heavy powder, crud, or crust, where the skis have to be almost (or) completely released from the snow surface in order for a direction change to be made. One other exception for this type of "up — turn — down" skiing is on extremely steep slopes where very tight turns are required to maintain control. Here the velocity is very slow and the radius of the desired turn is on the order of magnitude of 10 or 20 feet. No possibility of a carving phase is possible at any part in the turn — only during the traverse in between the turns.

In his book *Pianta Su*, Ruedi Bear infers that a "pole, up" motion is an essential preface to a modern racing turn. He has several excellent photomontage sequences to support his argument. It should be emphasized, however, that the strong "pole, up" movement is more important *at the end of the preceeding turn* than at the beginning of the turn in question. In any sequence of turns (most turns follow in a series), it is difficult to determine which movements are most necessary to which turn. The easier, older style of "up-motion — turn — down" is probably one of the most limiting factors which present a ceiling to the typical recreational skier's performance. Once that habit is perfected, it is extremely difficult (as well as more strenuous on the thigh muscles) to convert to a "down-motion — turn — up" modern style. Normal pleasure skiing requires so little emphasis on either of these techniques that it is difficult to determine which the skier is actually using. When the terrain, speed and snow conditions become more difficult, however, it is important to emphasize the more modern technique.

Synchronization of Up and Down Motion Caused by Terrain

A good skier should be able to make any radius turn at any point on the slope. However, since vertical body motion and temporary force changes can be caused just as much by terrain changes as by action of the thigh muscles, it follows that there are better and worse places to make a turn. The best example is at the top or on the downside of a convex surface to start a turn and at the

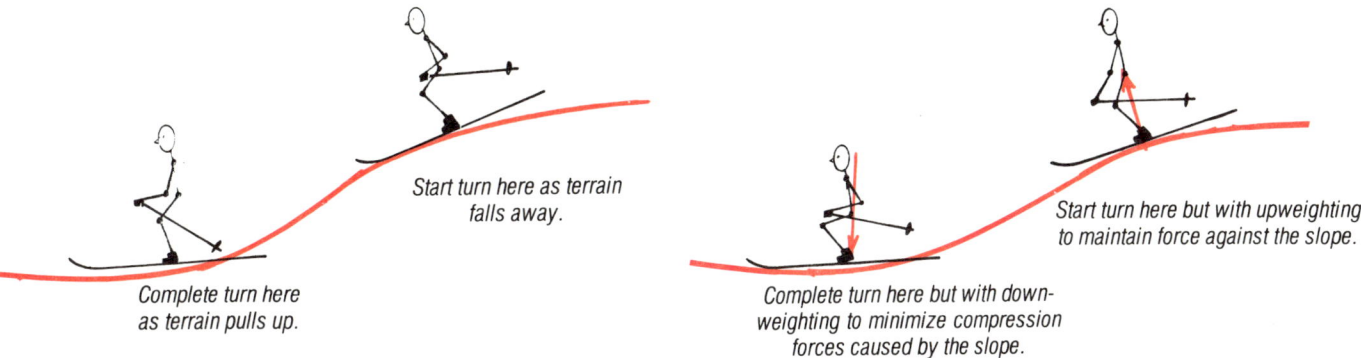

Start turn here as terrain falls away.

Complete turn here as terrain pulls up.

Start turn here but with upweighting to maintain force against the slope.

Complete turn here but with down-weighting to minimize compression forces caused by the slope.

Figure 11—3
Terrain changes can produce temporary vertical force changes. It's usually, therefore, easier to start a turn at the top or down-side of a fall-away surface where the force is minimal, and complete the turn in the concave area where the increased force will improve edge holding.

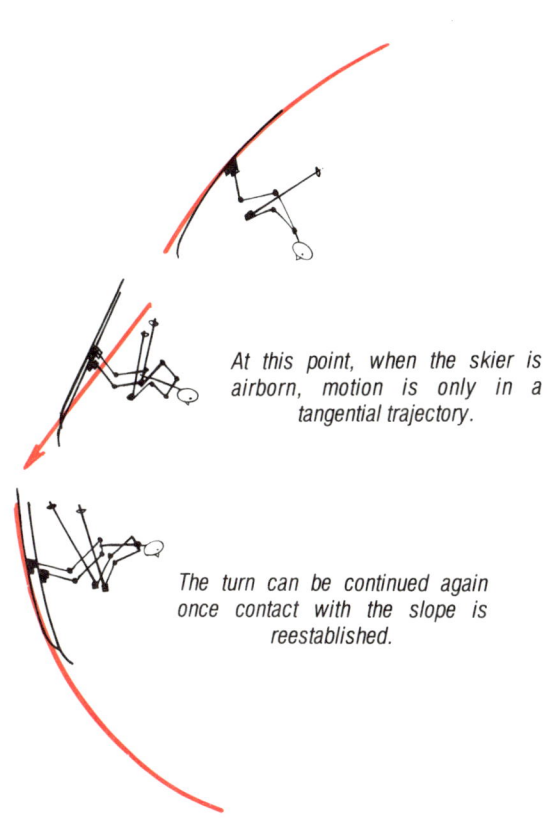

At this point, when the skier is airborn, motion is only in a tangential trajectory.

The turn can be continued again once contact with the slope is reestablished.

Figure 11—4
From the moment that a skier becomes airborn until he regains contact with the ground, no turn can be made and he can travel only in a tangential trajectory.

bottom or the upside of a concave surface to finish. In this way, the lessening of force against the slope desired at the beginning of the turn will be enhanced by the falling away of the terrain, and the increase of force against the slope in the opposite interaction will improve edge holding at the end of the turn.

The natural unweighting by this change of terrain alone might be sufficient at the beginning of the turn and for edge holding at the end. In other words, down-unweighting and up-weighting with the thighs, if added simultaneously, would provide *too much* unweighting and subsequent weighting. In fact, if the terrain changes were sharp enough (combined with higher speed which magnifies this effect), the muscular forces applied by the thighs might just have to be reversed in order to compensate somewhat for the terrain changes.

This contradiction is typical of skiing. There are few hard and fast rules. It is up to the expert skier to understand the forces involved so that he can best use them to his advantage. If very soft or very hard snow were added to the problem described in the above situation, this additional complexity would finally determine what force the skier should best exert against the slope at each part of the turn.

The skier might even desire to be airborn at some part of the turn. But at the instant the skier is airborn, no turn can be made since there is zero lateral adhesion supplied by the snow/ice surface.

If the critical holding, carving part of the turn is desired to be precisely at a fall-away point in the terrain, then it is especially important to emphasize the "down-motion — turn — up-motion" with the thighs. Since the skier is normally light at the instant

Figure 11—5

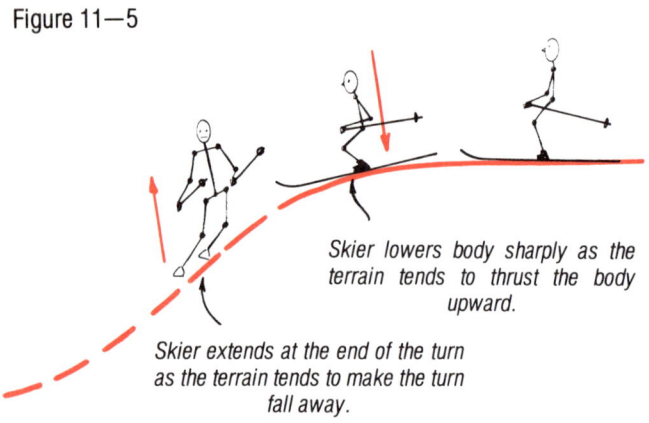

Skier lowers body sharply as the terrain tends to thrust the body upward.

Skier extends at the end of the turn as the terrain tends to make the turn fall away.

the ground falls away, he must be able to compensate for this with a sharp up-motion (upweighting) provided by the legs.

It is a lack of proper use of this synchronization of terrain forces and thigh forces that really gets the older style "up-motion — turn — down-motion" type of skier into trouble. His skis are so lightly forced against the snow at the critical point of the turn that he can't help but skid sideways. In addition, he is already so tall from his up-motion prior to turning that he can't possibly add any angulation just at the point where he needs it most.

The message here is that if there is a turn to be made after a knoll or where the ground starts to fall away sharply, the good skier will make an extra effort to lower his body position prior to the turn, especially at the instant the knoll would tend to launch him into the air.

Synchronization of Skidding

Most all turns have some amount of skidding added to the carving of the ski. This is the way the actual radius of turn is controlled by the skier and differs from the theoretical carved turn radius. In chapters 9 and 10 the theory showed that the carved turn radii were usually quite large — larger than the normal turn made by recreational skiers (but not longer than the typical racing turn). This is so because it is easy to skid a ski into a tighter turn than the ski is trying to carve. It is quite unusual, but not unknown, to skid a ski into a longer radius turn than it wants to carve.

We will begin this subsection discussion by considering the traversing ski which, at low velocities and shallow hill angles (low α), is really carving an uphill turn but at a very large radius. This is one way we first think of skiing — tracking fairly straight across a long pleasant traverse while we enjoy the scenery. With modern carved-turn skiing, however, we want this same ski to carve crisp, sharp turns down a steep, mogul-filled, possibly icy slope. This contradiction in design requirements has been alluded to frequently in this book. The result, in real life, is that the majority of turns are made at radii tighter than the ski wants to carve; especially at the beginning of the turn where the traverse angle (β) is shallow and centrifugal force and gravitational force are opposing each other. In other words, it is just at the beginning of the turn that the ski tends to carve the longest radius turn or won't carve at all for certain combinations of velocity and hill angle. At

Figure 11—6 ▶
Most turns are made at radii tighter than the ski wants to carve; particularly at the beginning of the turn where the traverse angle (β) is shallow and where the centrifugal force and gravitational force oppose each other. Hence, what skidding is used in modern skiing occurs in the top half of the turn. Consequently, the width of the track decreases from very wide to very narrow.

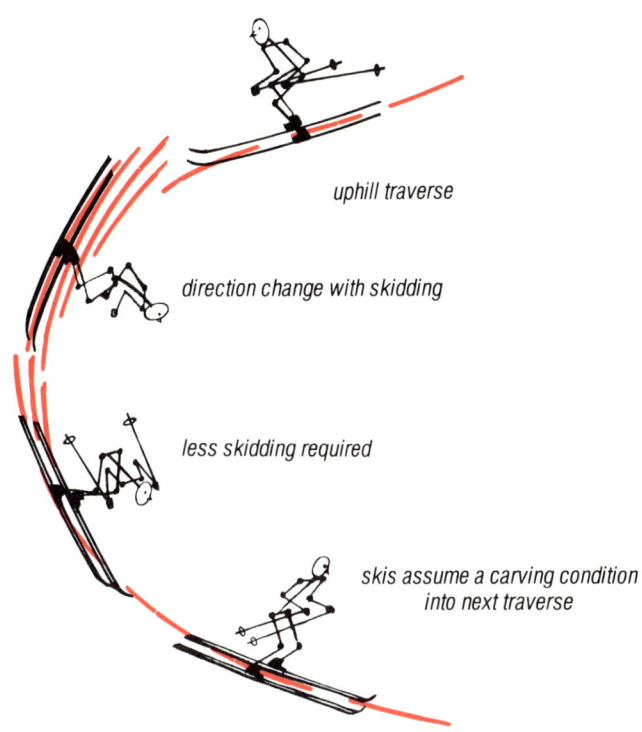

uphill traverse

direction change with skidding

less skidding required

skis assume a carving condition
into next traverse

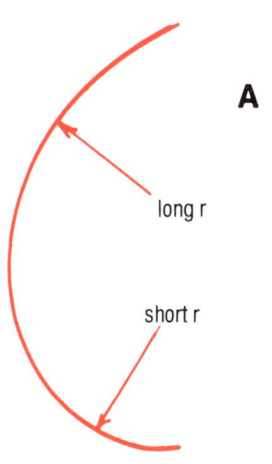

A

long r

short r

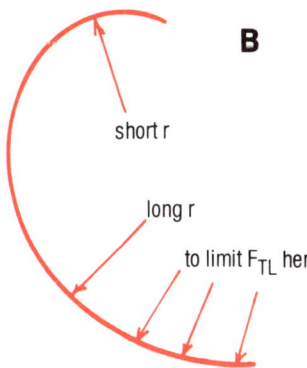

B

short r

long r

to limit F_{TL} here

Figure 11—7
Mechanics and ski design dictate that the path of a true carved turn [A] begin with a long radius and end with a much shorter radius. In real life situations, however, it is more advantageous to make turns that begin with shorter radius and end with a longer radius

the end of the turn, the carved turn radius has decreased, and it is also usually desirable to increase the actual turn radius to reduce the total lateral force (F_{TL}) against the snow. Furthermore, the velocity at the end of the turn has most likely increased since the skier has been near the fall line for some length of time. It's most likely, therefore, that the ski will come closest to a true carving condition at the end of the turn. The synchronization of skidding and the turn would then appear as in figure 11—6.

This synchronization of skidding coincides nicely with the down motion unweighting at the beginning of the turn and the up motion unweighting at the end as the skis begin to carve cleanly. This synchronization also coincides with the objective of having a tighter radius early in the turn when the total force (R) and edge angle (Θ) are small. The larger radius at the end of the turn is better as (R) and (Θ) increase and a critical point of lateral adhesion and/or thigh strength is approached.

It is unfortunate that the true carved turn tends to decrease in radius whereas the normal turn, all things considered, is better if it is increasing in radius. Ideally, the expert skier and racer will find the right combination of speed, angulation and ski design to find agreement between the desired actual turn and the true carved turn in a majority of turns as he descends the hill.

In figure 11—8, the true carved turn at A would usually be of a much longer radius than is desired. Also, in some cases as

Figure 11—8

Since the radius of a true carved turn would normally be longer at [A] than the skier wants to make, the skier must use muscular effort to induce a skidding of the skis and, thereby, achieve the desired change of direction to initiate the turn. If, once the turn has been started, the desired turn radius is longer than the true carved turn radius of the ski, the shovels of the skis must be skidded.

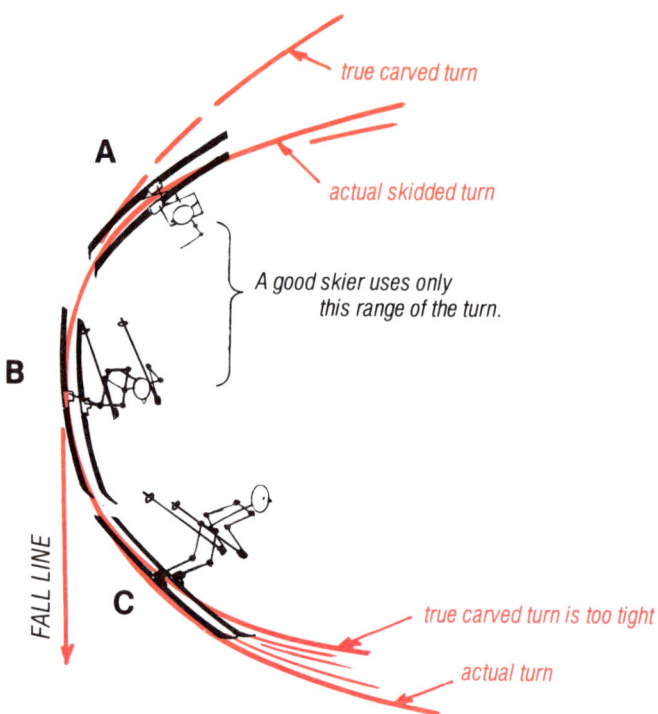

true carved turn

actual skidded turn

A good skier uses only this range of the turn.

A

B

FALL LINE

C

true carved turn is too tight

actual turn

explained in chapter 10, it may not be possible to carve a turn at all. At this part of the turn some type of muscular effort is required to achieve a direction change of the skis to start the turn. Even after the turn has been started, the desired radius of turn is tighter than the true carved turn, so the skis must be skidded *at the tail* (overturned) to make the desired turn.

As a higher traverse angle is approached in B, it is more likely that the skier's desired turn radius can coincide with the true ski-carved turn. This situation usually holds true through the fall line as the traverse angle (β) reaches 90° and then begins to decrease. In the downhill quadrants in C, one of three things can happen depending upon the speed, radius of turn desired, ski geometry, hill angle, and edge angle:

1. At high velocities, the desired radius of turn and the true carved turn might coincide nicely, but the lateral adhesion of the snow/ice surface will not support the rapidly increasing total lateral force (F_{TL}). The result is a sideways skidding of the ski, but this skidding is usually different from that at A because the entire ski skids (or chatters) sideways, out of the skier's control. At A, only the tail of the ski skids sideways and the degree of skidding can be effected by the skier's desire to control the turn; ie. the greater the radius, the less tail skidding required, and vice versa.

2. A low velocities and tighter radii, the desired turn may be less

than the true carved turn radius and the skier can use the controlled, oversteered type of tail skid all the way around the turn. He never achieves an actual carving condition at any point in the turn, although if he has good angulation he can begin to carve as he enters a new traverse at C. This is probably the most common situation for the beginner-intermediate recreational skier. Because of his need for low hill angles, lower speeds and tight radii, he probably only experiences true carving on a traverse. This coincides nicely with the less skilled skier's conscious or subconscious desire to continually "skid off" energy to keep his speed down within a comfortable range.

3. For certain combinations of all variables involved, the skier may elect to allow his skis to carve the true radius all the way around through C and into the new traverse. This is certainly the most efficient technique for the racer and aesthetically the most pleasant for the advanced recreational skier who can handle the speed. He will probably have to make adjustments in angulation to reduce the edge angle at some point in the turn to let the skis carve from a tight radius into a longer traverse radius. Another possibility is to actually skid the tips of the skis to effect the new traverse direction **as shown in figures 11—8 and 11—9.**

This is an unusual situation, but is sometimes necessary when using shorter, high side camber skis at high speeds and on steeper hills. The need for this is felt by the skier when he notices that the shovels of his skis are too "hooky" or tend to climb uphill excessively. This is just another example of the compromise in ski design. This tight turning ski is not as comfortable for the long high speed traverses as the longer, straighter side-cut "cruising" type of ski.

This discussion of the synchronization of skidding is extremely important since it deals with what usually happens in real life. True carved turns are quite rare — but they need to be understood so that even if some skidding is necessary it can be minimized (or maximized) to achieve the desired control of turn radius and speed. The best way to control skidding is with angulation, fore and aft location of force, and the synchronization of temporary up and down forces as have already been described.

If a skier desires to initiate a skidding of the tails of his skis, he need only press forward and push his heels sideways. A great many recreational skiers use this "heel push" technique to excess and tend to substitute it too frequently for a carving technique controlled by angulation and independent leg action.

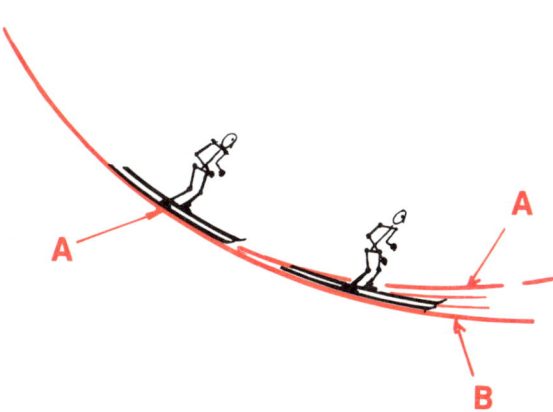

Figure 11—9
If the tips of the skis tend to 'hook' or climb excessively uphill, they can be skidded simply by shifting the weight back toward the tails. This problem is particularly noticeable when shorter skis with high side camber are used at higher speeds on steeper hills.

In this instance, the skis will tend to continue carving through arc [A], and in order to flatten the arc out into a traverse [B], the skier must shift his weight back.

Synchronization
of the Fore and Aft Location of Force

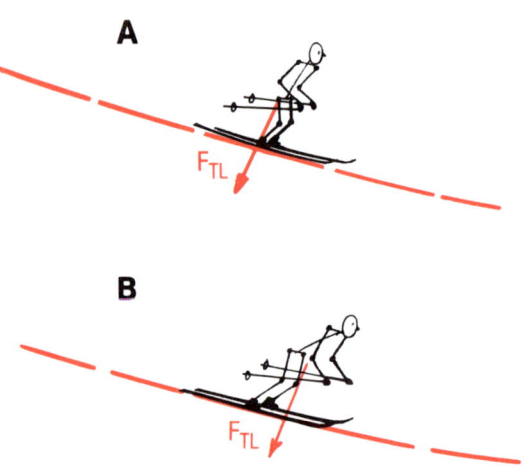

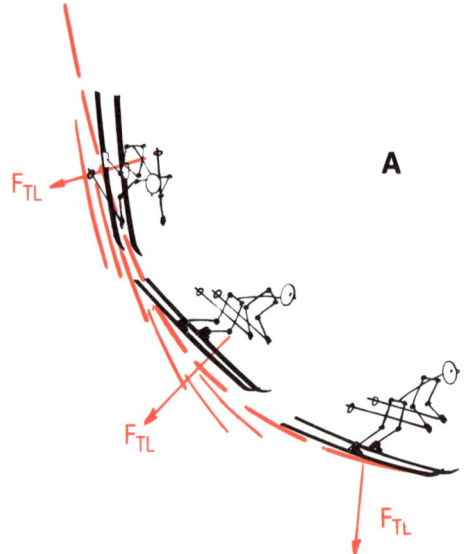

Figure 11—10
Leaning back, or pushing the skis forward, weights the tails of the skis [A]; whereas leaning forward, or pushing the skis back, weights the front section of the skis [B].

With modern boots and bindings, the skier has at his immediate disposal the ability to apply weight (leverage) to the front or back of the ski. Assuming there is sufficient lateral adhesion support from the snow/ice surface, if the skier weights the front of his skis (concurrent with proper angulation) the shovels will hold more than the tails and an oversteering, skidding condition can be induced or maintained. This presupposes, of course, that a turn has been started in some way and that centrifugal force (ie. a force sideways to the direction of travel — as in a traverse) is present. The position of the total lateral force (F_{TL}) is moved forward of the midsection of the ski and the tail starts to slide out into an oversteering, skidding condition.

If the skier positions his weight toward the rear, the total lateral force (with centrifugal force included) falls behind the boots and the tails will tend to hold more than the shovels. Depending on the degree of weight transfer and all the other variables, this rearward weight shift may only establish a true carving condition or it might phase into the shovel skidding-understeering condition described earlier.

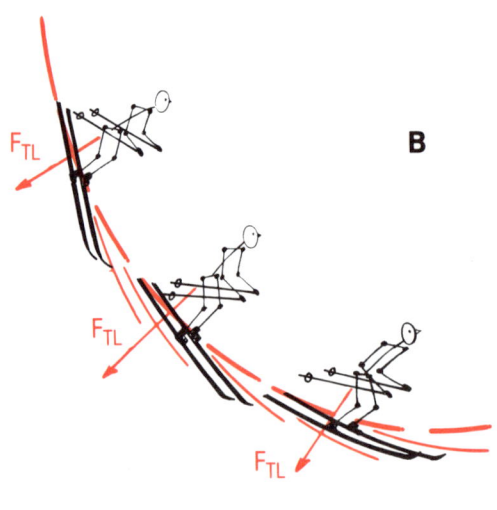

Figure 11—11
Once a turn has been started (thereby generating centrifugal force), weighting the fore-body of the skis will cause the tips to grip more than the tails, resulting in a skidding, oversteering situation [A]. If the skier positions his weight to the rear [B], the total lateral force (F_{TL}) falls behind the boots and the tails will tend to hold more than the tips.

Since it is usually desirable to have skidding at the beginning of a turn and carving at the end, it follows then that a forward weight shift is usually desirable at the beginning of the turn, followed by a rearward weight shift at the end. This is a dangerous statement if taken too dogmatically since there are so many exceptions to the rule. However, it is offered as the most common situation.

As the skier moves his weight back, the skis first try to carve their true radius. If this is all that is desired, then the weight transfer should be no more than back to the basic neutral position. If, however, an instability zone of borderline lateral adhesion is being approached near the end of the turn, the skier has two alternatives:

Figure 11—12
It's usually desirable to shift the weight forward (weighting the fore-body of the skis) at the beginning of the turn; and back to a neutral position toward the end of the turn.

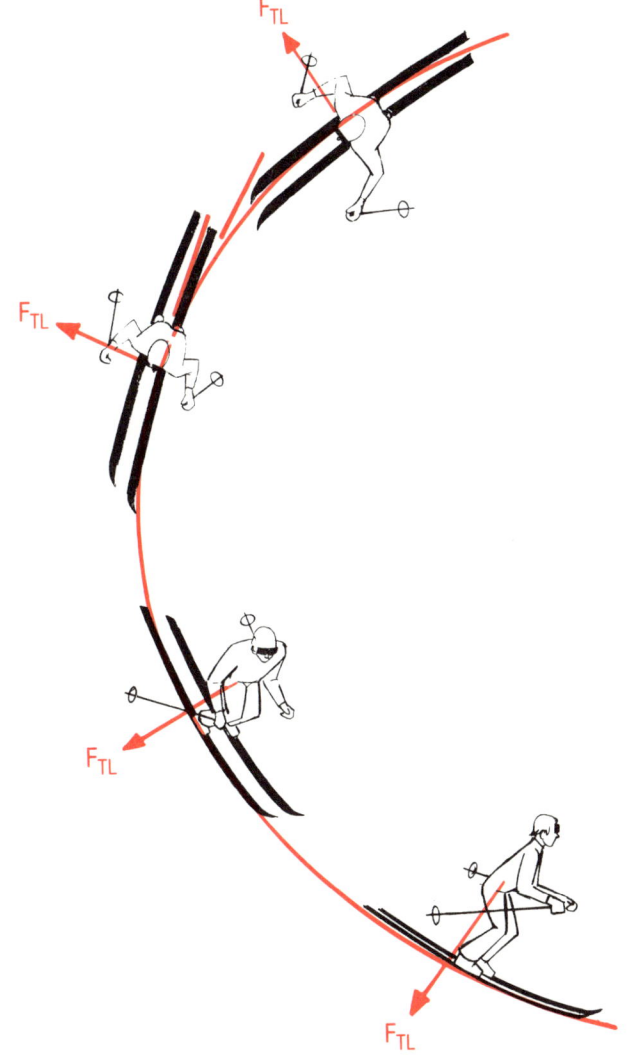

Figure 11—13
When the skis are about to lose adhesion toward the end of a turn, the recreational skier who wants to control his speed will shift his weight forward to insure that the tails will skid more than the shovels.

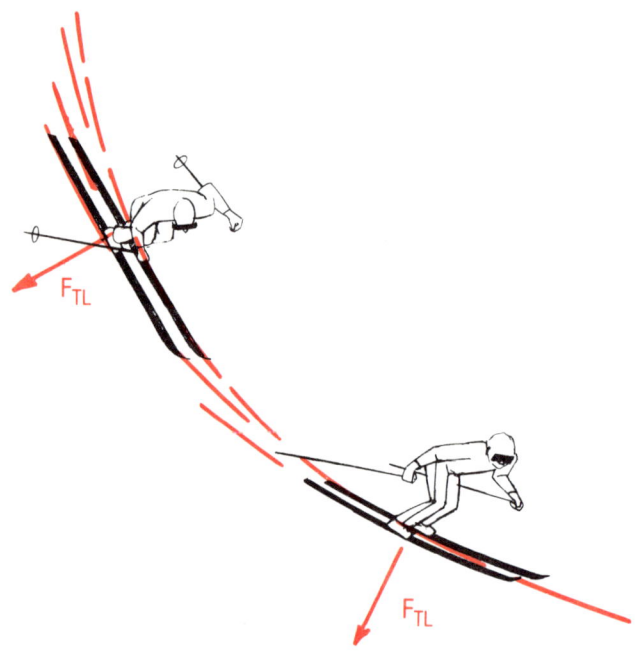

Figure 11—14
The racer will shift his weight back at the end of a turn to maintain his momentum and discourage tail-skidding.

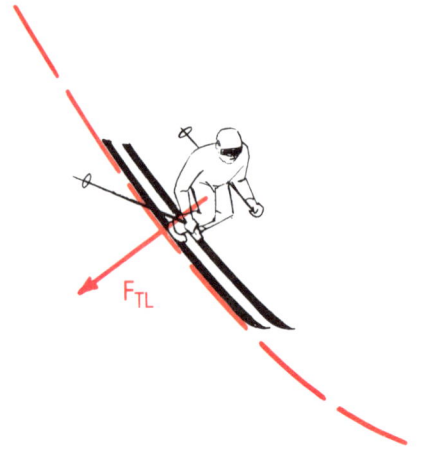

1. As a recreational skier wishing to control speed, he can keep his weight forward and insure that the tails skid first more than the shovels.

    In this case, the skier takes the risk of "spinning out." But this is usually more desirable than losing control in a straight down-the-hill attitude; especially if trees or other obstacles are in the way.

2. The racer desires to maintain velocity at all possible risk. He also has the strength and agility to step sideways when necessary. He will usually be stepping (lateral projection) anyway if he is at all competitive. He will, therefore, come back more onto the tails of his ski to insure that it holds more than the shovel and keeps the ski heading in a direction more down the fall line. In this way, he avoids getting sideways and "skidding off" his precious momentum.

    This movement back onto the tails of the skis at the critical point of the turn is analogous to the *"avalement"* forward thrusting of the skis that evolved in the 60's in the modern French technique.

Synchronization of Rotary Motion

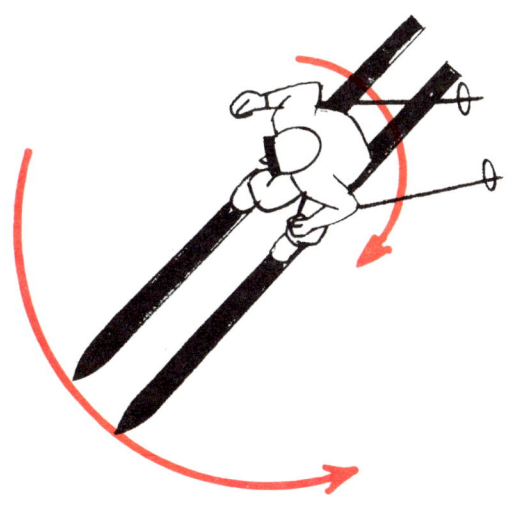

Figure 11—15
The clockwise twisting of the upper body induces a counter-clockwise twisting of the feet and skis, provided the skis are not held firmly against the ground.

The skier has at his disposal the ability to instantaneously apply a turning torque to his feet and skis. He does this by twisting his upper body in one direction. The equal and opposite torque tends to twist his feet and skis in the opposite direction.

This is a very handy turning force when used properly. Much has been written in the past about rotation, split rotation, counter rotation, anticipation, follow through, etc. All of these infer some type of rotary motion about a vertical axis. We will now try to sort out this slightly hackneyed subject in the framework of analysis presented so far.

A basic consideration is that; if the skis are firmly in contact on the ground in a flat position, or if they are carving on an edge, they *will not* rotate about a vertical axis, even with a twisting force applied by twisting the upper body in the opposite direction (counter rotation). All that will happen is that the upper body will end up being overtwisted and facing a substantially different direction than the ski travel. A twisting force resulting in counter rotary motion of the skis about the vertical axis is only possible if the skis are:

1. Light against the ground, by virtue of muscular or terrain unweighting.

2. Balanced at their center at the top of a convex surface.

3. Skidding or chattering sideways.

This is not to infer that the use of a rotary twisting force is unimportant. It does explain, however, why excessive emphasis on rotational forces does not usually provide the skier with instant turning ability. Counter rotary motion of the body around a vertical axis should be used to augment the more basic forces of turning and *not* be relied upon as the sole turning force.

The most likely place for additional counter rotation turning force to be needed during a turn is at the beginning of the turn concurrent with down unweighting and the required skidding to change direction. If the skier's upper body is properly facing downhill (or in the direction of the turn) prior to the instant of turn, he can add appreciable twisting force to his skis at the instant of turn by twisting his upper body in the opposite (or counter) direction.

The beauty of this technique is that in a series of linked turns the upper body is always properly positioned for the next turn and, in fact, appears to rotate very little as it is always facing downhill.

For normal skiing on harder, packed surfaces, very little up-

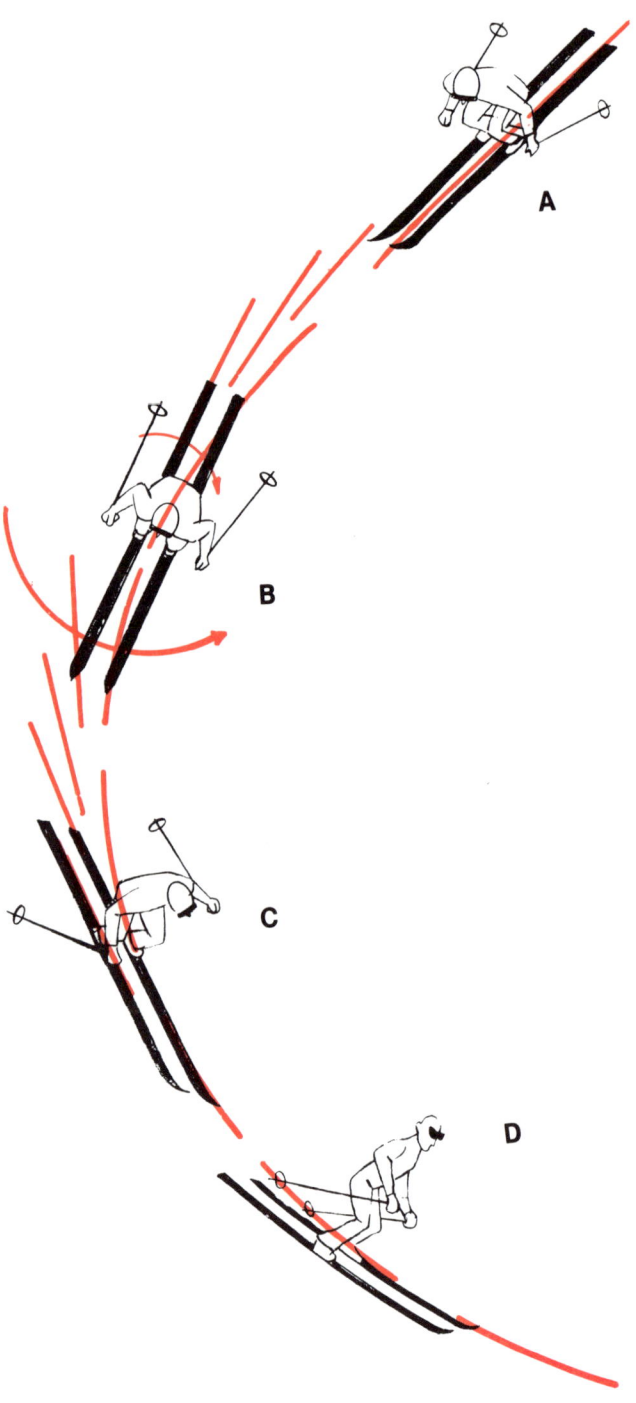

A

B

C

D

Figure 11—16
COUNTER ROTATION. With his body facing downhill prior to a turn, a skier can induce an appreciable twisting force to his skis during turn initiation by twisting his upper body in the opposite direction. In the traverse at point [A], the skier's torso faces slightly downhill. He rotates his upper body in a clockwise direction [B] to induce a counter-clockwise twisting force on the skis. As the turn continues [C], the skis enter a carving phase of the turn with the body again facing downhill.

Figure 11—17
In a series of linked turns, the upper body is always properly positioned for the next turn and appears to rotate very little as it always faces downhill.

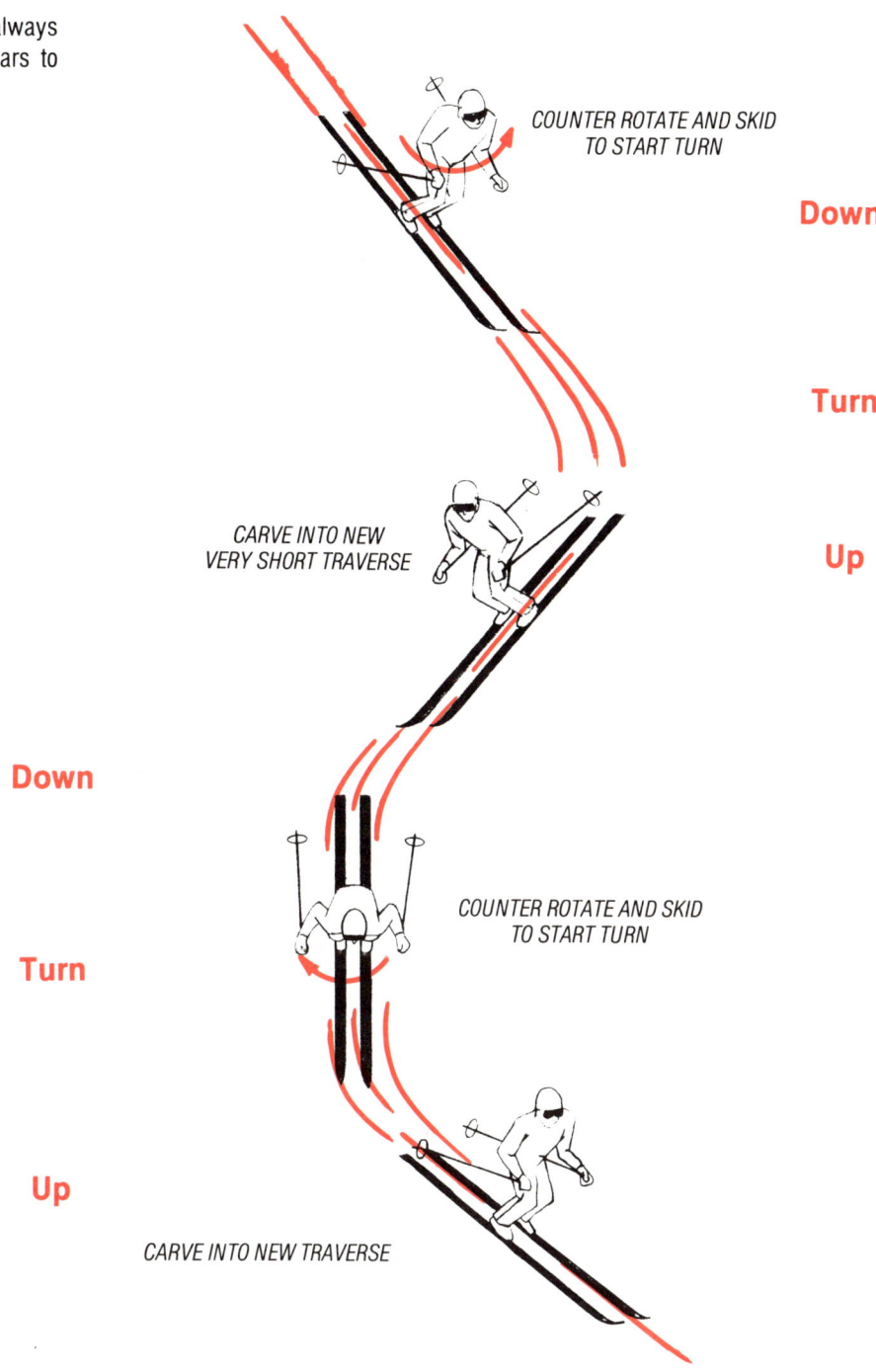

COUNTER ROTATE AND SKID
TO START TURN

Down

Turn

Up

CARVE INTO NEW
VERY SHORT TRAVERSE

Down

COUNTER ROTATE AND SKID
TO START TURN

Turn

Up

CARVE INTO NEW TRAVERSE

143

Figure 11—18
A high speed turn requires a quieter upper body with just enough counter rotation to faciliate angulation of the hips and knees.

per body counter rotation is required. This is especially true as the turns become longer in radius and approach true carved turn radii early in the turn. For true carved turns, the ski will make the turn and upper body counter rotation is not required. If the ski is at the limit of lateral adhesion near the end of the turn, additional counter rotation might just start the tails skidding, so it is more likely that the high speed skier or racer will maintain a more neutral upper body position with less emphasis on counter rotation.

For very soft snow and crud skiing, it is necessary to summon all the turning force available. It is, therefore, common to exaggerate the counter rotation of the upper body as the true turn is started. It may even be helpful to positively rotate the upper body in the direction of turn prior to the turn and then stop the positive rotation and begin counter rotation at the critical start of the turn. This technique is called *anticipation*, as the skier 'anticipates' the turn before it actually appears. He then counter rotates during the beginning of the turn, which could also be called 'split rotation' — ie. his rotation is split at the waist with the upper body and lower body rotating in opposite directions.

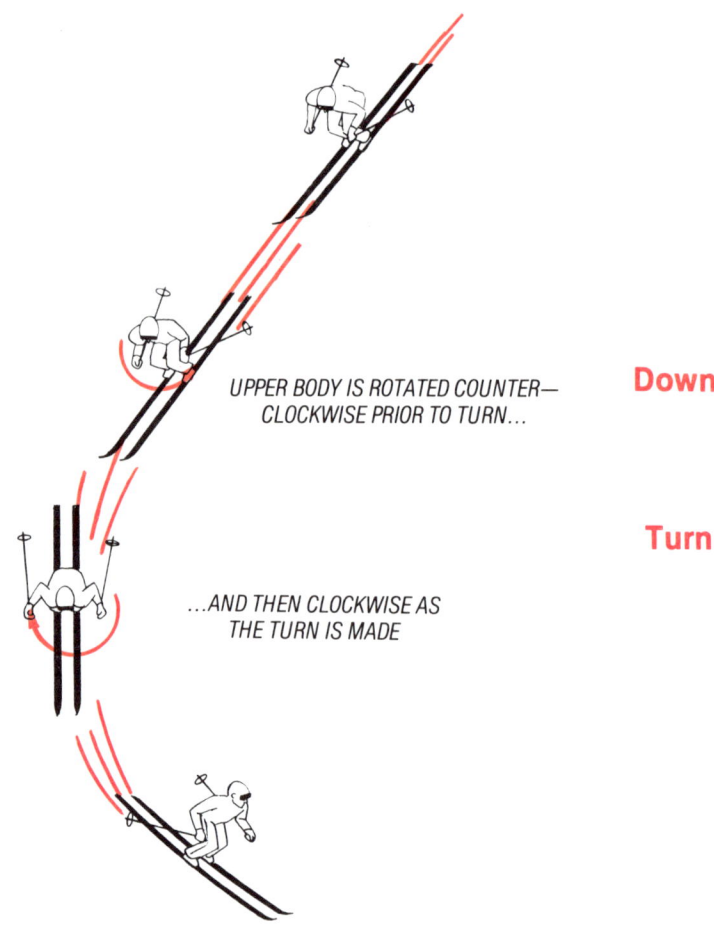

Down

UPPER BODY IS ROTATED COUNTER—
CLOCKWISE PRIOR TO TURN...

Turn

...AND THEN CLOCKWISE AS
THE TURN IS MADE

Figure 11—19 ▶
ANTICIPATION. In situations where it is necessary to generate as much turning force as possible (eg. powder skiing and 'crud' skiing), the skier can rotate his upper body in the direction of the turn prior to turn initiation, then block this rotation and counter rotate as the turn begins.

One last important point concerning rotation is that it is almost always dangerous to become over counter rotated; especially too early in the turn and in softer snow. If the skier uses up all of his available counter rotation force too early in the turn, and is essentially all 'wound up' even before crossing the fall line, he will have used up all of this available turning force and will not be able to complete the turn. If this happerns (and it sometimes does; especially with slower speeds, shallower traverses, and softer snow), the skier has no choice but to rotate back into a positive (facing downhill), downhill position and start the turn all over again from his new, steeper traverse.

Figure 11—20
If a skier uses all of his available counter-rotation force too early in a turn, yet doesn't achieve enough direction change to carry him all the way around the fall line, he won't be able to complete the turn.

Skier counter-rotates but doesn't generate enough turn to carry him around the fall line.

His skis slide straight down the fall line with his upper body twisted into the wrong position.

The difficulty of obtaining sufficient turning power via upper body counter rotation in soft snow is the primary reason it is easier to make turns from a steeper traverse; ie. closer to the fall line. The expert powder skier knows that it is best to start his run straight down the mountain and make the first turn right off the fall line. The more timid skier is used to more shallow traverses (across the fall line) and can't begin to generate the turning power, especially at slow speed, to make a complete turn in the soft snow. This is a puzzle to the poorer skier and he is in trouble until he can generate the confidence and strength to ski more in the fall line, thus requiring less direction change with each turn.

Synchronization of Angulation

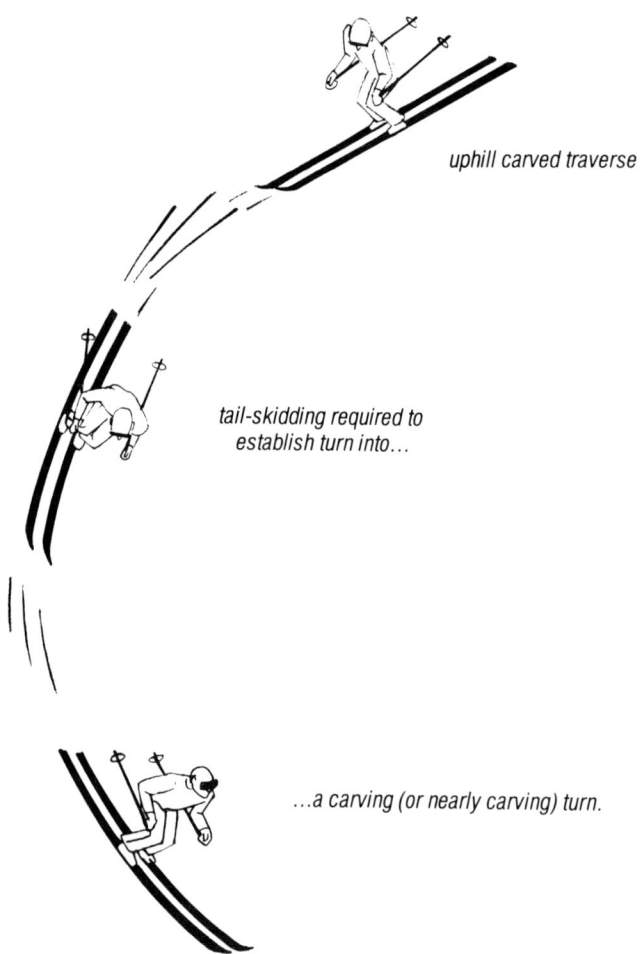

uphill carved traverse

tail-skidding required to establish turn into...

...a carving (or nearly carving) turn.

Figure 11—21
Oversteering or tail-skidding is required to initiate most turns — particularly turns started from shallow traverse angles and low speeds.

The argument has now been made that in most turns, an oversteering or tail skidding condition is needed to start the turn — especially from shallow traverse angles and low speeds. There are two ways to enhance this tail skidding mode that relate to angulation and the corresponding edge angle (Θ). Since they are opposite in their motion, they need to be clearly understood. Both require an edge change. The difference is the quickness of this change.

1. An elimination of angulation concurrent with the start of the turn will allow a foot swivel type of direction change

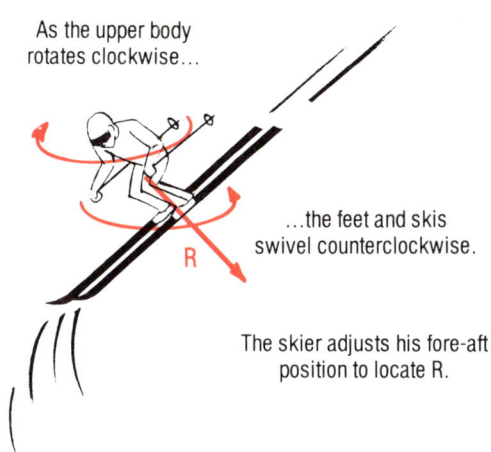

As the upper body rotates clockwise...

...the feet and skis swivel counterclockwise.

R

The skier adjusts his fore-aft position to locate R.

Figure 11—22
In a counter-rotation turn initiation, the inertia of the upper body about a vertical axis provides the counter-torque necessary to achieve a swivelling of the feet and skis into the turn. But this can only occur when a decrease in angulation reduces the edge angle to zero, and when the skis are unweighted.

either with one ski ('braquage') or with both skis ('vissage'). The preceeding section on the synchronization of rotary motion explains how the inertia of the upper body about a vertical axis can provide the counter-torque necessary to achieve a swivelling action of the feet and skis. This foot swivel can only happen when the decreased angulation has reduced the edge angle (Θ) to zero and the skis are temporarily unweighted by the thighs or terrain. The zero edge angle obviously occurs midway between the change in angulation from the uphill traverse to the new downhill turn. With this type of foot swivel, zero edge angle direction change, a concurrent forward pressure at the tips of the skis is not used. It would only restrict the swivelling motion of the skis. The direction of pressure through the skis should remain centered through the heel part of the boots.

This foot swivel type of turn is usually used at lower speeds and in mogulled terrain. It is especially easy at the top of a mogul. It is easy to completely change the direction of the skis before coming onto the new edges and finishing the turn.

The disadvantage of this type of turn is that during the foot swivel period there is a complete lack of directional stability to the ski. It is also easy to get the skis swinging too much in a rotary mode. The result is over-turning, excessive skidding at the end of the turn, and the distinct possibility of crossed tips. Another problem is that with any speed at all, the centrifugal force generated will tend to push the skier sideways since the flat skis cannot generate any lateral adhesion.

2. The better way to synchronize angulation to get into the turn is to use a very quick edge change combined with forward pressure on the skis. This angulation onto the new edge will force the tips of the skis to lead the ski into the new turn with much more control of the direction of the skis than in the foot swivel method. There still needs to be an edge change from the uphill edges to the downhill edges. The difference, however, from foot swivelling is that the edge change is much quicker and by being either on one edge or the other, without a long period with flat skis in between, the skier has much more control over his directional stability.

The reason for the forward leverage concurrent with the edge change is to induce some degree of tail skidding at the beginning of the turn. If no degree of tail skidding is desired at the beginning of the turn, then no forward pressure is required and the turn becomes a pure, carved turn right off the center and then the tails of the skis as the turn is ended.

Some coaches will tell their students to drive their knees toward the direction of the new turn. This conscious motion will automatically achieve both the forward leverage and the quick edge change required to make this preferred type of turn. This is a more dynamic, positive, and safer way to initiate a turn. The foot swivel type is a slower, longer method that encourages excessive skidding at the end of the turn.

It may be that the foot swivel and sideways skidding type of turn, which dissipates more energy, is more responsible for sharp, tight moguls *regardless of ski length*. The energy is dissipated in

Figure 11—23
The Foot Swivel and Quick Edge Change techniques of turn initiation are contrasted here. Both can be completed either by carving or by skidding. The advanced skier will use the Foot Swivel on occasion, but generally prefers to use the Quick Edge Change which gives him better directional control of his skis.

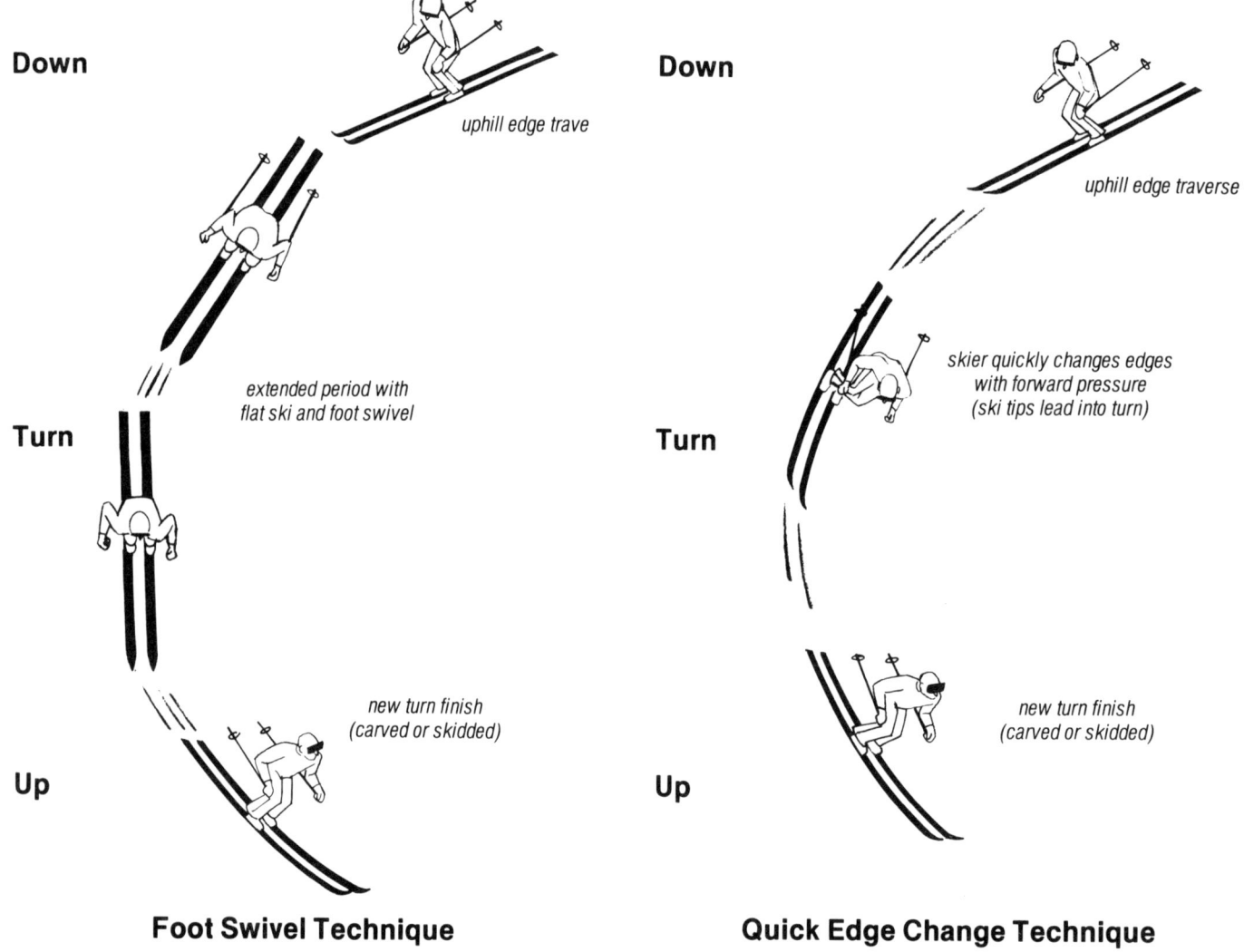

Down

uphill edge trave

Down

uphill edge traverse

extended period with flat ski and foot swivel

skier quickly changes edges with forward pressure (ski tips lead into turn)

Turn

Turn

new turn finish (carved or skidded)

new turn finish (carved or skidded)

Up

Up

Foot Swivel Technique

Quick Edge Change Technique

moving the snow sideways until a pile of snow (the next mogul) stops the sideways motion. This is not to infer that the advanced skier should never foot swivel. It is just recommended that he not rely on it as the foundation for his entire technique.

Once the turn is initiated by either method, it can be completed as a carved or skidded turn, depending upon the degree of angulation and forward pressure used. Continued forward pressure and good angulation will encourage tail skidding (oversteering) with the tips carving into a tight turn.

Continued forward pressure with decreased angulation will greatly encourage tail skidding and possibly allow the tips to skid out — also depending upon the speed and lateral adhesion available.

Neutral pressure (moving rearward) with good angulation will encourage the skis to carve into a tighter neutral radius.

Neutral pressure (moving rearward) with decreased angulation will encourage the skis to carve into a longer neutral radius but possibly skid sideways depending upon speed and lateral adhesion.

A

B

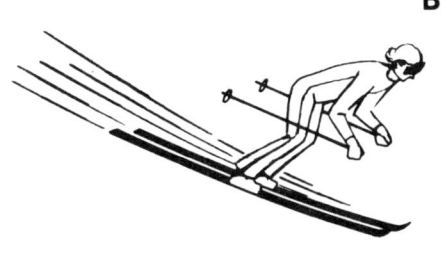

C

◄ Figure 11—24
The degree of angulation and forward / backward weighting define how a turn will be completed.

[A] Continued forward pressure and good angulation encourages tail skidding (oversteering) with the tips of the skis carving into a tight turn.

[B] Forward pressure and decreasing angulation greatly encourages tail skidding and perhaps also allows the tips to skid depending on the speed and degree of lateral adhesion.

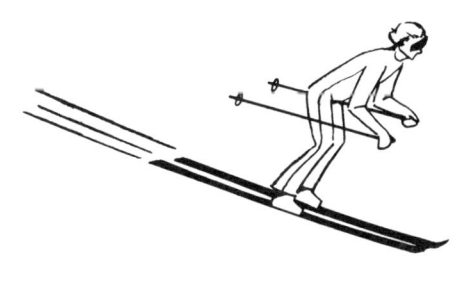

D

[C] Shifting the weight back to a neutral position, but maintaining angulation, encourages the skis to carve into a tighter neutral radius.

[D] Shifting the weight back to a neutral position and decreasing angulation encourages the skis to carve into a larger neutral radius. However, if the angulation is no longer sufficient to provide enough lateral adhesion, the skis will skid sideways.

Synchronization of Independent Leg Action

The 1960's can be characterized by the evolution of down unweighting and carved turns. The 1970's have seen the perfection of independent leg action as an integral part of high performance skiing. The powerful and positive direction changes that can be

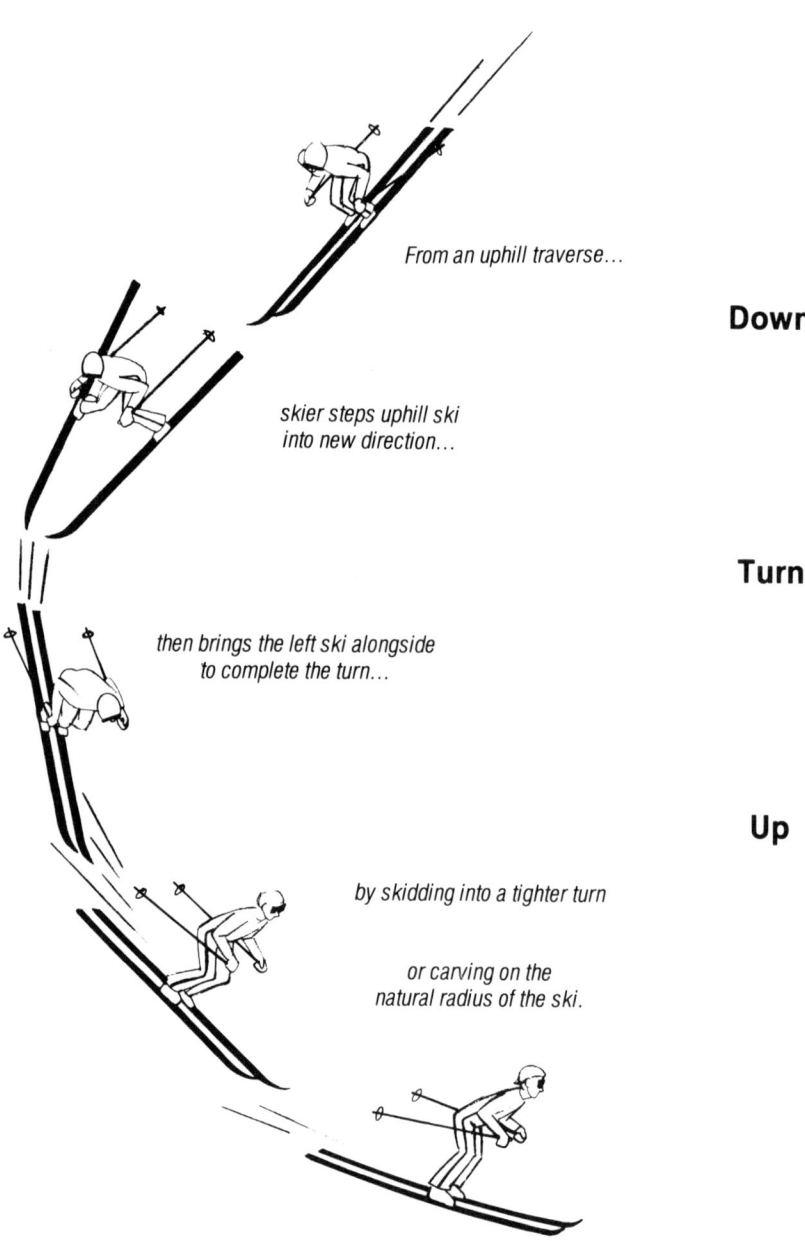

From an uphill traverse...

Down

skier steps uphill ski into new direction...

Turn

then brings the left ski alongside to complete the turn...

Up

by skidding into a tighter turn

or carving on the natural radius of the ski.

Figure 11—25
The uphill stem remains one of the best ways to initiate a turn because:
• It bridges the gap of the "instability zone" where, because of shallow traverse angles, turns are difficult to start.
• For the racer, it allows a lateral projection from the lower carving ski and with a minimum of energy loss.

Figure 11—26 ►
The downhill stem is a more passive or conservative maneuver than the uphill stem since it establishes a braking energy loss or 'platform' from which the turn is initiated.

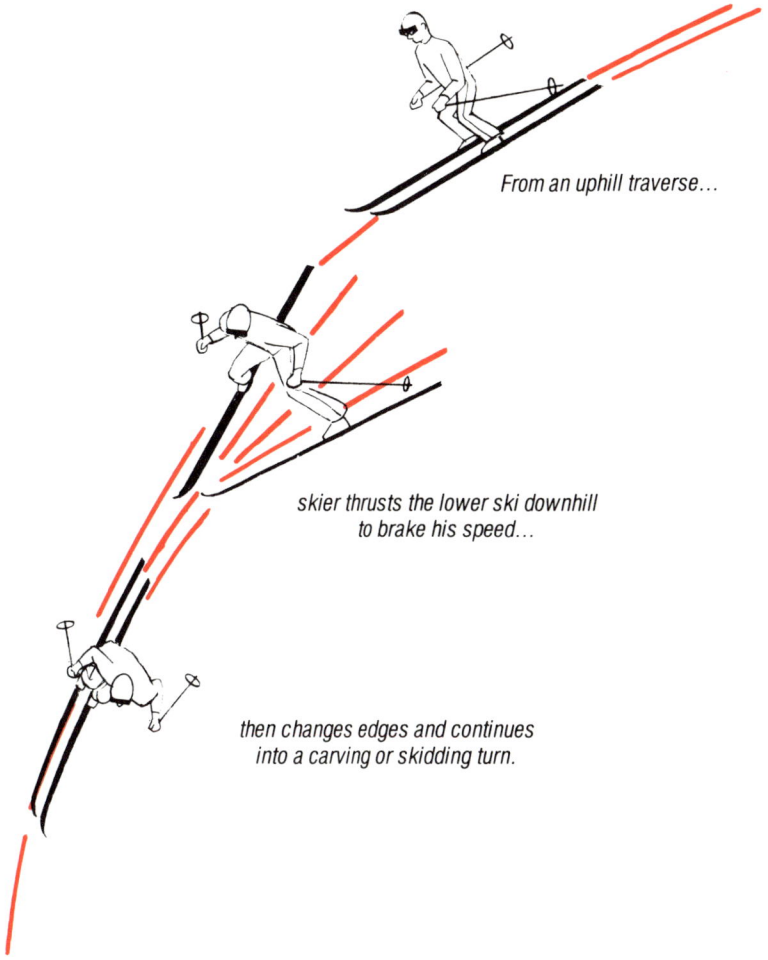

From an uphill traverse...

skier thrusts the lower ski downhill to brake his speed...

then changes edges and continues into a carving or skidding turn.

effected through independent leg action are absolutely necessary in modern racing. The advanced recreational skier can also expand his freedom of motion and agility by copying the racer and using both legs independently.

One type of independent leg action is much older and has been an accepted part of skiing since the end of the telemark days. This is the stem turn. To stem is to positively push or place one ski at an angle from the direction of travel.

An uphill ski stem is very effective because it immediately and positively establishes a new direction of travel. A turn and centrifugal force are commenced which can be followed by a carved completion (long radius) or a skidded 'christie' which can be followed by a carved completion (long radius) or a skidded 'christie' completion (short radius).

The uphill stem is still one of the best ways to start a turn because:

• It bridges the gap of the "instability zone" where, because of shallow traverse angles, turns are difficult to start.

• It coincides nicely with a lateral projection off the lower carving ski with a minimum of energy loss.

The downhill stem is more passive or conservative since it establishes a braking energy loss of platform from which to start the turn.

Both of these classic stem maneuvers are decades old but, in more recent years have been frowned upon in advanced skiing since they deviate from the ideal (?) parallel form. But with the advent of the lateral projection as an absolute necessity in racing during the 70's, variations of the uphill stem, in particular, should be reconsidered by all skiers.

In earlier chapters, the step turn or projection of the body laterally was clearly justified as a way of changing direction (eg. turn radius) without skidding while at the same time adding muscular energy to the kinetic energy of motion down the mountain. The synchronization throughout the turn would be as shown in Figure 11—26

Figure 11—27
The step turn (or turn with lateral projection) is a highly effective way of changing direction without skidding and can even allow a racer to add his own muscular energy to the kinetic energy of motion. In [A], the skier extends dynamically off of his outside (downhill) ski at the end of a turn. In doing so, he lifts his uphill ski and steps it into a higher track. The downhill ski is then brought alongside the uphill ski [B] followed by a change of edges and then a carving or skidding into the next turn [C] depending on the speed and turn radius.

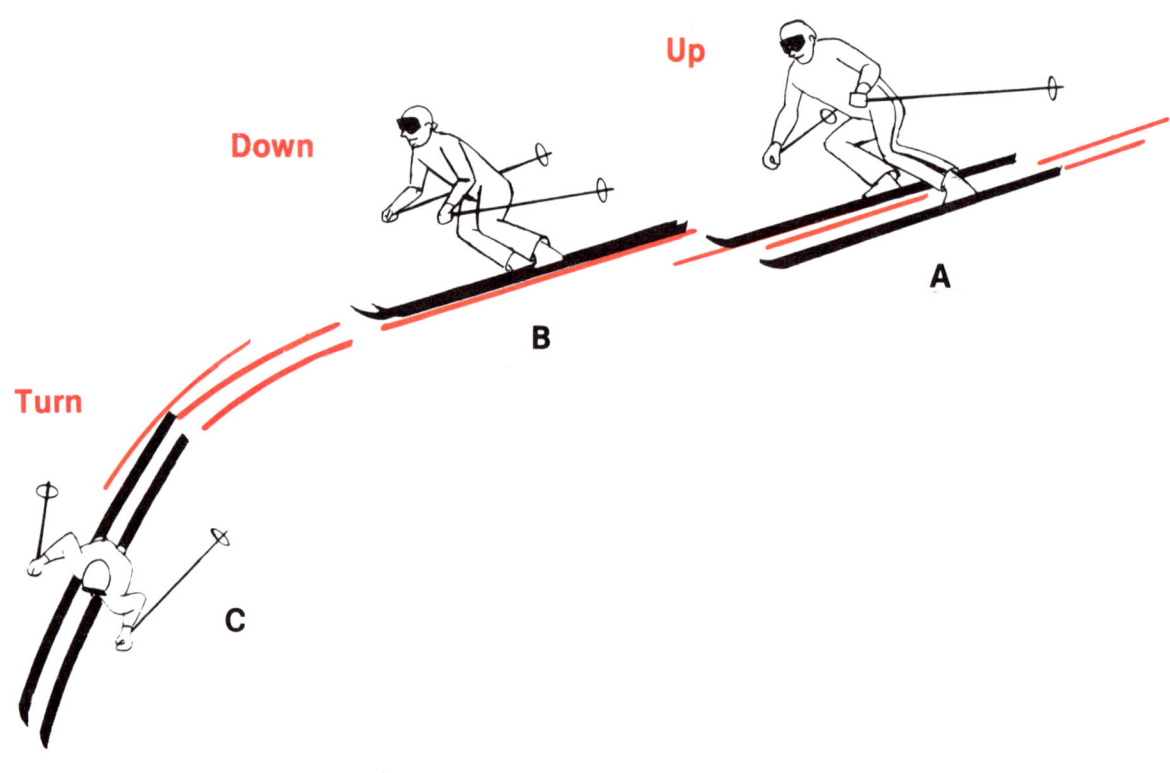

*Skier steps into a higher traverse,
but stays on his uphill edges
before carving into a new turn.*

Figure 11—28
Lateral projection is typically a far more dynamic maneuver than a turn initiated with an uphill stem. We normally think of lateral projection as a dynamic transfer of the body mass up the hill to achieve a higher line. Particularly when executed from a shallow traverse, this normally implies that the weight is transferred to the outside or uphill edge of the uphill ski. Nevertheless, a step or lateral projection can also involve a transfer of weight to the inside edge of flat surface of the uphill ski. A stem turn always involves a transfer of weight to the inside edge of the displaced ski but, as has been described earlier, the displaced ski in a stem turn is always placed at an angle to the direction of travel. World class racers often initiate turns close to the fall line by stepping to the inside edge of their outside ski. These maneuvers are often called step turns, but usually they are, in reality, stem turns.

The difference between this and the earlier uphill stem are subtle.

• The extension off the lower leg is much more powerful as the skier attempts to gain a higher line — not just change direction with the right ski.

• The newly established arc with the uphill ski might still be an uphill carved traverse with a turn to follow, or it might immediately begin a carved turn on the new (left hand side) edge.

Again, the power and versatility possible from independent leg action cannot be overemphasized. The only problem with skiing too much this way is that in very soft snow the sharp weight transfer will cause one ski to dive sharply and the other to rise. Soft snow and crud skiing require a softer, more delicate type of skiing using both skis together as a surfboard-type platform — like skiing on egg shells. A good analogy is water skiing. Advanced water skiing is much better on one ski than on two since independent leg action in the water could be disastrous. Water skiing is a buoyant phenomenon, like powder skiing, rather than a hard surfaced phenomenon, like skiing on packed powder or ice. All the force on one ski would cause it to sink sharply with respect to the other. This is why 'mono ski' skiing on snow will probably always be limited to deep powder.

Synchronization of Pole and Arm Action

By this point in the text, the lack of emphasis on the use of poles is probably conspicuous by its absence. This has been purposely done because it is felt that the use of the arms and poles (except as a counter balancing mass for foot and leg movements) should be de-emphasized. It is entirely wrong (albeit possible) to use the poles to generate a force to enhance turning. This is because the force would have to appear through the arm and upper body before it interacts with what's happening at the feet. A long-standing argument for the pole was to "trigger" the turn. This was especially true in the "*up — turn — down*" days where the very motion of touching the pole would force the body to rise up and over it as the planted pole passed by.

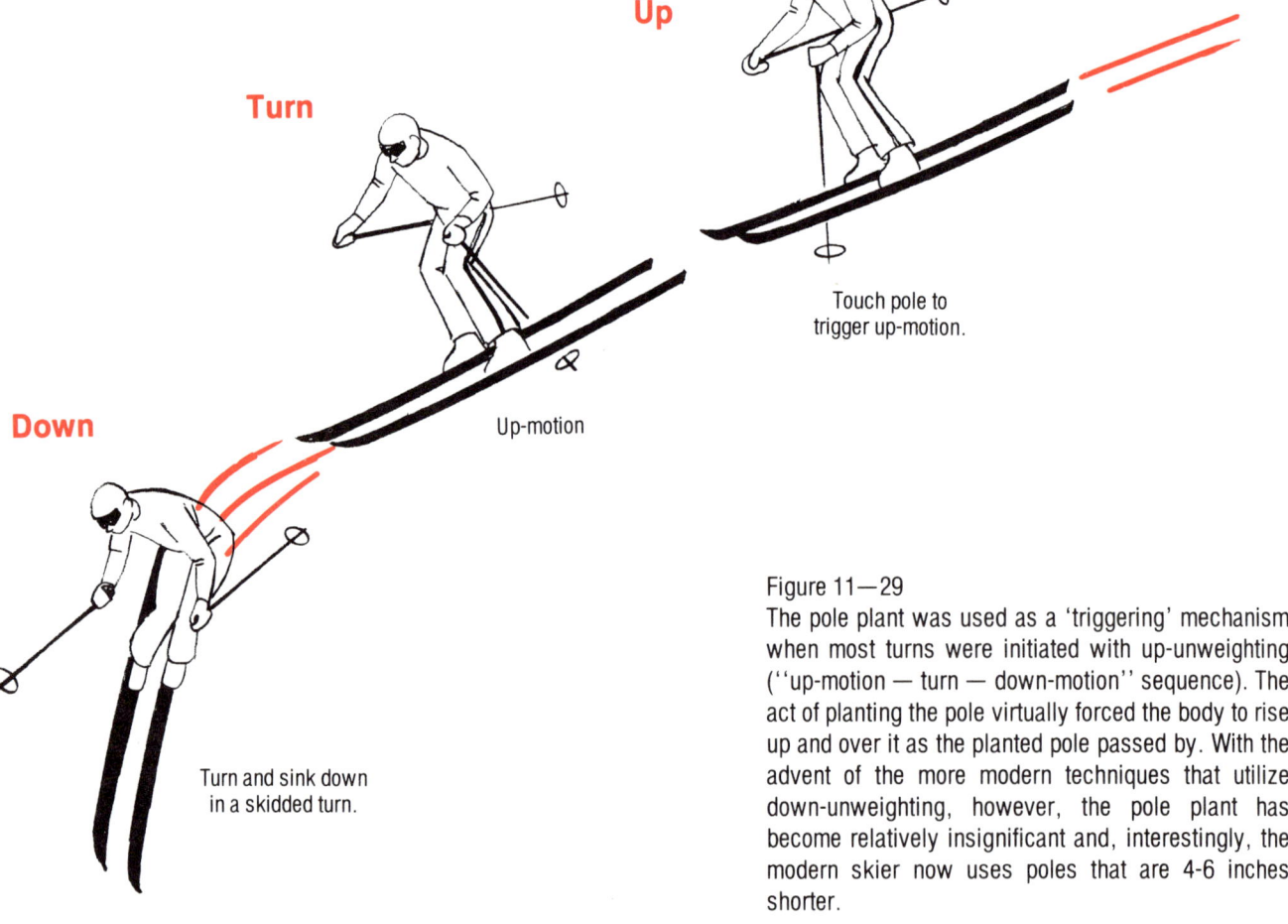

Up

Touch pole to trigger up-motion.

Turn

Up-motion

Down

Turn and sink down in a skidded turn.

Figure 11—29
The pole plant was used as a 'triggering' mechanism when most turns were initiated with up-unweighting ("up-motion — turn — down-motion" sequence). The act of planting the pole virtually forced the body to rise up and over it as the planted pole passed by. With the advent of the more modern techniques that utilize down-unweighting, however, the pole plant has become relatively insignificant and, interestingly, the modern skier now uses poles that are 4-6 inches shorter.

There are many conflicts between this traditional type of pole plant and a more modern turn.

- The pole plant interferes with the down motion to start the turn.

- The inside pole plant encourages a negative counter rotation *prior* to the turn which is just the opposite of the positive anticipatory rotation needed if extra turning power is required.

- The pole plant is precarious in moguled terrain or in soft snow conditions where it can sink in and pull the skier backwards.

- The pole plant is too rapid to serve any real function at higher speeds.

In addition, dragging the pole during the latter part of the turn should not be depended on in any way for providing balance or additional turning torque — (yet how many of us still revert to it now and then?)

Contrary to the above arguments against the use of the poles as an integral part of skiing, there are good uses for the poles that are consistent with the mechanics proposed in this book:

1. For starting, or at slow speeds, the poles obviously allow the use of the upper body muscle power (F_p) to add to the pull of gravity to provide the skier's motion. In cases where the hill angle (α) is shallow, the force possible from the arms and upper body (via the poles) can be substantially more than the ($F_g \sin \alpha$) possible from gravity. The total force available at *all* speeds to accelerate the skier's mass is ($F_g \sin \alpha$) plus (F_p) (plus any muscle force provided by skating or stepping).

2. In emergencies, when balance is temporarily lost, there is a good chance it can be quickly regained by adding a temporary outside force via the arm and pole. Every skier does this instinctively.

3. At a critical point in a turn where the lateral adhesion of the snow/ice surface is just on the verge of being insufficient to support the total lateral force generated by the skier, it may be possible to provide a few extra pounds of additional lateral supporting force with a timely pole plant. This usually coincides with the final upward weighting motion of the racer as he completes a turn.

It is this pole plant at the end of the preceeding turn in racing which can be easily confused as triggering an up-motion necessary

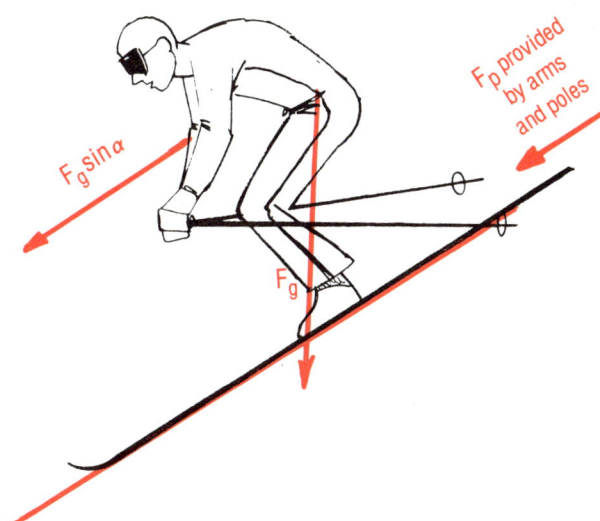

Figure 11—30
At low speeds, the poles become a potentially important source of propulsion. The total force available to accelerate the skier's mass is ($F_g \sin \alpha$) plus (F_p) plus any muscle force provided by skating or stepping. On very flat hills (low α) the force available from pushing with the poles (F_p) can be substantially greater than that from gravity ($F_g \sin \alpha$).

Figure 11—31 ▶

A properly timed pole plant can be used to provide a little additional lateral support when the lateral adhesion of the snow/ice surface borderlines on being insufficient to support the force generated by the skier. Racers will often use their poles in this way to gain a few extra pounds of lateral support during the final upward weighting motion as they complete a turn on an icy surface.

SIDE VIEW

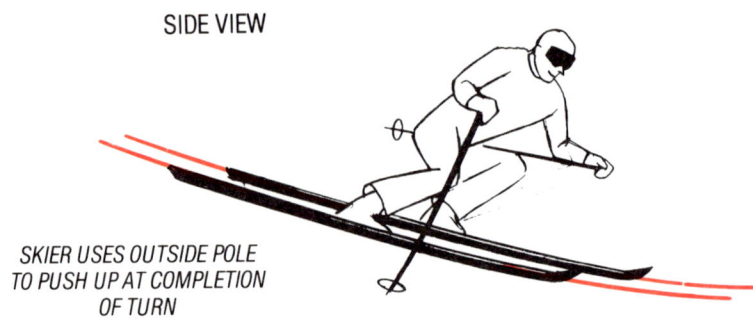

SKIER USES OUTSIDE POLE
TO PUSH UP AT COMPLETION
OF TURN

FRONT VIEW

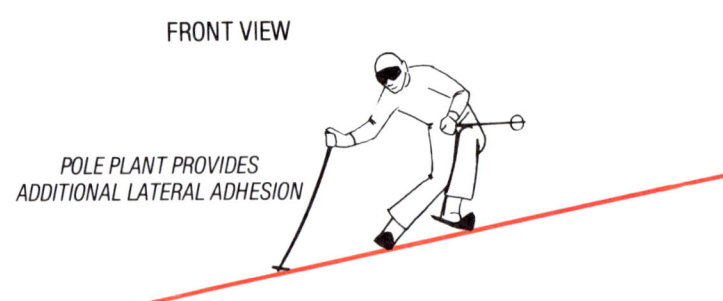

POLE PLANT PROVIDES
ADDITIONAL LATERAL ADHESION

for the next successive turn in a series. While watching racers on film, it is difficult to determine to which turn the pole plant belongs. It was not too clear in the fine book *Pianta Su* if the mechanics of this pole plant enhanced more the preceeding turn or the turn to follow. It would seem that the primary purpose of the pole plant is to enhance the upweighting motion that completes the prior turn. If the next successive turn were delayed a few seconds, it would best be initiated with a down unweighting, which doesn't need a pole plant to help start it.

Older books on skiing devote entire chapters to discuss the maneuvers of the pole plant, hand position, tip placement, etc. It is the contention of this author, that the pole plant should take a secondary role in modern skiing, and in most cases be eliminated entirely. This will insure that it is not being erroneously relied upon to provide some of the forces required for turning.

The position of the hands (on the other hand) is very important since they can contribute to and represent the balance of the entire body. Combined with the poles, they represent a considerable amount of quickly moved counterbalancing mass and wind resistance.

1. They should be held relaxed in front of the body and in a fairly low position to keep the center of gravity down.

2. The arms should be slightly bent so that movement can immediately be made in any direction.

Figure 11—32
The hands should be held in a low, relaxed position in front of the body and with the elbows flexed.

3. The hands should not cross in front of the body nor lag behind the body (except when poling). In these extreme positions, they would unbalance the upper body.

4. If additional rotational inertia is needed from the upper body to provide the turning power for foot rotation, then the arms and hands should be extended more out to the sides. This is especially effective as rotational inertia depends on mass and the radius of the mass around the rotational axis *squared* (Mr^2).

Likewise, the hands can be moved out sideways from the body for quick adjustments of balance just as a tight rope walker would do.

Synchronization of Fore and Aft Foot Position (Shuffle)

In Chapter 7 on traversing, the argument for "shuffle" was made. It follows that if the upper foot is ahead during one traverse

uphill traverse

edge change

new uphill traverse (completion of turn)

Figure 11—32 ▶
The skis should be "shuffled" at the moment that the edges are changed.

prior to a turn, then it must be changed to lag behind the new upper foot in the new traverse after the turn is made.

The question, then, is how does the change or shuffle synchronize with the turn? The answer is that presence and type of shuffle should agree with the edges that are being used; ie. if the skier is on his right edges, then his right ski is advanced, and vice versa. At the point in the turn where the new edge angle (Θ) is established, the skis should be shuffled slightly for two reasons:

1. To agree with the required knee and hip angulation.

2. To discourage the outer ski from carving underneath the inside (of the turn) ski.

Synchronization of the Forces Generated by the Ski

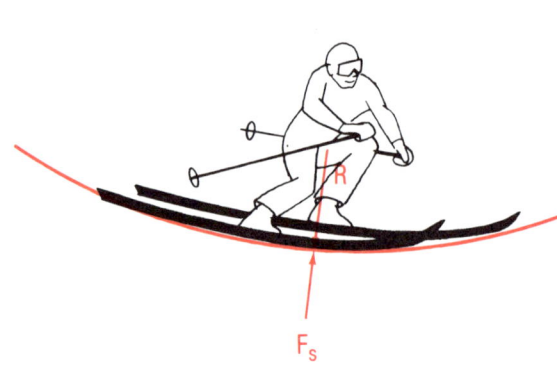

Figure 11—33
As long as the ski is held in a reverse bend, the bending force in the ski (F_s) pushes back against the skier. This force is considerably less than the total reactive force acting perpendicular through the skis (R), but can be used at the end of a turn by the skier to project him into the next turn.

Force is required to bend a ski into a reverse bend. This subject was covered in Chapter 9. As long as the ski is held into a reverse bend throughout the turn, the bending force in the ski pushes back against the skier.

The bending force in the ski (F_S) is usually less than the total reactive force (R) acting perpendicular through the skis. It cannot be greater than (R) nor can it be greater than the force required to bend the particular flex of skis used through the bending deflection (B_D) involved in this particular turn as defined by equation 9—5a. If both skis are weighted evenly, (R) is split evenly between both skis. If all the weight is on one ski, (R) is totally concentrated on that ski. The bending force in the ski, in either case, is still limited to the spring rate of the particular ski used (see Figure 9—1) multiplied by the bending deflection (B_D).

For instance, in the example given in Chapter 9, for a typical slalom ski (K = 195 ft), and an edge angle of 60°, we calculated that (B_D) = 0.519''. Then from Figure 9—1, we saw that a stiff ski (60 Newtons/cm spring rate) so bent would generate a force of 30#. This force is (F_S) and it pushes back against the skier constantly, as long as the edge angle (Θ) is at 60° and the ski is pressed into the reverse bend of 0.519''.

If the skier is careful, he can use this force at the end of the turn to help him project into the new turn. This phenomenon gives the ski, and the skier, a feeling of liveliness. The racer might say that the ski had "jetted" or "popped" at the end of the turn. When it happens, the feeling is unmistakable. If the ski is deflected into a concave rut, the bending deflection would be much greater than on a planar surface and (F_S) could be as high as (R), even when (R) is very high. In this case, (F_S) would be much higher than desirable and would actually project the skier into the air at the end of the turn. This is one reason a softer spring rate ski would be better in ruts; ie. it would develop less (F_S) for a given reverse bend.

With regard to synchronization throughout the turn, as long as good angulation and edge angle (Θ) are maintained *throughout the end of the turn*, the bending force in the ski will be returned to the skier after any temporary unweighting force (F_D) is completed. If good angulation is lost before the end of the turn, the ski might straighten out at either the tip or tail (depending on fore or aft leverage) and not only would the bending force be lost, but the ski could suddenly take off in some erratic direction.

If very high bending forces are experienced — as in a concave rut — then the thigh muscles must not be held rigid or extended at the instant (F_S) is very high. The thigh muscles should even be relaxed as in down unweighting at the instant the ski is flexed and starts to come out of the rut so that the high (F_S) does not act directly on the skier's mass and propel him into the air. Instead, the energy is absorbed into the thigh muscles. The coach might say, "be supple and absorb the rut rather than tensing and letting the rut throw you out of the course." Remember, it is the rut manifested as great energy absorbed in the ski that causes the problem. If the ski is softer, less energy is absorbed in the ski — and the ruts give less problem. The trade-off with very soft flex skis is that they give poor directional stability and sluggish response on planar (non-concave) surfaces.

Also, remember that flex and camber are interrelated. There can be as much energy and bending force in a high camber, soft ski as in a lower camber, stiff ski when both are deflected into a certain rut. The difference between the two design concepts is that the high, soft ski will be more sluggish in its response and more un-predictable in its direction as it flexes to extremes. It can readily carve into radically different turn radii depending on the bending deflection. An analogy is a very flexible tennis racket with which the player might say, "it feels good, but I don't know where the ball is going." This discussion points out the importance of mat-ching ski flex to skier's weight. Since (F_S) is working against the skier's weight (F_g), it is important that people with higher weights use higher spring rate skis in order to achieve the same effective ratio or balance between (F_S) and (F_g).

Chapter and Book Summary

This has been the longest chapter in this book because it represents the useful application and coordination of all the supporting theory presented in the earlier chapters. It should be clear by now that there is no one, single way to ski. Also, there are usually no singular, simple answers to questions regarding skiing. The complexity of the "playing field" and the wide variety of movements possible make total understanding difficult and somewhat contradictory. When the skier combines this situation with the different types of skis available, it is little wonder that there is disagreement as well as confusion.

The evolution of skiing certainly won't stop in the 1980's. New techniques and equipment will continue to make racers faster and recreational skiers more proficient and safer. It does appear, however, that the science of skiing is not now changing as rapidly or as widely as it has in the past. The recognized experts and teachers of the sport seem to be forming worldwide basic agreement founded on the universal laws of physics. Fortunately, to enjoy everyday skiing, the skier doesn't need to consciously or continually concern himself with these laws. However, somewhere in his skiing career, he needs to have been exposed to these if he is to advance to highly skilled levels. Hopefully, this book will make it possible for the racer to go a little faster and the recreational skier to enjoy even more the great sport of skiing.